Mary Russell Mitford

The Friendships of Mary Russell Mitford

In Two Volumes. Vol. I

Mary Russell Mitford

The Friendships of Mary Russell Mitford
In Two Volumes. Vol. I

ISBN/EAN: 9783744712972

Printed in Europe, USA, Canada, Australia, Japan

Cover: Foto ©Thomas Meinert / pixelio.de

More available books at **www.hansebooks.com**

THE FRIENDSHIPS

OF

MARY RUSSELL MITFORD

AS RECORDED IN LETTERS FROM

HER LITERARY CORRESPONDENTS

EDITED BY

THE REV. A. G. L'ESTRANGE

EDITOR OF "THE LIFE OF MARY RUSSELL MITFORD," AND
AUTHOR OF "THE LIFE OF THE REV. W. HARNESS,"
"THE VILLAGE OF PALACES," ETC. ETC.

"Whoever reads my letters, that is the letters written *to* me, will
find them interesting."—M. R. MITFORD *to* J. T. FIELDS.

IN TWO VOLS.—VOL. I.

LONDON:
HURST AND BLACKETT, PUBLISHERS,
13, GREAT MARLBOROUGH STREET.
1882.

CONTENTS OF THE FIRST VOLUME.

CHAPTER III.

CHAPTER IV.

CHAPTER V.

CHAPTER VI.

CHAPTER VII.

CHAPTER VIII.

CHAPTER IX.

CHAPTER X.

CHAPTER XI.

CHAPTER XII.

CHAPTER XIII.

THE FRIENDSHIPS

OF

MARY RUSSELL MITFORD.

————

INTRODUCTION.

THERE is something dear to us in every object associated with those we have loved or admired. The dwelling-place of a celebrated person, though now merely an ivy-covered ruin, possesses something of national interest, and the gift of a departed friend, be it but a faded flower, is treasured as inestimably precious. This feeling is sometimes purely sentimental, and exists even where the connection of the memorial with the person has been accidental and unimportant. But I imagine that in most cases there is some solid foundation for such emotions. As the mental characteristics of man are closely connected with his physical constitution, so are they also

VOL. I.   B

largely influenced by the surroundings of his daily life. Occasionally we can directly trace the bearing of some unexpected occurrence upon our future destiny, and the views of the most eminent people have been largely affected by the age and country in which they have lived.

Thus to those by whom the memory of Mary Russell Mitford is cherished, the letters which form these volumes will be interesting not merely as having been valued and preserved by her, but as having to some extent left an impress upon her mind. She sought to profit by the thoughts of others, and the bright mosaic-work of her own letters is largely formed of re-set gems. Here, also, we learn who her friends were, with what sentiments they regarded her, and what subjects they thought would give her pleasure. Beyond this the letters have an intrinsic value of their own as coming from the pens of some of the most successful authors of the day; and, as their character must depend upon the recipient as well as the sender, we may suppose that, being written to the authoress of 'Our Village,' they will not only contain literary judgments and opinions founded upon wide experience, but will also confide some more recondite and personal feelings.

We naturally inquire, first of all, how Miss Mitford, who lived in a secluded Berkshire village, and seldom visited London,[1] became acquainted with so many celebrities. More than one cause produced this result. She was a successful dramatist, the editor of an annual, a contributor to periodicals, and from time

[1] Except in early youth.

to time people wrote to her expressing admiration for her works. But mere literary success has never made any one socially popular, other attractions are requisite, and Mrs. Barrett Browning considered Miss Mitford's conversation to be even better than her books.[1] Thus we find that in the summer-time, when she gave strawberry-parties at her cottage, the road leading to it was crowded with the carriages of all the rank and fashion in the county. By example as well as precept she 'brightened the path along which she dwelt.' Her kindly nature did not exhaust itself in a girlish enthusiasm for pets and flowers, but went forth to meet her fellow-men and women, whose virtues seemed to expand and whose faults to vanish at her approach. 'There is,' she writes, 'an atmosphere of love, a sunshine of fancy, in which objects appear clearer and brighter, and from such I sometimes paint.'

Miss Mitford's friendships extended from the highest to the lowest classes of society, but her sympathies were especially enlisted on behalf of genius. Great thoughts and noble enterprises had a peculiar charm for her; hence she cultivated those eminent persons with whom her talents brought her into connection, and drew round her a brilliant circle of authors, artists, and politicians. Her playful humour and joyous enthusiasm cheered and refreshed their lives of toil, and they in turn reflected back upon her

---

[1] 'In my own mind, and Mr. Kenyon agrees with me, she herself is better and stronger than any of her books, and her letters and conversation show more grasp of intellect and general power than would be inferable from her finished compositions,' Mr. Fields says. 'Her voice was a beautiful chime of silver bells.'

an enduring lustre. Miss Mitford does not stand upon
a cold, isolated height, but will ever be associated
with the intimacies she formed and the society in
which she moved. She even carried on an affectionate correspondence with many persons whom she had
never seen.

It is not improbable that her sympathetic tendencies were partly hereditary, for both her parents were essentially sociable and fond of company. Her mother formed the centre of a little
homely coterie at Reading, and her letters to her
daughter invariably record some grand five-o'clock
dinner or select 'sandwich party' at which she had
been, or of some friendly gathering at her own house.
Her accounts of these festivities show considerable
observation, and are amusing both for her opinions
about the guests and for the minute details she gives
of the good fare at the entertainments.

MRS. MITFORD to DR. MITFORD.

Hans Place, June 2, 1802.

Sweet Mezza'[1] is hard at work doing a prize composition. She does not return to dinner till half-past
four, as her drawing-master attends at half-past three.
The paper does not, you will observe, give the same
account as you heard yesterday at Mr. Taplin's of
the Union Masquerade, but Rowden saw Lady Bes-
borough last evening, who was there, and who mentioned the confusion that prevailed in similar terms.
Her ladyship's own dress was demolished in the

[1] Miss Mitford.

scuffle. This, however, does not deter her from attending the masquerade at Ranelagh to-night, which, it is thought, will be better conducted. She mentioned the Prince supped alone with Mrs. Fitzherbert and another lady, and that their privacy was broken in upon by the mob ere they had finished their repast. Mrs. St. Quintin pressed me much to dine with her to-day, but I declined it. She and Miss Rowden are to dine with us to-morrow on the pig you are to send us.

Those who are at all acquainted with Miss Mitford's early history will remember M. St. Quintin, the French *émigré*, at whose school in Hans Place she was educated. The Mitfords became very intimate with his family, and sometimes stayed with them. Miss Rowden was the governess who married M. St. Quintin after the death of his wife.

Mrs. Mitford *to* Dr. Mitford, *Reading, Berks.*

Hans Place, June 3, 1802.

Dr. and Mrs. Harness called on us last evening, and sat near an hour. They wished us to dine there this day, as they had some captain—I forget the name— to dine with them, but Mary's lessons both before and after dinner furnished us with an excuse. I told you I had asked Mrs. St. Q. and Rowden to partake of the pig, and if M. St. Q. is not obliged to go into town he will also dine with us. Dr. H. saw Mr. Harley, and told him that we were at 76, Hans Place; he may look long ere he finds that number here; but I suppose he will have sense enough to go to 22 to learn where we are.

.   .   .   .

I have bought some salmon, and had a baked gooseberry pudding made, which, with my pig, will afford ample provision for our small party; and purchased a bottle of sherry. We only wish you were here to partake of it with us, as it would relish much better.

Mezza has got her little desk here, and her great dictionary, and is hard at her studies beside me, on which account and the warmth of the morning her little spirits are all abroad to obtain the prize, sometimes hoping, sometimes desponding. It is as well, perhaps, you are not here at present, as you would be in as grand a fidget on the occasion as she herself is. Adieu, God bless you.

Our most affectionate love is yours.

MARY MITFORD.

Postscript by her daughter.

Mumpsa[1] has been telling you a parcel of stories, for I do not care a brass farthing about the prize, and I am *certain* I shall not have it.

Dear Croppy sends you her love and good wishes.

MISS MITFORD *to* MRS. MITFORD.

Hans Place, Sept. 3, 1802.

M. St. Q. and some of the young ladies and the Wrights are going to Richmond by water on Sunday. They wished me to persuade you to join them there,

---

[1] A pet name for Mrs. Mitford.

but I rather thought you would prefer taking a snug dinner in Hans Place at five o'clock with Rowden and Mam Bonette (herself) to joining their Johnny Gilpin's excursion. M. St. Q. wished not to go, for he says that he should enjoy your company much more than the water-party; but as he is going soon to France, and could not go at any other time, and the young folks had set their hearts on the excursion, I persuaded him to go.

You are a dear flatterer, my darling, but I have heard that people always excel most in those things which they are fondest of; if so, I am sure that my *forte* must be writing to my beloved parents, for there is nothing when away from them that affords me so much pleasure as receiving and answering their dear letters.

Mrs. Mitford to Miss Mitford.

Reading, Nov. 14, 1802.

The concert went off extremely well, and the house quite full. We had no vacancy in either of our boxes, as Mrs. Terry (her sister not coming as she expected) applied to me on Thursday morning, and I was happy in giving her the only vacant place. For fear of consequences, I durst not put Monck and her in the same box, therefore we marshalled our company in the following order:—In the front row of the stage-box Mrs. Dolly, your aunt, and Mrs. Terry; on the back seat Mr. Annersley, Mr. Robinson, senior, and your father. The other box in front Mrs. Nicholl, Miss Valpy, and myself; and behind us Mr. Monck, Mr. Southgate, and Mr. Matthew Robinson took their

station. The party drank tea here, and Mr. D.'s
coach conveyed the female part of it to the theatre
a little before seven.   Mr. and Mrs. Lefevre were on
the opposite side of the house, so that we had no conversation till the concert was finished, when Mr. L.
came to pay his compliments to me and my friends,
and old dad went round to chat with Mrs. L.   When
the house was sufficiently cleared to afford me an
easy passage, I joined her also, and was agreeably
surprised to find that, during the time we were waiting for their coach to get up, Mr. L. had desired your
friend Monck to put his night-cap in his pocket, and
accompany them and us back to Heckfield. The
night was dry, though cold, and, being moonlight,
our drive was a very pleasant one; and we reached
their truly hospitable mansion before twelve. Sand-
wiches, negus, etc., was immediately brought in, and
after half an hour's pleasant chat, we separated for
the night.   I cannot attempt to detail what an agreeable day we had on Friday. The gentlemen dedicated the morning to field sports; the ladies accompanied me round the grounds, and afterwards we
took a ride round Lord Rivers' park before we dressed
for dinner, when there was an addition to our num-
bers of a Mr. Milton, his wife, and two daughters; the
youngest of whom, Miss Fanny Milton,[1] is a very
lively, pleasant young woman. I do not mean to
infer that Miss Milton may not be equally agreeable,
but the other took a far greater share in the con-

[1] The Miss Fanny Milton above mentioned afterwards became
the celebrated Mrs. Trollope. Her father was Vicar of Heckfield,
near Reading, three miles from Swallowfield.

versation, and, playing casino great part of the evening with Mr. S. Lefevre, Mr. Monck, and your old Mumpsa, it gave me an opportunity of seeing her in a more favourable light than her sister.

The next letter was written during Miss Mitford's visit to the north.

Mrs. Mitford to Mary Russell Mitford.

Bertram House,
Saturday Evening, Sept. 27, 1806.

It appears as if Providence kindly favoured the wish of your friends to give you an agreeable impression of Northumberland. The weather is quite heavenly. You smile at local attachments, but I think the enthusiasm of your character will kindle into affection when you behold the spot that gave birth to a parent you have so much reason to love and revere.[1] Dooley is vastly well, but is suspected of having killed one of the Dutch teal; either himself or the old cat did it. The most suspicious circumstance against the poor baronet is that he was caught with one of them in his mouth some days before. I am grieved at the accident, and shall suffer your pet to be as little in the garden as possible, and keep a strict eye over him. He is certainly much more anxious to go there than he used to be.

I am half sorry that you did not see the Marquis of Exeter's in your way down. So lovely a place would have had additional charms from the fineness of the weather, and it may be tinged with November

---

[1] These encomiums are very creditable to Mrs. Mitford, and probably had great influence with her daughter.

gloom when you return. Her Majesty came by Three Mile Cross, and so up by Dr. Jones's and the church at Shinfield, on her return from Sir William Pitt's to Windsor on Wednesday; but the showers had induced her to substitute their coach for her own sociable, and as Lady Pitt, according to etiquette, waited on the queen, the next morning she went in the royal sociable, and returned in her own carriage. Our worthy Dr. and Mrs. Perry dined that day with Mrs. Brocas, so were not at home when her majesty, with truly royal speed, whirled by their cottage, which she did at the rate of twelve miles an hour at least.

I went past them between Bernard Body's and the Cross, and did but just get in time to Heckfield Place. The two ladies received me in great spirits. Mr. Lefevre got down to his own room the day before, and Mrs. S. L. had been out a short airing with him in the carriage. We were soon informed dinner was upon the table, and Mr. Bulley, senior, joined us in the dining-room. We had some delightful eels at the top, soup in the middle, and a haunch of Lord Stowell's venison at the bottom, a boiled chicken on my side, and what was on the other I do not recollect. Some venison was sent in to Gog,[1] but he thought it very bad, and sent for some chicken. We had after, a brace of partridge at top, a very fine rabbit at the bottom, a dish of pease in the middle, tipsey-cake on one side, and grape tart on the other. Except some pease, I dined on the fish and venison, and tasted nothing else. Their greenhouse grapes, which now

[1] Mr. Shaw Lefevre.

succeed the hot-house, are admirable, and we had some very good peaches, a pine, pears, and walnuts. The pine, not being tasted, Mrs. Lefevre ordered it to be put in my carriage, with many apologies for its not being so large as she could have wished. As Mr. Bulley was engaged to a sandwich party at Mrs. H. Marsh's, Mrs. Lefevre, as soon as she left the dining-room, rang to order the servants to get tea and coffee by seven, as she thought Mr. Bulley would wish to be off soon after. Magog, who had gone to visit her good man, returned to us to say that Mr. L. hoped I would excuse his *déshabillé*, and begged we would take tea and coffee in his room, and on the old lady ringing again for the butler to tell him to take it thither at the hour she had ordered, he told her his master had directed him to bring it in immediately, so we repaired thither without delay. I am happy to say our good friend looks better than I expected, and was in excellent spirits. He; as well as the ladies, begged to be most kindly remembered to you both.

The Mitfords were liberal in their hospitalities at this time. In a letter, dated March, 1806, Mrs. Mitford writes to her husband: 'Will you purchase a dozen and a half new doileys, as ours are getting too shabby for company. I mention eighteen, as when a party amounts to fourteen or fifteen, which ours sometimes do, it does not look well to see them of two different sorts. And, if you conveniently can, bring six pounds of wax or spermaceti candles.'

The following lines, written by Mrs. Mitford during

the absence of her husband and daughter in the north, will give some idea of her simple and affectionate nature :—

Though Mitford's absence causes many a sigh,
And tears unbidden fill his consort's eye,
Detained at Kirkby waiting for his friend
Till dark November's gloomy fogs descend,
Yet has that month to me superior charms
To those when summer's sun our bosom warms,
For in that month was born the friend most dear,
The constant partner of each joy and care;
And faithful memory, with grateful lay,
Shall fondly hail her husband's natal day.
Some little votive wreath to deck her strain
Of every Muse she asks, but asks in vain.
She seeks no flowers a garland to prepare,
They bloom not when stern winter chills the air;
Nor needs her Mitford ornaments like these,
Secure by genuine worth all hearts to please.
But unassisted by the tuneful Nine
Can she attempt his virtues to define;
Depict his ardour when, at friendship's call,
From distant lands he flew to yonder hall?

In calm domestic scenes his worth revere,
See the kind husband, the fond parent here!
May each revolving year behold him blessed
With peace, best inmate of the human breast;
The cheerful glow of health his cheeks adorn,
Whose eyes still sparkle like the brilliant morn;
And many a season pass unmarked by care
In social intercourse with friends most dear.
Oh, may his darling child, his soul's delight,
As now with sweet affection meet his sight!
And should some virtuous youth obtain the fair,
Making her happiness his constant care,
Will not her father, pleased though loth, resign
Parental rights at wedlock's sacred shrine?

Mrs. Mitford *to* Dr. Mitford.

Oct. 6, 1806.

Much has been said in the public prints of the sum expended by the Mayor and Corporation of Liverpool in entertaining the Prince.[1] There is a tale in circulation here—whether it may have reached Northumberland I know not—that his royal highness asked for three things during dinner, which were not to be found amidst the innumerable profusion of delicacies which were provided for the occasion. Of the various kinds of fish the Prince chose salmon, and called for some salad to eat with it; but, to the great dismay of the mayor and aldermen, salad there was none! With that politeness for which he is so distinguished, he said it was of no consequence—a little cucumber would answer the purpose just as well; but that was no more to be obtained than the other. So, after graciously receiving the apologies of the mortified host, he called for a stand of cruets, and mixed up some oil and vinegar to eat with his fish, and the Body Corporate began a little to recover from their embarrassment, when unfortunately he asked for a glass of soda-water. This completed the climax of their distress. Had I learnt to make embellishments to plain, simple matter of fact, I might add that his worship the mayor could not sleep for three nights in consequence of his vexation, and that half the Court of Aldermen fell ill from the same cause; but my story ends with the glass of soda-water, and I shall dismiss the subject with remarking that no genteel

[1] The Prince of Wales.

family in Liverpool will in future admit salmon at their table without offering salad and cucumber to their guests at the same time, and it would not be at all wonderful if, instead of liqueurs, they should hand round soda-water at the conclusion of their great dinners, and whoever should dare to refuse it will at least not be considered as a Prince's man.

Mrs. Mitford to Miss Mitford.

Tuesday, Oct. 21, 1806.

Your letter of the 16th, my beloved, I have just received, and, encompassed as I am with all the horrors of an election before my eyes, it is the greatest cordial that can be. Nothing can exceed the madness of the people in Reading for your father's return. I own I hope his squire will keep him where he is till he bring you both back: to have you and your dear 'ittey' obliged to return with election speed such an immense journey when probably everything will be settled before you could arrive is what by no means I can reconcile myself to. Impatient as I am to embrace you both, I should apprehend a thousand ill consequences from the fatigue of so long a journey taken in such a manner.

. . . .

John, Simeon, Edward, and Dick are canvassing in all directions, and the bells are ringing most merrily; the people, men, women, and children, were standing about in all directions, and never were two poor souls so stared at as Victoire and myself as we drove through the town. I think, from the earnestness of their gazing at us, they expected to see your father pop his head out of the chaise, and I was obliged to bow on all sides to return the salutations of the multitude, though convinced no particular respect was intended me, as I could see a look of disappointment in some of their faces at seeing only two females in the carriage. Chamberlayn was assailed by inquiries when his master would be back. He stated the immense distance, and said his return was very uncertain, but they were all sure he would be back as soon as the news reached him.

Right Hon. Lord Charles Aynsley's,
    Little Harle Tower, Northumberland.

Dr. Mitford returned from Northumberland at full speed for this election, and Miss Mitford piteously complains of being left to travel back alone.

MRS. MITFORD *to* DR. MITFORD, *Richardson's Hotel, London.*

Wednesday, 4 o'clock.
Feb. 26, 1808.

I was doubtful, my dear Mitford, whether to write to you to-day or wait till we heard from you, which I hope and trust we shall to-morrow morning; but, receiving a letter from Bocking, the post determined me. Her ladyship[1] has been in a very grand bustle, as the King of France, Monsieur the Duke d'Angoulême, Duke de Berry, Duke de Grammont, and the Prince de Condé, with all the nobles that composed his majesty's suite at Gosfield, dined at the deanery last Thursday. Mr. and Mrs. Pepper (Lady Fitzgerald's daughter) were asked to meet him, because

---

[1] Lady Charles Aynsley, Miss Mitford's cousin.

she was brought up and educated at the French
Court in Louis XVI.'s reign. General and Mrs.
Milner for the same reason, and Colonel, Mrs., and
Miss Burgoyne—all the party quick at languages.
The storm alarmed Lady C. not a little; it prevented
the carrier going to town, in the first instance, and in
the second, she began to fear the king might not be
able to come, after all the preparations made for him.
The Milners were so anxious about it that the General,
who commands at Colchester, ordered five hundred
pioneers to clear the road from that city to Bocking.
On his majesty's approach the Bocking bell proclaimed
it, and, on driving up, the full military band which
Lord C. had engaged for the occasion struck up 'God
Save the King' in the entrance-passage. In his
majesty's coach were Monsieur and the Dukes d'Angoulême and Berry.   All stood till dinner was announced,
when our cousin handed his majesty—Lord C. walking before him with a candle.   The king sat at the
top of the table, with Lady C. on his right and Lord
C. on his left.   Mrs. Milner's and Mrs. Pepper's French
butlers were lent for the occasion.   The bill of fare
was in French top and bottom, and the king appeared
well pleased with his entertainment.   They were all
dressed in stars, and the insignia of different orders.
They were three hours at dinner, and at eight the
dessert was placed on the table—claret, and all kinds
of French wine, fruit, &c., a beautiful cake at the top,
with 'Vive le Roi de France' baked round it, and the
quarterings of the French army in coloured pastry,
which had a novel and pretty effect.   The three
youngest children then entered with white satin mili-

tary sashes over their shoulders painted in bronze,
' *Vive le Roi de France—Prospérité a Louis dixhuit.*'
Charles, on being asked for a toast, immediately gave
' The King of France,' which was drunk with the
utmost sensibility by all present, and one of the little
girls came up to his majesty, and, with great expression, spoke ten lines in French composed for the
occasion. Louis soon followed the ladies into the
drawing-room, when again all stood, and Lady C.
served her royal guest with coffee, which being over,
she told him that some of the neighbouring families
were come for a little dance in the dining-room, and
that perhaps his majesty would be seated to cards.
He good-humouredly said that he would first go and
pay his respects to the company in the next room,
which was the thing she wished; therefore handed
him in, his family and nobles following, which was a
fine sight for those assembled, in all sixty-two. At
the king's desire, she introduced each person to him
by name, and, on the king sitting down, the band
struck up, and Monsieur, who is supposed to be the
finest dancer in Europe, led off with Lady C., who,
spite of Lord Charles's horror and her own fears for
her lame ankle, hopped down two country dances
with him, and they were followed by Charlotte and
the Duke d'Angoulême. I have hurried over this
account from her ladyship's letter, and the Chelmsford
paper, which, having been interrupted whilst writing,
she sent at the same time.

Feb. 17, 1809.

I would not omit writing, my dearest husband, though in our still-life way nothing has occurred since I wrote to you yesterday. You would have supposed Bertram House was turned into the Hall of Criticism had you seen the number of books with which the dining-room has been bespread all the morning; in the first place, the Bible and Mrs. Trimmer's Sacred History, next Johnson's folio dictionary, Guthrie and Adams' Geographical Grammars, &c., &c. When I tell you our treasure transcribed the whole canto in the course of yesterday, though you knew she possessed the pen of a ready writer, you will allow she has outdone her usual outdoings. The notes she has left to poor Pill Garlick to transcribe, and I have not yet entered on my task, though I have been scolded divers times this blessed morning for not setting to it. Pity me, for I must grub away all the evening to get it accomplished. We have read it over three several times, and at each reading discovered new beauties. The only fault to me perhaps originates more in my family pride than that any other person might consider it as a defect, but I feel rather grieved that my illustrious relation, Lord William Russell, is, as it were, smuggled in between the old Grecians, when he might have been so conspicuous a figure on the canvass, and would have afforded, through the medium of his friends, Monmouth and Cavendish, an undeniable proof that friendship glowed with as bright an ardour in British hearts at that period as in any of the most renowned ages of antiquity. I the rather wonder that our fair friend let slip so good an opportunity for a tribute of just praise to the ancestor of the Devonshire family.

Mr. Horne, in his edition of Mrs. Barrett Browning's letters, tells us that Miss Mitford's father was 'a jovial, stick-at-nothing, fox-hunting squire of the three-bottle class," a tolerably correct description, if we substitute 'coursing' for 'fox-hunting' and 'doctor' for 'squire.' His daughter says he was the 'handsomest and cheerfulest' of men, and it appears from incidental notices that he had a keen relish for fine wine, and that indulgence in it did not invariably make him the better. Miss Mitford, no doubt, owed to him much of her natural buoyancy of spirit and some of her predilection for country pursuits and for the canine race, of which greyhounds were his favourites. Children and dogs loved him, and so did others who did not understand him, or refused to see his faults. Women have generally represented Dr. Mitford as amiable and pleasant; there was something cheering and hearty in his familiarity. The character is not uncommon; he was one of those good-looking, profligate spendthrifts who, reckless of consequences, bring misery upon their families and remain dear to their mothers and daughters. 'We often like the foolish better than the wise,' writes Miss Mitford, thinking perchance of her own fireside. The man of pleasure is generally acceptable at the moment, and, although he may be thoughtless and unjust, he is seldom calculating or severe. Dr. Mitford often did kind actions, which it is unfair to ignore; he seems even to have had some sort of generosity, and the ease with which he parted with his money was one of his most unfortunate weaknesses. But Miss Mitford's appreciation of her father was mostly due to filial devotion. Never was affection more severely tried. She had to see thousands, seventy thousand pounds, passing out of his careless hands until he became dependent upon the small pittance she could earn by arduous literary labour.

While Mrs. Mitford was making up little parties at Reading, the doctor was indulging his social proclivities in a wider field. Except to attend a coursing match, he seldom cared to visit the country,[1] but lived

---

[1] Mrs. Mitford, May 12, 1806—

'Your teal are all hearty and alive, and wash themselves twenty times a day at least; I visit them constantly to see that they are all there. The laburnums and lilacs are stealing into bloom very fast, the weeping and double-flowering cherries fully out; everything is looking very beautiful, and one of the espalier apple-trees in the garden is a perfect picture, the blossoms are so large and handsome; but I fear it will have lost all its charms before I have the happiness of showing it to you.' And in 1806 she writes:— 'Let not our darling, my dear, generous husband, betray you into an' excessive purchase on my account. You can bring no present half so valuable to me as yourself, were you to buy all the rich things the treasures of a nabob could command.' In another letter in 1808, in which she says that she is glad he went to Gosfield and had an interview with the French monarch, she adds, 'We walked to darling's (Miss Mitford's) favourite hill last night. The nightingales were singing most beautifully, and the face of the country was altogether lovely. How we wished you had been a partaker of our walk! I fear the lilacs will be rather going off before you see them; they have been very handsome; the guelder

a reckless bachelor life in London, scattering his money among gamblers[1] and 'good fellows,' and associating with Whig politicians. Even his connection with M. St. Quintin[2] proved disastrous. That gentleman, though not very proficient in his scholastic duties, was astute in financial affairs. He induced the doctor to enter into partnership with him in the coal trade, and furnished accounts of the business which would have deceived a much more cautious and scrutinizing man. Large profits were apparently being realized until the doctor refused to advance more capital, and then the whole speculation collapsed and no assets were forthcoming.

Not content with involving the doctor in these difficulties, St. Quintin introduced him to the Marquis de Chabannes, one of the Legitimist refugees of the old *régime*, who visited at Hans Place, and of whom, with their powder and puff, high heels, and fine manners, Miss Mitford gives such an exquisite description. Chabannes was descended from an ancient and illustrious family in France, had fought under the great Condé, been decorated with the Order of St. Louis, and now in exile his active mind had turned from campaigning to speculation. His plans and projects

roses are coming on very fast, and the laburnums are in the very height of their bloom.'

[1] Miss Mitford says that he was considered one of the best six players in London at piquet and whist, at which he lost large sums in St. James's Street.

[2] A French refugee. He had been secretary to the Comte de Moustiers, one of the last ambassadors of Louis XVI. to the Court of St. James.

were curious and plausible, ingenious in conception, and unfortunate in result. He had an improved method for lighting London ; but the most remarkable enterprise he engaged in was that of substituting in France our small and fast stage-coaches for the cheap and commodious diligences.

Dr. Mitford's financial connections with St. Quintin and Chabannes seemed to have commenced as early as 1805, and not to have terminated in 1820. The following correspondence is somewhat interesting and characteristic, showing the nature of these transactions, the artifice of St. Quintin, and the confidence of the doctor, not entirely destroyed even at the last :

M. St. Quintin to Dr. Mitford.

Paris, April 10, 1820.

My very dear Friend,

I deferred a few days answering your last letter in order to write to you by the opportunity of our friend Mr. Monck, who leaves Paris sooner than he expected, owing to the meeting of Parliament. It is impossible to recall to my recollection the various money transactions that have taken place between us, excepting in two instances, the first when you were in durance vile, and I got you some money on your paintings to get you out immediately, and the second when I got £50 for you under my own guarantee. I know I went several times to ask money for you, and was sent by you when you did not like to call yourself, but I know likewise that most of my applications were vain . . . You remember, of course, that I paid to Messrs. Robins £626 3s. out of the

£2,488 I received from your brother for your account. What was that sum for?

Chabannes' fate does not at all astonish me. His whole life has been a long series of imposition; by his alluring prospects held out of great profits he has taken in the longest heads and deepest calculators. I can only deplore and regret that he has so shamefully succeeded with me, who have neither a long head nor deep foresight. I do not so much regret it on account of the £800 I lose by him as on account of the much heavier sum you lose. I have had a very long conversation with your friend, Mr. Monck; we are both of opinion that you could live even in Paris at half the expense you must necessarily incur even at Reading in old Bulley's house, which I understand you are going to take. Of course, I am rather partial to your coming here with your family, and as such I am not so impartial a judge, but Mr. Monck will tell you that the Deans managed to live here very respectably with £200 per annum. Living anyhow is better than being pestered with calls from creditors. Poor Mrs. Q. says she is in heaven since she *hears*[1] no more the single knocks at the door. You have here all the English books and newspapers that you *would*[1] have in a public library at Bath or Cheltenham, and need not *lose*[1] a word of print if you do not like it. Give our best regards to Mrs. M. and our love to dear Miss Mitford, and believe me most sincerely yours,

DE ST. QUINTIN.

---

[1] These words are put in; the original is torn.

M. St. Quintin to Dr. Mitford.

Paris, May 16, 1820.

My very dear Friend,

I did not answer sooner your letter of the 13th of April last, because I was in daily expectation to hear from you in answer to the letter I gave to Mr. Monck for you, the contents of which I read and explained to him. As this has not been the case, and I have not heard a syllable from you, it behoves me to give you the information you require. I can make many allowances for your feelings and for the pressure of circumstance that weigh you down. Nobody feels more and sympathises more with you than I do. Yet there are limits to everything. And since your mind is impressed with feelings on my account that you cannot either reconcile *with friendship or integrity*, since you believe Monsieur de Chabannes, who never spoke a word of truth in his life, in preference to me, it is high time that something conclusive and definitive should be done in this unpleasant affair, for too long have I been represented to your family as the cause of your ruin, and out of mere friendship to you have I suffered this impression to remain on the minds of Mrs. and Miss Mitford, whose good opinions I always valued, and still value very highly. It is, therefore, with much pleasure I shall see your friend, to whom I shall be happy to give every information and every explanation in my power. In the meanwhile I send you the name of our adversary and the names of the attorneys, as you require it.

With best regards to the ladies, believe me, in spite of everything, most truly yours,

De St. Quintin.

Dr. Mitford *to* M. St. Quintin.

Shinfield, near Reading, June 12, 1820.

Dear Sir,

I have received both your letters : the first by my friend Monck—in answer to which I deny you have any claim against the estate of the Marquis de Chabannes, for I paid the £300 which you say you paid. Perhaps it may have escaped your memory that you wrote me from Paris a strange letter respecting this very money. I have not, however, forgotten it. You had not the means of raising that sum at that time.

I can likewise prove that you won upwards of £2,000 of General Hompesch, when you wrote me you had not ; in consequence of which you had from me upwards of £100, according to the agreement you forced upon me. If you had been paid by General Hompesch I was entitled to £300—this you know. You engaged to pay the difference of my loss with Madame Eonbleon, and I paid both principal, and, I fear, more interest than was due to her, with Mr. Corbett's bills ; and you know I am entitled to be paid my loss and expenses respecting the money you paid Mr. Corbett, which ought to have been paid to Mr. Aubery. The loss I sustained by your not paying this properly amounts to upwards of £60, and with the deposit, which you had for my brother, makes a very considerable sum.

Now I come to a very extraordinary business. In the account of Messrs. Robins I find several hundred pounds said to be paid to you ; this, of course, requires your seeing the statement. I have no knowledge of many of the sums.

I have written this in perfect temper, and am ready for any explanation: but this must take place. It is a very remarkable circumstance that you admitted before the marquis and myself, that there was property to the amount of £1,400 in dispute: you afterwards stated it at £1,200, and in your last letter you make it £1,000.　How can this be?

With kind regards to Mrs. St. Quintin—dear Mrs. St. Quintin,

I remain yours,

G. MITFORD.

P.S.—I have not to a human being stated the contents of this letter.　I will leave the whole to Monck.

M. ST. QUINTIN to DR. MITFORD.

Paris, July 21, 1820.

MY DEAR DOCTOR,

When I received your letter of June 12th, I was very ill in bed with an inflammatory fever of a dangerous nature, which was succeeded by a severe fit of the gout, from which I am not yet free.　Its perusal gave me a most painful sensation, and, therefore, I perused it but once; nor did I consider it as requiring an answer farther than obeying your injunctions of not making any compromise with the person who disputes us the £1,000.　This I have done, though much against my will.　The law must, therefore, take its course, and most likely it will be a very long, and, for a certainty, a very expensive course.　If I have stated to you that there were £1,500, not in the French funds, but in security, it was because Chabannes told me so; but I told you since this sum is reduced to 24,000 francs, which remained on the purchase of Madame de Chabannes' house in the hands of the purchaser to pay an annuity of 1,200 francs to an old priest, the old woman's confessor—by Chabannes I understood at one time that there were two old maids. This priest has now been dead one or two years ago, and I have attached the money in the hands of the purchaser, who, of course, will not pay it until the law will have decided to whom it is to be paid. The letter which Mr. Monck has delivered to you fully explains how the law stands in this respect, and what is for or against you. *How this difference can leave on your mind very unpleasant conjectures attended with feelings most acute* I am at a loss to conceive, unless you suppose that I reduced the £1,500 to £1,000, and put the rest into my pocket. But there are public law documents to prove the whole, which must convince the most incredulous. You have, you say, several hundred letters of mine: I am very glad of it, I am sure they contain nothing but the truth, or, at least, what at that time from the representations of Chabannes appeared to be the truth. I have kept but a very few letters of yours; but among them I find the copies of three important ones I wrote to you, to which I refer you as an answer to the other parts of your two last letters. One of them I wrote to you December 28, 1805, the second, September 23, 1807, and the third, November 16, with no year affixed to it, but from its contents I suppose was written in 1808 or 1809. If you have not those letters, let me know, and I shall send you copies of them.   At present I am too much pressed by the post, and I will not defer any longer my answer.

From these letters and the accounts in my hands it follows that you have embarked in that unfortunate concern £2,800, and I £700, in the whole £3,500 ; you say now that I had not then as many pence.   This may be true ; but I had above £7,000 of Mr. Slaney's money, and as you would not advance another shilling on Chabannes' account, and I had given my acceptances, I was obliged to pay them, and to re-imburse Mr. Slaney I was obliged to return him the bond he had given me for an annuity of £100 settled on my life and Mrs. St. Quintin's.   This capital, with profit and interest, has produced the large sum Chabannes owes us.   Let me see now how much you have received on account of this sum :—

First money received from France	£90
From General Hompesch on account of Chabannes ...	1,360
From Taylor's money on account of Ravelli ...	192
	¹1,842

So that within £1,000 you have received back your capital exclusive of profit and interest.   Besides, you have received for several years £50 per annum for his bond of £1,000.   After this statement, which is pretty correct, what becomes of the belief that is entertained against me that I have ruined you by this unfortunate speculation : nobody can be more sorry than I am that I should have induced you to make it.   I myself have been prevailed upon since to make two speculations, which have cost me nearly

¹ A remarkable calculation for a schoolmaster.

£10,000, and, thank God, every farthing is paid ; but I do not lay the blame on those who induced me to make them . . . . .

With best regards to Mrs. and Miss Mitford,

Believe me, my dear friend, most truly yours,

DE ST. QUINTIN.

In a final letter St. Quintin assures the doctor that he will do his best to obtain repayment from Chabannes 'by threats and persuasion, and by secret influence over his d——d heart.'

CHAPTER I.

POLITICAL FRIENDS OF DR. MITFORD—LETTERS FROM MR. SHAW LEFEVRE—POEM BY MISS MITFORD—LETTER FROM S. J. PRATT —LETTERS FROM COBBETT.

THE only advantage which seems ever to have accrued to Dr. Mitford from his extravagance and political activity was that of introducing him, and consequently his daughter, to some of the leading politicians of the day. In this manner they became acquainted with Shaw Lefevre, who lived near them at Heckfield, and represented the borough of Reading. Miss Mitford appears to have known little of this gentleman before her leaving school, but sufficient, nevertheless, to have hoped that he would preside at the race ball, where, on first coming out, she would have to dance with the steward. The doctor, who was fond—not always wisely, as I have heard— of showing off his daughter's powers of writing and recitation, sent Mr. Lefevre from time to time specimens of her poetry, to which there is some allusion in the following letters :—

C. Shaw Lefevre, M.P., *to* Dr. Mitford.

Spring Gardens, June 18, 1805.

My dear Friend,

Report, I am aware, is always busy, and has probably by this time conveyed to Bertram House a full, true, and particular account of my indisposition, with all its etceteras. Certain it is that I have had the gout for these ten days past, and that I was during a week of that time confined to my bed at Heckfield. In short, I was in a sad state during the whole of our stay there, and what added to my mortification was the impossibility of adding to the majority against Lord Melville. I do most cordially congratulate you on the event of these proceedings, highly honourable to the Opposition, and also to Lord Sidmouth's friends. The law will now take its course, and I am confident that justice will be tempered with mercy when the noble peer is brought up for judgment in the Court of King's Bench. You see, I have already concluded that he will be convicted; his own confession is enough against him. I am told he made his case much worse by his defence.

As to your noble friend, the D—— of A——, I hear most serious arguments against his claim; but he has so many votes with him that I suppose he will succeed. The canvass in his favour is irresistible. He has all the ladies of fashion in town on his side, and they leave nothing unturned upon this occasion.

We have little prospect of getting to Heckfield for these next six weeks, and then only with room for half our family; we shall, however, have the use of

the kitchen, and hope you and the ladies will partici-
pate with us in beans and bacon.   As to ragouts, &c.,
they must be postponed till we entirely open house
again.   Give our kindest regards, and tell Miss M.
that I hope she is not idle at this sweet season for
poesy.   The muses are never more propitious than in
spring.   If you come to town, let me know before-
hand.

Yours most sincerely,
C. SHAW LEFEVRE.

C. SHAW LEFEVRE *to* GEORGE MITFORD, Esq., *Bertram House.*

House of Commons, July 2, 1806.

MY DEAR FRIEND,

I forwarded your letter to Mr. Ogle yesterday,
and will execute any other commission for you in
return for the exquisite lines you enclosed on Mrs.
Mitford's birthday.   Mrs. L. and my wife are delighted with them, and I really think they surpass all Miss
M.'s former productions.

I hope very soon to thank her in person for them ;
at present I have work enough here till our assizes,
though some holidays ought to intervene.   In the
city everything to-day is peace.   Mr. Fox is certainly
better, but his case is said to be alarming.   Excuse
haste.

Yours most sincerely,
C. SHAW LEFEVRE.

The poem referred to in the above letter was the
following :—

To my dearest Mamma on her Birthday.

Hail, lovely June! thy genial suns
  With plenty crown the smiling land,
The rip'ning fruits their treasures yield,
  The beauteous blossoms wide expand.

Fair are the flow'rets Maia boasts,
  'The primrose pale, the violet blue,'
But none can match thy lovely rose
  Bright sparkling with the morning dew.

Yet not thy brilliant rose, sweet June;
  Thy lily fair, thy cistus gay,
Would ever deck my humble song,
  Or ever tempt my native lay.

But my lov'd mother's natal day,
  This dear, this blooming month has blest,
And all its soft, its genial pow'rs
  Are centred in her glowing breast.

Vain were the task her mind to paint,
  Her modest, timid genius tell ;
Vain were the task to paint that heart,
  Where the sweet female virtues dwell.

Yet grant, ye heavenly powers, my prayer!
  May bliss in that dear heart still live,
And may she in December's gloom
  Taste ev'ry pleasure June can give !

M. R. M.

The following letter is from a man who was opposed to Dr. Mitford in politics, but was a favourite poet with his daughter in her girlish days.[1] Originally a bookseller at Bath, Samuel Jackson Pratt first attracted notice by a poem entitled 'The Tears of

---

[1] Speaking of Pratt's 'Contrast,' she writes: 'The poetry is good, the politics are execrable.'

Genius, occasioned by the death of Doctor Gold-
smith,' and he endeavoured to imitate the style of
that celebrated author.   He published 'Gleanings'
and many other works, and preceded Southey as
Laureate.   But his name is little known at the present time, and many contemporary critics spoke lightly
of 'the Gleaner.'

S. J. Pratt to Dr. Mitford.

10, Tottenham Court New Road,
Jan. 4, 1806.

Dear Sir,

Nothing but the dread I feel of hazarding the
appearance of neglecting those to whom I owe respect and gratitude could induce me to take up
the pen for any purposes unconnected with the
solemn offices which I have been lately called on to
perform consequent on the death of Mrs. Pratt, whom
I had a few days before her illness gratulated on a
redundance of health I neither ever did, nor ever shall,
enjoy.   We have long been separated for inevitable
reasons, as to mere personal intercourse, but we have
for upwards of twenty years exchanged the most
cordial and confidential amity, both as a habit and a
principle.   We were gladdened to visit, converse
with, and consult each other ; and I am now consoled
only by reflecting that attention to the sick-chamber,
the last pressure of the hand, the latest direction of
the will, and the last collected expression of kind
remembrance, were given to myself.   I remember
among my consolements, also, that to me and a
dear female relative, Cordelia Skules—the lady who
wrote in 'Gleanings' and 'Harvest Home' under the

signature of a Sibyl—devolved the last duties when life was no more.

This communication will, I am persuaded, be to you, as it must be to a great many other friends, a sufficient explanation for delays which were unavoidable ; and I do assure you, dear sir, nothing short of such a cause could have withheld me from pouring forth the sensibility of my heart for the very lovely verses your amiable and ingenious daughter has offered to my muse. Thank and bless her for them, and may her talents and virtues be long a blessedness to you and to all who partake her duty or her love ! With this prayer, which I do assure you is one of ' earnest heart,' I subscribe myself, dear sir, her and your obliged and devoted servant,

S. J. PRATT.

Dr. Mitford's friendship with the celebrated William Cobbett commenced at a coursing match,[1] and was increased by the doctor's appreciation of the Olympic games established by Mr. Cobbett at Botley. There was also much political sympathy between them, and the families eventually stayed on visits at each others' houses. Cobbett's letters reflect his character. On one side we see the ardent lover of the country, the sportsman, and horticulturist ; on the other the political

---

[1] Dr. Mitford met Cobbett while on a coursing expedition near Alton, gave him a greyhound, and invited him to another coursing meeting near Reading. The Mitfords were introduced to a variety of company at Cobbett's house, ' from the earl and countess to the farmer.' Miss Mitford gives an amusing account of an encounter at Cobbett's between Mrs. Mitford and a lady to whom the doctor had once been engaged.

D 2

combatant, the giant wielding the club, and dealing heavy blows upon his antagonists. It will be best to give his letters without omissions, so as to retain all the force of his style, and the characteristics of the period in which he lived.

WM. COBBETT to DR. MITFORD.

Botley, November 17, 1807.

MY DEAR FRIEND,

To go to Hilsley will, I foresee, be impossible for me, unless I most shamefully neglect my most important concerns; namely, those of planting. The keeping off of the frosts kept the leaves so long on that I have not been able to stir a plant until within these two days; and at the very soonest I shall not be able to get done what I must see done before the end of this month. I need not say how much it vexes me; but so it is, and I cannot help it. If I were to neglect this most essential concern, I should never forgive myself. To give you a specimen of my seriousness in these matters: I stopped at Ludgershall, in the rain too, to gather the seed of an ash-tree (the only one with seed that I have been able to find this year); and, after much difficulty, did, with the aid of the parson's ladder, fill a sack full, which sack I tied before our knees upon the gig, and thus we took it to Botley, to the no small amusement of those who saw us pass, and to my great satisfaction; for I can even now hear of no ash-tree in the country which has borne seed this year. After having taken so much pains with my plants, I cannot bring myself to risk the loss of them, and therefore I hope you will

consider my absence from Hilsley as absolutely unavoidable . . . . Mrs. Cobbett and Nancy join me in
affectionate remembrances to Mrs. and Miss Mitford.
God bless you.

WM. COBBETT.

WM. COBBETT *to* DR. MITFORD.

Botley, December 13, 1807.

MY DEAR FRIEND,

My wife is much better, but is not well . . . .
Give me some news about dogs. D——n politics! Is
Snip with pup yet? a matter of far more importance
than whether the Prince of Asturias be hanged or
not; or whether his silly father be in a madhouse; or
what grenadier is the gallant of his old punk of a
mother. We are well set to work truly, to pester our
brains about these rogues! It matters not a straw to
us whether Napoleon hang them all, or send them
a-begging. And as to our fellows at Whitehall and
Westminster, we shall be sure to do right if we hate
them all. Lefevre indeed, as far as the spaniels go,
is of some importance; and, though he has played
you foul, I hope he will live till we have got that
more valuable part of the creation out of his hands.

Miss Mitford, you owe Nancy a letter, and she is
not of a vein to suffer herself to be defrauded with
impunity. So pray make haste and pay her. Let it
be a letter about all manner of things but politicians
and fashions, which are the silliest things now going.

When I send about dogs (which are always the
main subject) I will send you some seeds by way of
episode. God bless you.

WM. COBBETT.

Wm. Cobbett *to* Dr. Mitford.

Botley, January 13, 1808.

My dear Friend,

I cannot indeed imagine how the letter should have miscarried. I shall get rid of three at least of my dogs, and shall be ready to receive, with many thanks, those which your goodness intends for me; but of those which already exist, give me leave to say that it will be very desirable (if attended with no inconvenience) that they should have the distemper first. The spaniels I should very much like to have; but I will put up with the want most cheerfully rather than subject you to anything disagreeable in the obtaining of them. I was extremely sorry to hear of Mr. Webb's misfortune: and, when poor Nancy heard that the beautiful blue bitch was amongst the dead, she could hardly refrain from crying.

I have been frequently out; but our sport has not frequently been good. I wish you and Mrs. and Miss Mitford a happy New Year, and in this wish I am cordially joined by my wife, and daughter, and boys. James always hears what you say of him, and always spreads your fame amongst those who do not know you, and to whom he prattles. As far as I can now judge, he will be just such another fellow as myself; and, were it not too much to indulge the hope of, I would fain flatter myself that he will cause the *Register* to live when the first author of it shall mingle with his native dust. As we proceed in life, the objects of our pursuits and our enjoyments change; the change proceeds as we proceed towards the grave; and, even in our last moments, there is, in general, something to comfort us. Yet do the mass of mankind talk of the Author of this wise scheme as if he were no better and no greater than a partial politician. Poor James has led me into this digression, who is now at the other end of the table, making scratches upon paper, which he calls 'drawing,' quite unconscious. Nancy has received Miss Mitford's letter, which she will answer very soon. I know not when we shall stir from this place; for, as to London, I hate it with a fervency equal to that of Saint Francis towards the devil.

I remain always most faithfully yours,

WM. COBBETT.

WM. COBBETT *to* DR. MITFORD.

Botley, May 13, 1808.

MY DEAR FRIEND,

I thank you for your letters, and beg you will excuse my not answering them sooner. The truth is I have been so constantly engaged between my *Register* and my timber cutting that I have not had a moment to spare. I have succeeded in shutting up my footway, and I have now one hundred and fifty acres of woods and corn-fields, into which no one but myself has a right to enter. The water bounds it on two sides, the Titchfield Road on one side, and I can easily make an impassable fence on the fourth. Here I will, if I live, have a stock of hares and pheasants. The timber will be cleared out, and all will be as tranquil as possible. I shall this fall have my labourers' cottages here and there all round it, and I will not suffer man or dog to enter for the purpose of sporting till I have well stocked it. The rest of my land on the other side of the Titchfield Road (now about two hundred and fifty-six acres) I will sport upon, and it, which consists two-thirds of covers, will soon be well stocked too. There will be no coursing amongst these coppices; but it will be pleasant to have plenty of hares; and I daresay I shall get some one to give me a few brace of young ones .... If Snip be ready, I will send for her, with my best thanks to Miss Mitford, for whose sake I will take particular care of her. In a parcel to the care of Mr. Wright (with directions to send it to you immediately) I this day send some Indian corn. It must be sown in pots, in a hot-bed, two seeds in a pot, suffered to get four inches high, and then be planted out at four feet asunder, in good ground and a warm situation .... We are very sorry to hear of the death of a friend; but you and I must be clay again, and it is useless to repine. While life lasts, however, let us be kind to one another, and amongst the objects of our kindness we beg you to be assured that there are very few indeed that have the precedence of you and Mrs. and Miss Mitford.

Yours faithfully,
Wm. Cobbett.

P.S.—I am flattered by what you say about my *public letter.* Nothing was ever more *read,* I believe; and I am not without hope that it will produce some effect. I may be a very illiterate fellow; but I certainly am more than a match for all those pretenders to learning and philosophy. There is a damned cant in vogue, which, when attacked by plain sense and reason, discovers its weakness.

The commencement of the following letter refers to a visit the Mitfords were about to pay at Botley.

Wm. Cobbett *to* Dr. Mitford.

Botley, August 29, 1808.

My dear Friend,

Be it then on the 19th of September; but on one account I regret the postponement, and that is, that we shall have little or no Indian corn or melons which we have had and have now in an abundance so great, or to make it a shame for us not to have made some money of the latter. I have actually cut one hundred and twenty pounds' weight of melons. Those remaining would weigh nearly as much, and the corn is full as fine as ever I saw in Pennsylvania. The summer has been fine, to be sure, but I verily believe that my mode of culture, and my man Robinson's surpass all modes and all men in this kingdom. The pheasants are all well, both nids, and I have great hopes of success in stocking my woods.

The two Yorkshire pups are completely recovered and doing exceedingly well. If the one comes from Northumberland, I shall be glad to have it; but beyond that (except the two pups of Fawn) I have no desire for more dogs of any sort, and have only to thank you for your new and obliging offers. I care little about the colour of the dog puppy. Choose you for me. They must be good, be their colour what it may. I will try the yeast when the hour of necessity comes. Well, we saw Fonthill, but, even if I had the talent to do justice to it in a written description, ten such sheets as this would not suffice for the purpose. When I see you, I will at times give you an hour's account of it. After that sight, all sights become mean until that be out of the mind. We both thought Wardour the finest place we had ever seen, but Wardour makes but a single glade in Beckford's immense grounds and plantations. The grass walks at Fonthill, fifteen feet wide, if stretched out in a right line, would reach from there to London, upwards of ninety miles; there are sixty-five men and ten horses constantly employed in the pleasure-grounds, a thousand acres of which, being the interior and more private part, are enclosed with a wall of squared stone from ten to twelve feet high, with an oak palisade at top pointed with iron. Scarcely any soul is permitted to enter here, and, from what we had heard, we had not the least expectation of it; but Johnstone insisted that, if I wrote a note, we should get admittance, and we did. But not to see the house, which no one as yet has seen the inside of. The outside we approached very near, and, like the rest, it sets description at defiance.

After all give me Fairthorn, and the hares, and the pheasants when I can get them. *Apropos* of the hares, when I read the account of poor Lord Clanricarde's death, 'There, said I, expired the hares of that country.' I have met Poulter (whose name should receive the addition of an *er*) who, you know, is a parson, brother-in-law of the bishop, prebendary of Winchester, rector of four parishes united into two, a chaplain of the bishop, a commissioner of taxes, and a justice of the peace. But you know him. This fellow met me as I was coming from Robinson's (whose poor wife is very ill indeed), and he spake me thus: 'Mr. Cobbett, I am happy to meet you. I was just telling the farmer (a sly-looking fellow who was with him) that of the two manors of Eaton and Stoke (adjoining that of Warnford), myself and Sir Thomas Champneys (a famous cuckold) have now got the deputations from the Chapter of the college in consequence of the death of Lord Clanricarde, who kept them unjustifiably to himself. And we mean that that tyranny shall no longer be exercised, but that any gentleman or farmer shall take their pleasure upon them when they please.' Oh, d——d Levite! thought I to myself, so you would fain persuade me that I shall have better sport when the farmers have killed the hares, and you have stuffed your hoggish parson's guts with them than I had when they were preserved and when the whole neighbourhood was stocked with them by my Lord Clanricarde? I was a base dog for not telling him this; but my wife was with me, and the thing was sudden. I leave you to guess (the manor of Warnford being closely circumscribed by these manors) what a chance the poor hares will now stand. By the 1st of October there will not be a brace left alive in these manors, and then, there being no one at Warnford House, rush they go, the pot-hunting crew, into that manor, and the hares will be heard squeaking like rats on the breaking up of a wheat-mow. Oh, d——d prebendary! thy maw will now be crammed, and sportsmen may hunger and thirst over the barren downs. What a base dog to curry favour with the rascally curmud-geons of farmers by these means!

This is truly an unfortunate event. Nobody will feel the effects of it more than I shall. Robinson will feel it too, but not so severely as I shall. Do you know the proprietor of *Crawley?* That is a fair place, and plenty of hares are within reach of us when you come. A couple or three days there are worth a month elsewhere. Cannot you get leave for High-clere? If so, we could have a good day or two there, at any rate. Mrs. Cobbett begs the ladies to accept her kindest regards, to which you will please to add those of

Your faithful and most obedient servant,

WM. COBBETT.

WM. COBBETT *to* DR. MITFORD.

Botley, October 10, 1808.

MY DEAR FRIEND,

This is a letter of *deaths*. The pup from York-shire, the smallest of Cox's spaniels, and the three you bought me last are *all dead*, in spite of care and pains infinite. I do assure you that I am absolutely unable to encounter the chance of seeing this misery and suffering again. The piteous looks of the poor little things pierced my very heart. Another puppy under four or five months old I will never have again as long as I live. If you have got the spaniel dog puppy for me, and will be so good as to put it to anyone to keep, I will gladly pay for it; I mind no expense, but upon my soul I cannot bear the anxiety and mortifi-cation. It is really making a positive addition to the miseries of life. The pain outweighs the prospect of pleasure, and oh! how many times, while the poor little, tender things were moaning, did I reproach myself with being the cause of their unmerited sufferings. We have *no right* thus to punish any living creature. How is Miss Mitford's *eye?* We are very anxious to know, and pray most heartily that ere this it may be well. I do hope that you will all come as soon as it is recovered. Though we shall no longer have a warm *sun*, I showed you ample means of having a warm *fire*, and you will have something still more cheering, as warm a welcome as heart ever gave. God bless you.

WM. COBBETT.

WM. COBBETT *to* DR. MITFORD.

Botley, October 16, 1808.

MY DEAR FRIEND,

I was yesterday at Winchester, where I learned, with some surprise, that there was a requisition going on for a meeting, on the part of Sir Thomas Miller and others of a pretty good stamp. Lord Folkestone will be at your meeting, and I hope you will carry the thing with a high hand. The king's answer to the address of the Londoners is the most insolent thing of the kind that any King of England ever did. But do not they deserve it? Ay, that they do. He has three hundred thousand red coats to keep us down. Why should such a king be at all delicate? As long as the Londoners flattered him it was all very well; but the moment they attempted to advise, they got a good snap. Well, we deserve it, and ten thousand times more at his hands. The nation is a base, rascally crew, and he knows it. Has he not three million of droits of Admiralty now in his pouch? Has he not done act upon act that I need not point out to you? Is he not exempted from the Income Tax? Well, then, who can blame him? Snails should be trod upon. Smash them, old fellow, they deserve it all. Ay, and they will love you the better, too. Oh, what a base and degenerate nation! Do you feel any great anxiety about the result of this war for Ferdinand? I do not, and do not care which way it goes. I said from the very first that our people dreaded nothing so much as to see freedom establish-ed in Spain. We are now fighting against freedom as much as we are against Buonaparte. We are taking a part in the war with a view of preventing the *people* of Spain from giving an example to the *people* of England. This is the real motive. All the rest is sham. We are spending our money and our blood for the old race of kings against the people. We deserve to be treated like dogs, and like dogs we are treated. Adieu.

Faithfully yours,
WM. COBBETT.

WM. COBBETT *to* DR. MITFORD.

Botley, November 8, 1808.

MY DEAR FRIEND,

By heaven, I cannot leave here! This is the very time when my exertions are most wanted, and though this base nation has no fair claims upon any exertions of mine, or of any other disinterested man, I cannot go a-coursing and see the people cheated and abused without an effort to open their eyes. The Court of Inquiry is the greatest of all humbugs, and I must endeavour to make it seem what it is.

Adieu.

WM. COBBETT.

WM. COBBETT *to* DR. MITFORD.

Botley, January 22, 1809.

MY DEAR FRIEND,

I have waited to be able to give you certain intelligence of our movements.

26th.　We go to Oxford.

27th.　Remain there.

28th.　Call at your house, and perhaps sleep.

29th.　Return to Botley.

Depend upon nothing as to time of day. A dish of tea will always do for my wife, and a hunch of bread and cheese for me.

I *feed* my wild pheasants in the woods. Shall I get the pied ones? Our kindest respects to Mrs. and Miss Mitford. God bless you and damn the minister.

WM. COBBETT.

WM. COBBETT *to* DR. MITFORD.

Botley, March 16, 1809.

MY DEAR FRIEND,

I shall be delighted to see the dogs in a picture, but as to you, I like better to have you in a ' tangible shape.'　.　.　.　.

I send by the man:

Eighteen Chinese roses.

Four tree carnations.

Twenty white pinks.

Twenty pheasant-eyed pinks.

They must all be put in rich soil, mixed up with some rotten dung, and in a good aspect. The pinks are the finest by far that I ever saw. I had several of the latter that measured, when put on a card, four inches over; but, to keep them to their size and beauty, they must be piped every year . . . . .

The duke will go notwithstanding the powers of corruption. Indeed, to send him going is the only chance that corruption has left. It is a strange scene! Coke's speech is the best of all. I thought he was too far gone in the whiggism to be worth a farthing. I have worked like a horse at this affair. If the cause does not triumph, it will not be my fault. I shall owe the duke nothing, at any rate.

I am sincerely yours,
WM. COBBETT.

WM. COBBETT *to* DR. MITFORD.

Botley, January 7, 1810.

MY DEAR FRIEND,

Your letter of yesterday is greatly important to me. If you have occasion to write to me again on the same subject do not write your friend's name at full length; and, indeed, if you say, 'my friend,' it will be better than putting even the initial; for the damned rascals see all our letters inside as well as out; or, at least, they have the power of doing it. I propose going to London in the last week of this month, when of course I shall remain there until the thing is over. Write me a line to say whether you shall then be in town. Your being there will be a most agreeable thing to me, besides the real important service it may be of. Mark well! Say nothing about the matter anywhere. The success of all our preparatory measures depends almost entirely upon our being close. All that truth wants is fair play, and I hope we shall get that. I beg my kindest regards at home, and am sincerely yours,

WM. COBBETT.

WM. COBBETT *to* MISS MITFORD, *Bertram House, Reading.*

London, March 18, 1810.

MY DEAR MISS MITFORD,

Your good and kind father has just given Nancy a copy of a little volume of poems, in which I find the verses on Maria's winning the cup at Ilsley inscribed to me, and for which honour I beg you to accept of my best thanks; an honour which I value the more because these verses are in company with those elegant and truly pathetic strains, addressed to your dear mother, which, unlike most other poetical effusions of praise, contain nothing but what is founded in truth.

Mrs. Cobbett joins me in kindest remembrances to Mrs. Mitford, and she begs to be as kindly remembered to you. My prose-writing daughter will thank you for herself in her own way.

I am your faithful friend,
And most obedient servant,
WM. COBBETT.

Miss Mitford speaks of Cobbett as 'a tall, stout

man, fair and sunburnt, with a bright smile, and an air compounded of the soldier and the farmer, to which his habit of wearing an eternal red waistcoat contributed not a little.' Some of the reviewers twitted her on her admiration for him, and said she derived it from her father. This she jealously denied. In politics she was no doubt led by her surroundings, but Cobbett's love of animals and of country life would always have awakened her sympathy, even if he had not been a man of genius.

A dispute between Mr. Cobbett and another gentleman, in which Dr. Mitford became involved, separated the families. Miss Mitford nevertheless continued to admire his talents, though admitting his violence, and spoke highly of his endearing domestic qualities. 'Milder thoughts attend him,' she writes; 'he has my good wishes, and so have his family, who were, and I daresay are, very amiable, particularly his very plain, but very clever and very charming eldest daughter.' This lady is still alive, and retains all the qualities attributed to her by Miss Mitford except the first.

CHAPTER II.

WE now begin to lose sight of Dr. Mitford and his political importance, while the talent of his daughter becomes more conspicuous. From her early years he had endeavoured to awaken an interest in her, and, much against her will, to exhibit her as a sort of infant prodigy. Now, when his extravagance was producing its results, and the sinews for party warfare were failing him, he sought to obtain consideration, if not fortune, by means of her poetical gifts. Almost the only persons of distinction with whom he henceforth corresponds, though not himself a man of study, are authors and editors, and the subjects of discussion are the merits of his daughter's literary compositions.

S. J. PRATT to DR. MITFORD.

10, Tottenham Court New Road,
October 2, 1810.

DEAR SIR,

Your kind present came at the end of a long

illness, and of more than as long deep application in preparing for the press my forthcoming poem (the last of length I shall ever offer to the public) on the deeply interesting subject of Lord Erskine's Bill and 'speech' to prevent wanton cruelty to animals; and in course of the notes I have taken occasion to illustrate the arguments, or rather the descriptions, by a quotation from your neighbour Dr. B——'s excellent sermon on bull-baiting.

Your daughter's very amiable and interesting book is quite a refreshment to my spirit, wearied on the one hand by labour and on the other by pain; for it would be in vain to tell you how I have occupied my mind on the before-mentioned theme, and this was the very volume to lead me sweetly and softly from myself to many charming scenes, conducted by the hand of virtue and genius. Where all are amiable, it is hard to select, but the poem addressed to yourself (page 70), and that part of the 'Epistle to a Friend' which continues the subject beginning with the line, 'How true the wish, how pure the glow,' to the end of the passage, went nearest to my affections.

And now I want to interest your benevolence and repay your bounty by making you acquainted with the specimens of a most extraordinary young man, who is author of the accompanying volume of poetic specimens, which I have edited. Dr. Valpy, who thinks very highly of him, contributes his guinea, but I wish you to withhold yours till you have seen, read, marked, and understood their merits. I told you some of the truly affecting points that attach to the very interesting and, I fear, dying young bard, who has been the object of my tender and alas! unavailing care for near a twelvemonth, and is meeting honour and golden opinions from all sorts of people, and everything but health, which is worth them all. My illness and literary occupations have thrown me deeply in arrears of engagement for most of the present week, and towards its close I am going for change of air to my friend Mr. Dallas's and some other families in Chelsea; but I will assuredly make my first long walk in the course of that time to Mount Street, in the neighbourhood of which I owe almost as many visits as a fair lady after an accouchement—with whom, indeed, I assimilate just now, as my muse has recently been delivered, and I ardently hope, for the sake of my poor brutes whose cause I advocate, it will not be a labour in vain . . . . . Requesting you will express my sensibility of Miss Mitford's goodness to me, I am, dear sir,

Your obliged and obedient,

S. J. PRATT.

REV. J. MITFORD to DR. MITFORD.

Benhall Parsonage, Saxmundham,
February 4, 1811.

SIR,

I beg leave to acknowledge the receipt of a volume of poems which Messrs. Longman transmitted to me a few days since, and for which I am indebted to your politeness. I have been very much pleased with Miss Mitford's poems generally, and many passages I think excellent. In particular I was delighted to see her muse busy in Northumberland, the

scenery of which in many parts is well worthy of a
poet. The counties near London are now become
almost its suburbs, a circumstance which is of considerable disadvantage to some of our old poets, particularly to Thomson and Akenside, whose favourite
spot was Richmond Hill—a place that will not, I
suppose, be again celebrated in verse till the revival
of the City Laureateship. Miss Mitford seems peculiarly to excel in descriptive poetry, which, after all,
is the poetry that pleases most and clings closest to
the mind. For myself, I would give whole pages of
Dryden and Young for one of Milton or of Cowper.

I beg my best wishes for Miss Mitford's success,
and if anything should lead you or your family to
Suffolk, I hope you will do me the favour of not forgetting my address.

I am, sir,

Your obedient servant,

J. MITFORD.[1]

The Mr. Davenport who indited the letters[2] next in
order was a prolific author, wrote a continuation of
' Mitford's History of Greece,' a ' History of Biography,'

[1] This gentleman, the Rev. J. Mitford, was a cousin of Miss
Mitford and a literary man. He wrote a volume of poetry, and
contributed the lives of the English poets to the Aldine edition.
Several classical works in the British Museum are enriched by
his MS. notes. In the ' Village of Palaces ' there is an interesting
account by him of old-fashioned gardens. Strange to say, he
wrote in the *Quarterly* an unfavourable critique on Miss Mitford's
poems.

[2] Mr. Davenport's letters are beautiful specimens of caligraphy,
being written in a clear, minute, round hand worthy of an
engraver.

and other works. He was also the editor of an inter-
mittent periodical called the 'Poetical Register.' Dr.
Mitford generally carried about in his pocket a bundle
of his daughter's poems for the benefit of friends or
chance acquaintances, and certainly took every opportunity of producing them, though her statement that
his ' charming·manner' was their principal recommendation must have been a fond delusion. In this
way Mr. Davenport became acquainted with Miss
Mitford's poetical talent, and he determined to make
use of it to brighten the pages of his 'Register,'
which, although supported by such names as Scott,
Moore, and Milman, was somewhat insipid and uninteresting. It was tinged with classical pedantry,
and abounded with lackadaisical sonnets, in which
mournful swains apostrophized their mistresses under
such titles as Chloe and Myra; but it was not un-
favourably received in its day.

R. A. DAVENPORT to MISS MITFORD.

Twickenham Common, January 17, 1811.

DEAR MADAM,

It has been said by some snarling cynics that
ladies have a propensity to indulge fears which have
no foundation. I do not give my assent to this libel
upon the sex; but, if I did, I should certainly quote
you as a proof of its justice. You tell me that you
fear the size of your packet is calculated to make me
repent of my request. Now, never was there any fear
(from the first moment when fear was expressed down
to the present moment) which was more completely
groundless. The plain proof of its being so will be

the appearance of all your pieces in my seventh volume. I shall not find it 'expedient to throw' a single one of them 'on the fire.'

I ordered Rivingtons to send Dr. Mitford a copy of the last volume, and I understand they have sent it. I will now give you, as far as I know them, the names of the anonymous contributors.

I believe you are aware that in all cases the letters R. A. D. are the initials of an inveterate scribbler of the name of Davenport . . . . . 'Moderate Wishes,' page 139—very moderate wishes indeed! This poem is by Mr. Hodgson,[1] translator of 'Juvenal,' and author of 'St. Edgar,' 'Lady Jane Grey,' &c. The epigram in page 160 is not from 'Montreuil,' but from 'De Cailly.' Sonnet, page 182, is addressed to the eternal pamphleteer and fingerer of the public money, John Bowles. 'Why did not you put his name, sir?' 'Because, madam, in this country truth is a libel!' Ode, page 252, I believe is by the Rev. J. Owen, of Fulham. 'Address to Poverty,' page 264, is either by C. Lloyd or C. Lamb. 'Mortality,' page 275, and the 'Death of Joshua,' page 475, signed S. F. are, I rather think, two of Southey's early pieces. Ode, page 304, by Mr. Courtier, author of the 'Pleasures of Solitude'. . . . 'The Golden Age' is by the Rev. Dr. Laurence, brother of the late Dr. Laurence.

I have now given you all the names with which I am acquainted. You will find that not many of the correspondents of the sixth volume remain anonymous.

I am, dear madam, with respect and esteem,

Your obedient servant,

R. A. DAVENPORT.

[1] Byron's friend, and afterwards Provost of Eton.

R. A. DAVENPORT *to* DR. MITFORD.

Twickenham Common, March 20, 1811.

MY DEAR SIR,

I may say to you as Falstaff says to mine hostess Quickly, ' One knows not where to take you.' Twice within these five weeks I have been in town, but without being able to find you. Yesterday was the second time of my visiting London. At Russell Street they told me that you had not been in London for the last fortnight; at the Mount the waiter first told me precisely the same story, and then retracted, and said that you were in town, and that he expected to see you in the evening. ' Who shall decide when waiters disagree ?'

At Rivingtons, during their absence at dinner, I yesterday found a packet and kind note to me dated Monday evening; but whether last Monday, or the Monday before, or the Monday before that, ' this deponent saith not.' You will see that your packet left me as much in the dark as ever with respect to the question of your being, or not being, in London. The Rivingtons not being visible, I could get no supplementary information upon the subject. By-the-by, if you wish me to receive within a century anything which you may have to forward to me, never send it to the good folks in St. Paul's Church-yard. I may say with much truth, ' Carelessness, thy name is Rivington.' In spite of a thousand entreaties to have my letters immediately forwarded, I yesterday found in St. Paul's Churchyard no less than five letters buried, and (like dead friends) forgotten among a pile of old bills, orders, &c., &c., in Rivington's counting-house.

Many thanks for the composition signed 'Arion.' You tell me I must not give the name. At present there does not appear that there is any probability of my giving it; and for this irrefragable reason that you have taken good care that I shall not. Fielding, in 'Jonathan Wild,' speaking of a jailor, says, 'He, first barring and locking the door, took his prisoner's word that he would not go forth.' You have locked and barred the door; you have not told me the name of the author.

I have just written to Miss Mitford to thank her for her kindness in sending Dr. Russell's poems, with which I was much gratified, and which I shall certainly insert in my next volume .... How goes on 'Christina'? I have not heard a single syllable respecting the lady. I hope the paper-maker, printer, &c., are strenuously exerting themselves to usher her into the view, and consequently the admiration, of the public.

I should have made more attempts to see you, but alas! I have been miserably bound down to my desk, whenever I could sit at it; and have, moreover, been exceedingly ill. I am not now well. A literary man has great occasion to study the Book of Job.

I am, dear Sir, truly yours,
R. A. DAVENPORT.

The following letter is that above alluded to, in

which he thanks Miss Mitford for sending him some
of her grandfather's[1] verses.

R. A. DAVENPORT *to* MISS MITFORD.

Twickenham Common, March 20, 1811.

DEAR MADAM,

Dr. Russell's verses are very highly welcomed.
I like them very much. There is great simplicity,
neatness, and elegance in them. The whole of what
you have sent me will find a place in my next volume.
I hope that the fund is not exhausted. If not for my
seventh, at least for my eighth volume I mean to take
the liberty of drawing on the poetical bank of Russell
and Mitford, and my experience of your kindness tells
me that my drafts will be honoured. There is, at
all events, one partner in that bank whose poetical
funds are inexhaustible.

.　　.　　.　　.　　.　　.　　.　　.　.　.

There is a story told of a little stunted Italian,
much, I suppose, about my own age, who, finding
some difficulty in mounting his horse, prayed to Our
Lady to help him. Having put up his prayer, he
made such a vigorous leap that he went *over* the
horse, and saluted the ground on the other side.
When he got up, he shook himself, and exclaimed,
' By Jove! Our Lady has helped me *too much*.' But

---

[1] This Dr. Russell was the man who penned the fanciful proposal of marriage which appears at the commencement of ' The
Life of Mary Russell Mitford.' From a portrait in the possession
of the editor, it would seem probable that his personal appearance
may have recommended his suit. He was a student of Christ
Church.

now I think I hear you say, ' Well, sir, what does this silly story mean? How do you intend to apply it?' Have patience a moment, my dear madam (patience is a female virtue); have a moment's patience, and you shall know. You have expressed a hope that in the next volume of the P. R. you may meet with the name of a certain rhymer quite as frequently as you did in the last. Now I really think that, when the next volume makes its appearance, you will find yourself in a similar situation with the before-cited Italian. You do not know what you will have to encounter. Besides all the little scrub poems meant to fill gaps, you will find a mortal long epistle, three hundred lines, partly descriptive, partly satirical. Is it not time for you to repent of your unwise hopes, and to exclaim in the words of the poet, ' Prayers heard in vengeance by the angry skies?'

To use a familiar phrase, I have a crow to pluck with you. In your beautiful lines on the death of Sir John Moore, there is *one* line which grates discord, not upon my ear, but upon my mind. You speak of the ' slaughtered victims of *degenerate* Spain.' Against the justice, or rather the injustice of this line, I must, my dear madam, enter my strongest protest. It is impossible for me to admit your charge against the Spaniards. Perhaps I am now biased by a long established prejudice in their favour. I confess that I have long esteemed them for their firmness, their sedateness, their generosity, their honourable scorn of meanness and insincerity. Even their faults have grown out of virtues. The very pride with which they are reproached is the noble failing of a high mind brooding, with a melancholy satisfaction, over the remembrance of happier days and departed glories, which,

'Lost in its *own*, reverts to *former* days.'

Never did a Spaniard descend to deal in that fawning insincerity, that smiling ruin, which degrades the character of his Gallic neighbours; never could it be said of him, as of them, that

'Bid him go to hell, to hell he goes.'

It is the curse of party that it destroys all candour, all generous sentiment. A party man will allow no merit in any individual belonging to the hostile party. I have often smiled in scorn on reading the attacks of the newspaper oracles of Queen Anne's time upon the great Duke of Marlborough. Those actions and conquests of which we are now so proud, they represented as trifles unworthy of notice. When, under the eyes of the French army, he reduced the fortress of Bouchain, they declared that he had done little more than conquer a pigeon-house. Party is still the same! My prejudices are against the Wellesley family, but I must say that our opposition papers have behaved with a scandalous want of justice to Lord Wellington, who, in my poor judgment, has manifested a high degree of military talent.

I shall break off now. Mercy on us! On looking back I perceive that I have positively written a whole volume of dry, dull politics. Well! so much the better. It is a very wise provision of Providence that every fault produces, in one way or other, its own punishment. You have done wrong to my favourite Spaniards, and what is the consequence?

that you are punished by a tedious letter of remon-
strance. Punishment enough, in all conscience!
May it induce you to come forward with a palinode!
I shall be truly happy to hear a lyre worthy of the
subject sounding the praise of Spanish patriotism.

It is time to return home after this fatiguing excursion. I hope that Christina is rapidly advancing
in her progress. I anticipate, with great pleasure,
her introduction to the public, and am only sorry that
it did not take place sooner.

I am, dear madam,
With the sincerest esteem, yours,
R. A. DAVENPORT.

This letter seems to have suggested Miss Mitford's
poem 'Blanch of Castille.' Refering to it she writes to
her father on March 22, 1811: 'I have had a most
delightful letter from that delightful man Mr. Davenport; he meant to write to you by the same post, and
was much pleased with my grandfather's poems. He
accuses me of gross injustice to the Spaniards. I
shall try to make amends by writing a poem on a
Spanish subject. Perhaps I may do more injustice by
my friendship than by my enmity.'

R. A. DAVENPORT *to* MISS MITFORD.

Perry Hill, Sydenham, January 8, 1813.

MY DEAR MADAM,

Though we have heard of 'Letters from the
Dead to the Living,' it seems to be pretty well ascer-
tained that dead men do not write letters, and, consequently, this epistle will convince you that I am

still breathing the gross and foggy air of this world,
which world, as Sterne observes, really does appear
to have been made out of the fragments and fag ends
of all the other planets. After all, I don't know that
I ought to say 'I'm alive,' for at best I am only cor-
poreally alive, having been this long while mentally
and spiritually dead. You are, therefore, to receive
this as a letter from a lump of animated clay, and now
you know what you have to trust to. You must certainly have thought that both work and editor were
as dead as a doornail. Indeed, so convinced was I
that you would think so, that I daily expected to see
an epitaph either upon the book or the maker of it.
But, alas! my hopes were vain ones; not a single
'melodious tear' did you give to my supposed un-
timely fate. However, as I said before and proved,
I *am* alive, though not over and above merry; my
work too is alive, and, I flatter myself, will give some
pleasure. I send you a copy, which you will do me
the favour to accept as a very small but sincere token
of my thanks and esteem.

If I remember right, you once wrote me word that
you were pleased to know the *names* of the *anonymous*
writers in the volumes. I will give you a key to those
in the seventh volume as far as I can. R. L. E., pages
16, 20, 32, 47, 79, 91, 160, 213, is Richard Lovell Edg-
worth, whose name must be familiar to you. R. W. W.,
page 56, is Mr. Wade, a stockbroker. E. C. K., pages
71, 175, is a Mrs. Kerr. W. R., pages 240, 439, is, I believe, Mr. Roscoe. Horace in London, Messrs. Horace
and James Smith, authors of the celebrated 'Rejected
Addresses.' These gentlemen are also the writers of

the pieces with the signatures H. and J. on pages 322, 337, 361, 417, 487, 529, 542. L. A., page 254, Miss Lucy Aikin. Anacreon in Bow Street, page 396, Mr. Dubois. J. M., page 323, Mr. Montgomery. Two heroic epistles, pages 387, 403, Dr. Richard Laurence. Avran, page 533, is either Mr. Hodgson or Mr. Bland, but I think the latter. Now you are as wise as myself.

I am busily employed preparing for my eighth volume, which is to be published *next* May. You laugh! Yes, by heavens you do! In my mind's eye I see you laughing outright, and I think I hear you exclaim, 'Ay, my good friend, two years ago you told us the same kind of story with respect to the *seventh* volume, and lo! the seventh volume is, even now, but just published! Well, all this is true—''tis pity 'tis true, and 'tis true 'tis pity.' But *now* I shall do better. Fortunately sinning once does not imply sinning always. I *will* publish in May; that is to say, if I have 'all appliances and means.' As to means, I must humbly crave you to furnish me with as large a portion of them as you can. Indeed I can prove it, under your own hand, in black and white, as the vulgar beautifully express it, that you gave me an authority, which has not been revoked, to draw upon the poetical bank of Mitford and Russell. I know the firm to be a rich one, and, therefore, the world ought to 'set me down an ass,' if I neglected to avail myself of my credit. Really and truly, I speak it with perfect seriousness, you will confer a great obligation upon me by your early aid. My interest and my pleasure both prompt me to a speedy publication of the next volume, and when interest and pleasure combine to stimulate exertion the power must be great . . . I hope that you are as well, and in as good spirits as you are wished to be by,

Dear madam,
Your obliged friend and servant,
R. A. DAVENPORT.

J. P. SMITH *to* MISS MITFORD,

April 9, 1812.

DEAR MADAM,

If I do not answer your letter now, it will probably be delayed till you will justly deem your knight a recreant from his word. I shall not condescend to rate you for your artful flattery in calling me by that wicked nickname, a *genius*, but admit that you are right in believing that there is a sympathy necessary to make a reader of feeling, as well as a writer who can command the feelings. This is true philosophy, and evinces your knowledge of the'human mind. With respect to my poetry, I have written but little and published less. I have within me a passion for literary fame, but I have many other passions also; have long devoted myself to the study of the law, which has not been very profitable; and am embarrassed with the cares of providing bread and cheese for a wife and family, from whom I have known nothing but affection and delight mixed with anxieties: I must not, therefore, presume to call myself a poet. I am only an occasional versifier for amusement when a strong fit seizes me, and I can get the strait-waistcoat off. I have written, let me tell you, all my offences in this way—a few odes, some epigrams, some love verses, some election squibs, one satire, two or three translations; planned one tragedy; translated one serious opera of Metastasio, with songs, which was rejected; have published three volumes of 'Cases in the King's Bench,' law reports innumerable from the daily journals; and am now printing a strange book on a subject which has made me mad for some years, and sets all the world mad besides, except you who live retired and, I hope, will never suffer much anxiety from anything. What is it, say you? 'Tis *Money*. I am actually printing a book to teach the world the nature of money. And you will think me more mad when I tell you that the world seems to me to know less of this than they do even of poetry. I will confess further. Could I write as fast as I could wish, I would now instantly write on two other subjects—namely, the Parish Register Bill and the East India Charter; and I would write to shield from calumny a man whom, as a politician, I dislike, *George Rose*.

Now, my dear little muse of Berkshire, observe how I have severed the order of things. I have placed you, who are as innocent as the sweetest nun that ever graced a cloister, into the chair, and I, who to be seen should be taken as the father confessor, have knelt before you to be *shriven* at the confessional. I have done it to let you see that I am without guile towards you, and that I feel flattered by your confidence. As to the verses you enquire for, the 'Ode to Fancy' is in the Annual Register, 1806, the one published by Otridge and Co. The 'Eclogue of Fox' is in the Gentleman's Magazine for January or February, 1797, for it was written in December, 1796. The ‘Life of Fox’ was written by me, as well as Pitt’s, and I had to flatter both, but by dealing a little too plainly in telling an anecdote of Lord Carington, I offended one of my employers, and compiled no more for them. My satire was published, but though rather general, as I published myself, I did not advertise. It was little read, and the copies got into the hands of the assignees of my bookseller, who was a bankrupt. It contains, however, some good lines, but very little poetical feeling. I have lent a volume in MS. to a lady, very fairly written out for my wife, and she has forgotten to return it, or I would send it to you.

Let me now change character, and talk to you a little as a critic. I approve of your plan very much, except that I should like to see ‘Blanch’ published now, in spite of the critics. I would try Longman, or Cadell, or some one who publishes more generally than Rivington. He is the parson’s bookseller, and they are rather a cold set of readers, and affect not to like ladies’ poetry, and, indeed, to like no lady but our Mother Church. If it could be published with engravings like Scott’s ‘Lay’ and ‘Marmion,’ so much the better, and there are scenes which would give full scope to the painter’s art. The tournament is almost a common scene for a painter; the banishment might make a good scene; the lover at the window in the serenade; so would the fall into the stream, and some other passages. I recommend to publish now because it is a *Spanish Tale,* and the *Spanish* is all the rage—I mean the Spanish taste, not money, which, you know, is vulgarly called 'the Spanish.' Perhaps next year *Spain* may be our enemy, and *John Bull* may rap against your *Dons* most violently; for John is very fickle, very proud, and very spiteful against all his enemies. I repeat that the Scotch reviewers have done wonders for Campbell and Scott; the former I think rather forced, the latter is a mannerist. The nationality of the Scotch has done all this. Moore writes pretty music as well as loose verses. He is absolutely the Anacreon of demireps; he has therefore a certain sect of his own, independent of all the singers. Now I should recommend you to make a party amongst the ladies, and steal into their hearts through their ears also by getting some knight or page of musical skill to set some of your songs to music. If you could set up a *Ladies'* review, you would soon beat Scott, or at least ride behind him, or before him, on a pillion or a pillow. By the way, there is an epigram of mine on Moore in a monthly publication three years ago, called the 'Cabinet,' new series, and several in the 'Monthly Mirror,' signed J. P. S., particularly a legal critique on Shakespeare and Massinger, also 'Love's Metamorphosis' in the 'Cabinet.'

The story of 'Blanch,' when the poem becomes fashionable, will be dramatized, and Kemble, who has just learnt to ride, will mount the horse, and run a tilt at Young or his brother Charles. I cannot help thinking it would make a good drama. The story is busy and pathetic. For the two small poems I thank you much. That to Lord Redesdale is most striking to me, and it is a just tribute to feeling where one would least expect it. As I have praised my friend McKinnon's brother, from a public feeling that tells me that praise is but a just tribute to great merit, you do right in cherishing that kind-heartedness which Lord R. has shown by this bill of his, and which I admire the more because men who have cards in courts, and made fortunes by the gainful practice of the law, are apt to have their hearts steeled against misery. It is the proper business of poetry to rouse the feelings, to awaken men to a sense of humanity, to sound the charge that shall animate them in the warfare of life; and, when you do this, you seem to me a little angel, to whom the triumph of fame has been consigned, for wise purposes and most noble uses, by the hand of a presiding Deity.

What shall I say when you sound the horn in pursuit of the timid hares? What but repeat Collins, who, in his 'Ode to the Passions,' describes you under the name of cheerfulness, and says that you

> ' Blend an inspiring air that dale and thicket rung,
> The hunter's call to fawn and Dryad known ;'

and in truth, my dear madam, you are the prettiest defender of what I have long thought a mere relic of barbarity. But I yield to your genius; I cannot admire cruelty in sport; but, if wild animals must be killed, I know not how they are to be killed with less cruelty than hunting, and giving them a run for it; for catching them in *gins* gives them a lingering death, shooting often wounds without killing, and, as you say, the hare often escapes, and, when caught at last, it is but one of the modes of death. The act of running perhaps bereaves her of pain, and relieves her anxiety with frequent transitions of hope. Is not this a picture of life? Are not we poets hares, and are not the critics dogs, bloodhounds, and all that is horrible to us? and when they kill us, do they not say, 'Ha! ha! it is but one of the modes of death'?

Your 'Sisters' is marked with the same character as all your other writings—the same power of description, the same views of nature, the same fluency of style—but it left off just where I would go on. Just as I had worked myself up, and begun to be in love, and to make love as I used to do, you left me, and dissipated all the sweet delusion of your scenery. It is really only the beginning of a poem, and as I had not my pencil in my hand, and did not note the few words that struck me, I shall not at present criticise further than by remarking you have repeated the figure of the diamonds as descriptive of dew-drops, whereas I prefer Collins' *gemm'd* with morning dew as more general, or *brilliants* as a softer word, and that you have used the word *lit* instead of light-ed. By the way, let me observe that there is not quite incident enough for your description. Poetry merely descriptive is like mere landscape in painting without figures, or a fine scene in a tragedy, which, when you have gazed on it for a while, you begin to wish for the actors.

Now, as I have, I presume, nearly fatigued you, I must beg you to excuse a hasty scrawl, in parts not strictly grammatical, and subscribe myself, with

many thanks in your character as a muse especially,
your true knight and admirer,

J. P. SMITH.[1]

Miss Mitford dedicated her 'Poems on the Female
Character,' including 'Blanch,' to Lord Holland in
1813, and, as it appears from the following letter, sent
them in manuscript for his approval :—

LORD HOLLAND *to* MISS MITFORD.

MADAM,

I am really ashamed of not having answered your
very obliging and interesting letter, and not having
acknowledged the receipt of the pretty poem which
you have done me the honour of submitting to my
perusal. The fact is, I have been confined to my
room for several days, and, though I have run through
your entertaining MS., I have by no means given
that attention to it which it deserves, and which alone
would entitle me to give you an opinion upon it.
Indeed you allow a very flattering partiality for me
to overcome your judgment when you ask me for
my opinion. I can, from the very cursory perusal
I have hitherto made of it, say very truly that it gave
me great pleasure, and is both an elegant and poetical
work, but it would require a critic more conversant
than I can pretend to be with the public taste, and
more capable of discerning the true merits and defects
of a poem, to decide how far it is likely to succeed
greatly with the public, and what slight alterations
would tend to defeat the severity of that criticism

---

[1] John Pye Smith, known for his works on legal subjects.

which uniformly attacks modern productions, especially when they are professed imitations of the most popular writer of the day. The loose metre which Mr. W. Scott has adopted, and which you very naturally follow him in, is unquestionably very favourable to narrative, very convenient to the poet, and very happy for the simple expression of tender sentiments. But it is apt to betray the writer into small inaccuracies, and perhaps it is the best advice one can give to an imitator of Walter Scott to avoid as much as possible his incorrectness in phrases, rhyme, and metre. For these reasons I will, with your permission, keep your MS. for another perusal, and will venture, where an expression strikes my ear as unusual or incorrect, to pass a pencil-mark under it; but, if I do so, I must entreat you not to consider the marks as intended to do more than to bring the expression once more to your notice, as it is at least full as likely that so incompetent a critic as myself should be incorrect in his observations, as that you, who have such a command of verse, should be faulty in your expression.

I am, madam, with many acknowledgments,

Your obliged, humble servant,

VASSALL HOLLAND.

This third Lord Holland was a distinguished Whig politician. He was Lord Privy Seal in the Administration of All the Talents, and was three times Chancellor of the Duchy of Lancaster. From his early years he was fond of writing poetry, and he published a memoir of Lope de Vega. His partiality for Spanish literature, and perhaps his connection with

the Chamberlayne family, led to this dedication of
' Blanch.'

Miss Mitford's earliest attempts, like those of many
authors, consisted of descriptive poems, and were generally addressed to some valued friend. Love of
the country gave the charm of Nature to her sketches
of rural scenery, and to the last she excelled in that
which first attracted her girlish fancy. Birds and
dogs, trees and flowers, were her delight, and we now
in 1812 find her joyously sketching the beauties of
Weston Grove, the country seat of Mr. Chamberlayne,
which she calls,

'A garland on the brow of Time,'

in reference to its overlooking the ruins of Netley
Abbey.

Mr. Chamberlayne naturally felt much gratified at
the compliment paid him by the young poetess, and
wrote as follows to her father :—

MR. CHAMBERLAYNE *to* DR. MITFORD.

Weston Grove, near Southampton,
November 7, 1812.

DEAR SIR,

Your delightful present reached my hands, I fear,
some weeks since, but I was then so much engaged
in an election contest, and my whole time since has
been so much occupied in business arising out of it,
that I am but just returned to the enjoyment of my
country life, and of those scenes which are only
excelled by the beauty of the picture which your
accomplished daughter has so kindly given me of
them. It is strikingly remarkable that her view of

Netley Abbey and its scenery coincides with that of
Lord Orford, written in 1755 in a letter to Richard
Bentley, Esq., and published in his works.   I have not
the book at hand, but think I recollect nearly the
very words of it :—' How,' says his lordship, ' shall I
describe Netley to you?   I can only by telling you
that it is the spot in the world for which Mr. Chute
and I wish—the ruins are vast, and retain fragments
of beautiful fretted roofs pendant in the air, and with
all variety of Gothic patterns of windows wrapped
round and round with ivy.   Many trees are sprouted
up amongst the walls, and only want to be increased
with cypresses.   A hill rises above the abbey, encircled
with wood.   The fort, in which we could build a
tower for habitation, remains with two small plat-
forms.   This little castle is buried from the abbey in
a wood, in the very centre, on the edge of a hill.   On
each side breaks the view of the Southampton sea,
deep blue, glistening with silver and vessels ; on one
side terminated by Southampton, on the other by
Calshot Castle and the Isle of Wight rising above the
opposite hills—in short, they are not the ruins of Netley, but of Paradise.   Oh, the purple abbots ! what a
spot had they chosen to slumber in !   The scene is so
beautifully tranquil, yet so lively, that they seem only
to have retired into the world.'

Have the charity to believe that I never meant to
compare this sketch of the peer, animated as it is
with the magic of the poetry with which I have been
so highly gratified in the finished stanzas on Weston,
though the objects seem in some particulars to have
presented themselves to both artists in much the same
order and point of view.

Would that I was among the number of those whose praise is fame ! No, the ‘ Berkshire Muse ’ has acquired that in the fullest abundance for *herself*, and requires no foreign aid. Have, therefore, the goodness only to express to her my gratitude for the delight which her genius has afforded me, and her kindness in noticing so humble an individual as myself. In most of her representations I scarcely know whether to admire most the fidelity of her portraits, or the creative powers of her mind. It is only when she is pleased to speak of *me* that I perceive the triumph of fiction over truth.

Had not the election contest run away with all my treasures, it was in my contemplation to have erected a column of Purbeck or Portland stone to the memory of Mr. Fox, at a moment when it seems forgotten by princes and people. Dr. Parr had kindly written a beautiful inscription in Latin for it, and I should have flattered myself with the hope that it would not have been an unpleasant subject to the feelings of the fair writer of ‘ Weston ’ to have introduced in a future edition of her incomparable poem—but we must wait for better days.

With best wishes for the health and happiness of yourself, Mrs. Mitford, and the ‘ Enchanting Muse,’
I am, dear sir,
Your obedient and obliged humble servant,
WM. CHAMBERLAYNE.

Referring to this letter, Miss Mitford writes to Sir W. Elford.

‘ You are right in supposing Mr. Chamberlayne to

be the gentleman who will succeed to the great
Dummer property at the death of Lady Holland.
Netley Abbey forms part of this demesne; and I
suppose its vicinity to the large estate, of which he
has so near a prospect, was one reason, joined to its
almost unrivalled situation, for his fixing on Weston
Grove for the site of his fairy palace.'

CHAPTER III.

SIR WILLIAM ELFORD was a friend, and Club-mate, of Dr. Mitford, who apparently first met him at Graham's Club in St. James' Street. He was a Tory, and belonged to a good Devonshire family, of old settled at Longstone, among the tors of Dartmoor, and there was a tradition that one of his ancestors had escaped the Roundheads by taking refuge in a cavity of Sheepstor known as the Pixies' house. Personally, the present representative was worthy of the line; for he was created a baronet by Pitt in 1800, and was an M.P., and Recorder for Plymouth.[1] Moreover, he was a man of taste and cultivation, though, but for an occasional pamphlet, he did not enter the field of literature. He was fond of poetry and painting, and some of his pictures appeared in the London exhibitions.

Sir William's acquaintance with Miss Mitford seems to have commenced in her father showing him some of her manuscript verses, for his first letter to her was

---

[1] He was a partner in a bank in that town.

to request that she would send him more of her poems. Her reply was the beginning of a close and remarkable correspondence between the young girl and the elderly gentleman,[1] from which, though much his superior in talent, she greatly profited. Not only did she receive useful advice from his experience, but she became accustomed to write full and interesting letters, and gradually formed the style for which she was afterwards celebrated. Sir William is occasionally alluded to in her letters to friends. She speaks of his ' having painted nearly every British bird,' and of one of his pictures being · destined for an apartment in Carlton House—a present to the Regent.' He stayed at one time on a visit with the Mitfords at Reading, and she says that ' he talks as much as a woman, and visits everybody in that enormous county. He is the kindest, cleverest, warmest-hearted man in the world.' She did not of course escape being twitted about her partiality for him, and she adds, ' he is perfect in everything but not being in love with me. I shall not marry Sir William Elford; for which there is a remarkably good reason, the aforesaid Sir William having no sort of desire to marry me; neither shall I ever marry anybody. He has an outrageous fancy for my letters, and marrying a favourite correspondent would be something like killing the goose with the golden eggs.' Referring to his correspondence, she observes, ' There is something of Horace Walpole's mixture of humour and courtliness about his style;' and she writes to him

---

[1] He had three daughters, older than Miss Mitford, one of whom became Lady Adams; he lived to a great age.

on April 22, 1812— 'I keep your letters as choicely as the monks were wont to keep the relics of their saints; and about sixty years hence your grandson, or great-grandson, will discover in the family archives some notice of such a collection, and will write to the grandson of my dear cousin Mary (for, as I intend to die an old maid, I shall make her heiress to all my property, *i.e.*, my manuscripts) for these inestimable remains of his venerable ancestor.' Miss Mitford's letters to Sir William Elford are well known, and we now propose to show the other side of the picture by printing some of his.

SIR W. ELFORD *to* MISS MITFORD.

18, Bury Street, April 9, 1812.

Your letter evinces how little attention ought to be paid to the most positive testimony, and that moss-roses which, when viewed at some distance from the place where they grow, appear to be white, are on closer inspection found to be of a maiden blush. Pray are you certain, however, of this fact? Were not Mr. Swallow's moss-roses white before your approach, and did not the blush proceed from *reflection?* You know that the purest bodies are sometimes suffused by involuntary reflections of another kind. I hope you consider this all very poetical and pretty; how-ever, I do not mean to let you escape from the trouble I intended to impose on you, and, therefore, I still beg you will be kind enough, the next time you go to Reading, to direct Mr. Swallow to send by Fromont's coach, to be addressed to me at Bickham, near Ply-mouth, four of the light-coloured moss-roses, and six or eight of the yellow roses, and two or three other cheap plants such as he would recommend, and among others some of the evening primrose which has been rendered famous by a certain songstress, and of which we have none in Devonshire. This commission being executed, you will be pleased to favour me with a few lines, enclosing Mr. Swallow's charge. So much for business, in which I make no scruple of employing my good and fair correspondent.

By-the-by, we are such good friends that there ought to be something of a free communication between us, and I shall inform you of a circumstance that happened to myself formerly, and which is known to very few people in the world. When on my travels in my younger days in the upper part of Ethiopia, an event occurred that almost recalls the 'Arabian Night's Entertainments' to one's mind. I was pursuing my way on the edge of a forest in beautiful rocky scenery, attended by my servant and a native guide, when, hearing the cries of distress, I pushed forward, and, dreadful to relate, saw an old, venerable-looking man under the paw of a huge lion, which seemed, like all the cat kind (*bathos*), to delight in tormenting its prey before it was put to death. I hastened, like a rash fool, to his assistance, and, with the aid of my two companions, rescued the sufferer by destroying the lion. He was so much injured, however, that I despaired of his recovery, and we had some difficulty to get him into his hermitage, which was situated in a cavity of the rocks very near, where in a few hours he breathed his last. Just before he died he presented me with an invaluable though

dangerons gift, the uses of which he shortly explained—it consisted of a small brilliant ball, with curious
characters engraven on it, which, when held in the
right hand, rendered the possessor invisible, and, in
the left, transported him whither he willed, and had
both operations when the two hands joined.

I have seldom ventured to use this wonderful talisman, but a fortnight ago, having employed myself in
reading White's ' Selborne,' and being extremely fond
of natural history, and, of course, highly delighted
with that book, I was seized with an insuperable
desire to see that village which Mr. White has, in the
eye of a naturalist, made classic ground, and, using
my means, I was presently transported thither, and
walked invisibly through the village, the Hangers, the
places where the beech woods had been destroyed,
and, in short, every part of that scenery which the
unaffected language and sterling sense of the author
has rendered so interesting. After having satiated
my curiosity, I proceeded on my return by slow steps,
and first having willed myself in an inn at Alresford
(for under the operation of this supernatural power I
am subject to extreme hunger), and having made a
good repast, I heard the names of Mr. and Miss Mitford mentioned, and, on inquiry, found they were
then actually in the town, and were those friends
whom I wished earnestly to see. Taking my brilliant
in my right hand, I walked to the house of a Mr.
Pollen, or Holland, or something very like it, and saw
you sitting in a neat little drawing-room alone, sometimes reading, sometimes ruminating; the apartment
was hung round with prints of various kinds, and

most neatly furnished.　You several times in contemplation spoke aloud, unconscious of being observed, and seemed to refer to Lord Redesdale and some poem, which, I suppose, you had lately produced, and which, from some lines you repeated, seemingly with a view to alter them, appeared to me to be exquisitely beautiful.　There was one part of your meditations which I could not make out, but which appeared to refer to some thing or person in which you were deeply interested.　You sometimes struck me as talking of a donkey,[1] then of the Mediterranean, from thence I heard something of a Quartermaster-General—in short, all this was like the incoherence of a dream, which is always the case with the waking reveries of those who are unconsciously thinking aloud.　I could hardly help laughing at your starting once or twice at a little bustle which my moving occasioned, and once particularly, as I approached so near as very slightly to touch you.　The weather was very bad, and I, being wet, was afraid the dripping from my clothes might tend to discover me, for they became visible on the floor, and I was just going out of the room when you said something of a friend of yours, one Maria, somebody to whose expected accouchement you seemed to be looking forward with some anxiety (by-the-by, I hope she has been confined, and is as well as can be expected in her condition).　Your father I saw in the street, more wet than myself, followed by greyhounds, and accompanied by other sportsmen.　By the time I returned to Bath I was tired to death, and shall not presently

[1] A reference, perhaps, to General *Donkin.*　See p. 176.

have recourse to my brilliant ball again. This
adventure is communicated to you in perfect confidence, and I desire you will not read the account of
it to your papa and mamma; but, with my best
compliments to them, believe me, my dear Mary's
faithful and affectionate friend,

W. ELFORD.

P.S.—I fear it is so late that I cannot get a frank
to-day. On looking at the fourth side of the enclosed sheet I found it beautifully blotted, but the
discovery was too late, so you must excuse it.

The story in this letter is to be explained by the
fact that Miss Mitford was at the time he mentions on
a visit at Alresford, the home of her childhood, staying in such a room and engaged in such occupations
as he describes. He obtained this information, which
he ascribes to a talisman, from an accidental meeting
with Dr. Mitford.

SIR W. ELFORD *to* MISS MITFORD.

18, Bury Street.
Sunday Morning, April 19, 1812.

I have just finished your poem of 'The Sisters,' and
tell you truly and fairly that I read it with an interest
and delight which I cannot express. I like it better
than anything you have done (am I right or wrong?)
and you have contrived to mix up poetical imagery
and expression with such a great degree of interest
as I have never before found in any poem. Have
you invented it all, or have you stolen it, or borrowed
it from some known or unknown tale? Not that it

signifies. Shakespeare is said to have borrowed some of his subjects, but he made them his own, as you have done. In short, it is, in my mind, quite perfect, with the exception of *two* or *three words*, which I don't like . . . .

Pray, my dear, can you tell me what I have done with your last letter? It is not in my right pocket or my left pocket, and I want to look at it, and can't find it, although I am quite certain that it is very safe somewhere, as I carefully preserve all your letters. Are you sure you have not taken it up?

Your papa was here just now, and swore through thick and thin that the two first stanzas in 'The Sisters' are not *quotation*. I, on the contrary, swore in a similar manner that they are so, having ' ' at the beginning of the first and end of the second; but at last he said they were from a song of your own, so that he was but a little perjured, and I not at all. The thought in them is beautiful, and quite new to me, and you are a dear little Mary, and a great poet, and you are also a little and a great flatterer in admiring my nonsensical talisman. You must know that I tried something like a similar experiment on a young lady (not a correspondent) to whom I had occasion to write about some business last year, and who had just before given a ball, which had been so far described to me, particularly as to a vase which stood in the middle of the table, and a man who appeared particularly attentive to her, as to furnish me with sufficient particulars on which to found a little fiction. She was a very good sort of plain, matter-of-fact person. She answered the business part of the letter, and merely remarked on the other part that I was mistaken in my inferences from the major's attention to her; and I am quite clear that she has ever since firmly believed that I possess an invisible girdle and wishing-cap like Fortunatus, and really appeared invisible at her ball—that's Irish! On turning the corner, I see my paper is very smutty, for which I humbly beg pardon.

I am very much obliged to you for executing my commission, and for your evening primroses, which I shall prize not a little. Your papa told me you had plenty, but I could not ask for them, as we were then in a plot against you. I had been getting from him some particulars on which to found my talismanic story, and, of course, was not to appear to have seen him, and the letter was also necessarily ante-dated. Such deceivers are men—take care of them, child. Your papa and I, however, are past being *.jay* deceivers.

By the way, I was not a little edified at the exemplary modesty you display in describing your humble and moderate choice of flowers, you having, I think, enumerated all those most admirable in the garden, the wood, and the field. I remember a similar instance of forbearance in a country Devonshire justice, who said that no man was less solicitous for the luxuries of the table than himself—give him a turbot of ten pounds, a haunch of venison, and a green apricot tart, and the devil might take all the beefsteaks and mutton chops in the world!

Sir W. Elford *to* Miss Mitford.

Bickham, June 18, 1812.

I'll tell you what, young woman, you are a little insidious, flattering gipsy, and want to evince your power of turning my brain by telling me that I can write letters, and that I have made a new observation about hanging madmen. I really believe that in this remark you are very much mistaken—at least, I am not at all aware of the merit of having found out anything new. Did not Cervantes or somebody tell a story founded on the same opinion, and which serves to corroborate it—a madman (mad on that one point, as far as could be discovered) used to amuse himself by walking about the streets of Madrid with a very large stone on his shoulder, and when he came near a dog he always let it fall on his head and crushed it to death. Having one day performed this operation on a favourite pointer, whose master was by, the owner attacked the madman, and gave him a most severe beating, calling out constantly, ' You scoundrel, that's for killing my pointer !' The next day the man, however, betook himself to his favourite diversion, and having killed a brace or two of dogs, was in the act of letting his stone loose on another, when he suddenly called out, ' Oh, that's a pointer !' and immediately desisted. So, you see, the opinion is quite as old as when Don Quixote was living, or at least when his historian was so. Now I have been thinking for at least a minute how to make an easy transition from this to another subject of your letter, and, not succeeding, I must do without it. Women understand this, as well as most other parts of letter-writing, much better than men, and slide from one topic to another without any of those rough jerks occasioned by sudden chasms.[1]

You talk of curiosity and women being related. I won't allow more curiosity to women than to men, and you only want to establish the fact in order to display the female character. Curiosity is only another name for a thirst of knowledge. 'Tis indeed applied opprobriously by wicked men when coupled with the female character, but very improperly certainly, especially as to the occasion which gave rise to your observation.

My two Devonshire words have done wonders in drawing out so acute and learned a commentary from you. It puts me much in mind of the voluminous commentators on Shakespeare, many of whom would have been spar'd wonderful pains had they been furnish'd with a correct copy of the author's performance. I have only one objection to your 'beautiful and ingenious solution of *daveid*, which I doubt not would have been quite just had the word been so, instead of *daver'd*, which was what I wrote, or meant to write. Perhaps (for you have heard of such a thing) the writing was not quite legible, which was certainly my fault, and not yours. ' Daver'd ' then, madam, you are to understand is the participle of a suppos'd verb neuter, to *daver ;* and, joking apart, is with us a very expressive word. A *daver'd flower* is in a state between faded and dead ; a corruption of

<hr>

[1] Miss Mitford, when making transitions in her letters, often uses a ∽, and alludes to Sir William's notion of jerks.

cadaverous. It is often applied to a person who looks very ill, and very *wish'd*, from which *wishness*, or *wishdness* is deriv'd. A *wishd*-looking man or woman is, in our conception, a poor, miserable, inergetic-looking person; but the substantive *wishness* is applied to things of a ghostly kind which cannot be distinctly describ'd; a *clear* and *well-appointed* ghost, that is a pale representative of some one departed, would be call'd a ghost; but if anyone is scar'd by he can't tell what, he is said to have seen *wishness.* Have I been able to describe these beauties in our language so as to be understood?

I had not despatch'd my last letter ten minutes before I recollected that I had not answered your kind query relative to the kind of stanza in which a song would be most welcome. I can only say 'in any that you like best.' We don't sing much, but whatever you send will be most kindly and thankfully received, and some tune will be adapted to it, or invented for it. I must leave off now, and finish another time. I am call'd to get into the carriage, and travel seven miles to dinner.

June 24.—From the date of the beginning of this letter, six days ago, you must necessarily have been expecting it for the last four days, and I am really sorry to disappoint you, but you may depend on receiving it within these four days to come, with which promise you will, I know, be quite *aisey;* and so I shall now tell you that I have been in the midst of an election at Plymouth, occasion'd by Sir T. Tyrwhitt's having accepted of the office of King's *Gentleman Usher of the Black Rod, and Daily Waiter,* for such is his style and title. Colonel Bloomfield[1] came, and had indeed canvass'd before, and a Mr. Longmead, a brewer, had long had his own consent to represent the borough, but as his father had once, by some strange conduct, got into the representation, and afterwards quitted it for a sum of money to Mr. Tyrwhitt, I determined as far as in me lay, as did many others, that the brewer should not *work* for us, and we have made him *hop* off. I hope you do not consider this as punning. I had the honour of proposing Colonel B., and, as he tells me, became his godfather for more than he shall be able to perform; and he was unanimously elected, the other having declin'd now and for ever. The canvassing therefore, the election, the various dinners, and lastly the great dinner on the great day, at all of which I have been assisting, aiding, and abetting, have taken me up so entirely that, although I have not forgotten my dear, and good, and kind correspondent, I have not been able to consummate my letter, and you see it is swelling in size beyond a single sheet, but that I don't care sixpence about, nor need you do so. The new member shall frank it, and this shall not be the last frank you shall get from him, as I have (*since his election*, which I mention to convince you I was not bribed) made him promise to direct all letters for you which I should send to him, ~~for which~~—I have scratch'd those words, as I am sure I don't know what they were to lead to. I should add that Bloomfield is a very old friend of mine, or I should not have made such a proposal.

[1] Afterwards Lord Bloomfield.

Apropos to Colonel Bloomfield (he is an Irishman), I have been, and am now, in the midst of reading Miss Edgeworth's 4th, 5th, and 6th vols. of 'Tales of Fashionable Life.' I don't enter into disquisitions about whether they come up to or fall short of her other works, but I am most highly entertained with them. Such admirable delineation of character and such excellent tendencies one seldom sees, and her stories are interesting, not from intricacy of plot, but from exact representations of Nature, and she has now and then evinced an extraordinary power—at least, so it appears to me—that of inventing a new character, and of marking it by making the person act so as he or she would act, with such propensities and objects as she attributes to him or her, in the situation in which they appear. Have I made myself comprehended, for I have expressed myself rather confusedly —in short, this is the female age, the men are beaten hollow by you; confound you all for your insolent usurpation. But let me rather say, God bless you all for the fund of delightful entertainment I find in your writings. Do tell me whether you have ever met with a novel called 'Anne of Brittany'; 'tis not of a high class, and is an historical story, but I know the author, and want your opinion. Have I anything else to say at this time? I am writing before breakfast, for you must know that I am a farmer, and an early riser. Remember me most kindly to your papa and mamma, and think me, as I am, most affectionately your friend

W. ELFORD.

Sir W. Elford *to* Miss Mitford.

November 1, 1812.

Did not you say something of your being a little of a democrat? I fancy you was once a good deal so (now can't I tell whether that's a provincialism or no?), but, like all other people of good sense, observation and experience render you otherwise; at least, it makes you think it necessary to appear otherwise. Now pray, Mademoiselle Democrate, what do you think of M. Buonaparte's situation? Is he on a bed of roses, or on a Moscow gridiron with the city cinders under him? Pray, as you are a well-wisher of his, desire them to put some pepper and salt—for a man like him should, in no state of his life or death, have any mawkishness or insipidity. Do you think he can return in post-chaises to Paris as usual, unless his army escorts him back? Come, tell me what you think.

Miss Mitford seems to have profited by the following advice :—

Sir W. Elford *to* Miss Mitford.

Bickham, November 25, 1812.

I sit down to begin a letter (to be finished as occasions offer) to my dear, good little correspondent, and to thank her for the long and most entertaining one I have lately received from her. Pray never refrain from writing much *because you want time and inclination to read over what you have written.* I would a thousand times rather see what falls from your pen naturally and spontaneously (that is in a letter) than the most polished and beautiful composition that ever went to the press; and so would you, I doubt not, from your correspondents. Upon this subject some very fine and trite sayings might be uttered such as how infinitely more beautiful to a naturalist (which I pretend to be a little of) is the ore in its native colours and crystallisations than the most polished state to which the pure metal can be brought.

SIR W. ELFORD to MISS MITFORD.

December 4, 1812.

Pope's maxim (if it is his) that 'easy writing is not easily written' is certainly true with respect to what is intended for the world as composition either in prose or verse, but is utterly false as applied to familiar letter-writing, of which his own letters— pretended to be warm from the brain, but in reality polished and revised for publication—are a striking proof. Write away, then, my dear, as fast as you can drive your quill, and abuse Miss Seward as much as you please; she deserves it for her abuse of our friend Dr. Johnson. Shall I tell you that you are a little like her in one respect—that is, you carry your censures on her to as great an extent as she does hers on Dr. Johnson; but then you do it in the proper place and in the right direction. I am called to breakfast, and when I begin again (an interval of time having passed) I shall not need a mark of jerkification on commencing a new subject.

December 5.—As this threatens to be a double letter it will wait for a frank, though I hope not long. You do yourself but justice in believing that you are in no danger with me of being charged with writing Miss-Nonsense about peace (observe Miss is spelt with a double *s*, and is not used as in misconduct, misfortune, &c., &c.), but still I must make a few observations. That peace in the abstract is better than war nobody can deny; in the same way as health is better than disease, or as plenty than privation. But what are the *great* trials and miseries (by great I mean extensive) of this world but war, pestilence, and famine. They have been so from the earliest ages of history, and, while mankind continues as they are, will occur to the latest. Nay, according to the course and construction of the animal world they *must* occur. All animals but men have some others that prey on them, by which means the natural tendency to inordinate increase is kept within due bounds, in the manner that wars keep down the human species. All animated nature is checked also by the other two causes—namely, disease and want of food. Now, dreadful as I allow wars to be, and dreadful as it must be to be eaten by larger animals, I freely confess that I should prefer those modes of extinction to disease and famine. The history of China within the last century affords a striking proof of the effect of the absence of wars. Since the Tartar Conquest, and the establishment of the dynasty of the great Emperor Cham-Hi (I believe that is the way the gentleman spelt his name) was the founder, the population has been very little exhausted by wars; but what has been the consequence? That several times (during the space of a few months' continuance each) famine, followed, of course, by pestilence, has swept off as many millions as one of the middle-sized states of Europe contains.

I hope you will not suppose me to be hard-hearted; indeed, I am sure you will not. I would venture to argue or illustrate what I think in this way with very few people indeed, because it would be mistaken. War, however, is a dreadful evil, although our insular position prevents our knowing much of the miseries of it. We always lose our money, and sometimes our friends; but what is this to being in the seat of war? Let us pray for peace, therefore, my dear little friend, but let us at the same time not forget to thank God that we escape the pollutions of wars, and that the nightingales are not driven from the groves of Bertram by the horrid din of arms.

Talking of arms puts me naturally in mind of hands (no jerk here), hands, of fingers, and fingers of pen and ink which I now see combined before me, and those of one of their results—namely, your good mamma's copy of your address for Drury Lane. Now, I'll be very candid. If I had never seen anything else by the same author I should have said, ‘This lady has very considerable poetical powers,’ but I think it as far above Lord Byron's as many of your own works are above it; I suppose your friend, Mr. Whitbread, prefixed the peer's in order to wheedle him and have his support in the new Parliament, upon the principle of all politicians—‘ rather to expend their means in buying enemies than rewarding friends.’ Now, remember, I don't attribute this maxim to one party more than to another.

I have never seen the volume of ‘Rejected Addresses,’

but have read some of them in the papers, which I
thought very good indeed. I am sorry the author
has outraged your nice feelings respecting your name,[1]
although not enough, it seems, to prevent your determination to keep it. I remember to have heard
formerly that ladies are induced to part with their
names rather by love than fear. By the way, I am
in the train of reading the 'History of Clarissa,' who
affords a notable example that fear is not the effectual
mode. Pray did you ever go through that work?
There is, indeed, tautology of sense—the same thing
said ten thousand times over. I should be glad to
hear your thoughts of that work. With much skipping I shall have finished it in two or three more
sessions. Now God bless you, my dear and good
friend. Write to me soon. Write me long letters,
and never read them over, because that would be
more than lost time. Tell me all that happens. Let
me know who is coaxing you to change your name.
Are you to be a Quartermaster-General?

Remember me most kindly to your papa and
mamma. Tell him (I like to have a little crack at
him about politics) that I fear he has lost ground in
the new Parliament, but he may perhaps fetch it up
in the next, with which consolation I beg to comfort
him, and you also, you dear little grey vixen, in
which words there is a deep meaning.

From yours affectionately,

W. Elford

---

[1] He gave the name of Mitford to a fireman: 'Whitford and
Mitford, ply your pumps.'

Bickham, December 23, 1812.

Having a quarter of an hour before dinner, and being dressed and seated in my own room (called in some families the lion's den) at my own round table, with my own pen and ink (which it is death for any-one to touch), I resolve to devote it to my own dear little friend, and to acknowledge the receipt of her letter by yesterday's post.

I am particularly glad that you have given up your custom of sending your publications to your friends, and I do assure you that nothing but delicacy prevented me hinting to you before now that it was a practice that you had very high authority for avoiding—among others that of Addison, who in a case somewhat similar when he got into office, was prevented from remitting a great number of fees to his friends and acquaintances by a suggestion that a great aggregate loss would be sustained, while each individual gained almost nothing.

I meant in my observations to make no particular reference to England or to the present war, whether just and necessary or unjust and unnecessary, but merely to state my opinion that in the system of the world generally there are various modes designed by Providence to restrain the inordinate increase of animal life besides natural deaths, and what may be termed accidents; and that this regulation, as applied to the human race, consists in the frequent recurrence of wars (which we learn from both sacred and profane history have existed from the earliest ages of society throughout the world), and, where those have for times been occasionally wanting, that famine and its concomitant pestilence have produced the same effect. I instanced China, and the excessive famines that have raged there within the past century, within which no wars have thinned the inhabitants, as a proof. Do I now make myself understood?

I am doubtful whether the opinion of the world is so much in favour of Richardson's talents as formerly. It appears to me that there is not one character in the whole work that has any natural trait in it, or any marks of distinction, which it required any considerable talents to depict. Many of them are known from one another only by some peculiar mode of expression in their letters or conversations respectively. There is no mind or characteristic feature portrayed, and no more skill was required to make such distinctions than a painter would want, who, finding a family each individual of which always wore a coat of a certain colour, should distinguish their portraits by the colour of their clothes, instead of the similarity of features. Clarissa is herself the only interesting character of the whole mass, and is on the whole a fine one, but God forbid that her virtue (as to chastity) should ever be considered as of a superior kind. What were her temptations? She knew her lover to be a man of free conduct respecting women. She was not irrationally in love with him, and, after she was in his power, was, by the peculiarity of her situation and her knowledge of his character, put most eminently on her guard. Any woman of common education and principles would have done as well in similar circumstances. I have one positive fault to find with her, which shows her to have come out of the same mint with Sir C. Grandison—who is a most infernal prig, and ought never to be admitted into gentlemen's company, nor ladies' either. I mean a seeming consciousness, which accompanies all she says or does, that it is said and done better than other people. There is a constant display, scenes, acting—in short, there is nothing of the rest of Nature. With regard to the Harlowe family, they are all brutal savages or contemptible idiots. Mr. Richardson may say that he intended them so, but that I deny. You are told indeed that they were fond, and loving, and doating on this daughter—for her piety, filial love, acquirements, and virtues generally, but throughout the work there is no mark of such feelings. . . .

Saturday.—As I have an opportunity of sending this off, I shall dispatch it with all its imperfections. Let me hear from you soon. I shall send to your papa some time or other a little book I once published, as soon as I can get a copy of it. It is on the subject of animals and vegetables, and was written in answer to a man who wanted to revive the doctrine of equivocal generation. I suppose it is more right to send it to you.

Yours most truly and affectionately,

W. ELFORD.

SIR W. ELFORD *to* MISS MITFORD.

Bickham, December 21, 1813.

As no one is less a theorist or hypothesis-builder than I am, it is not to be wondered at that it is only very lately, and by mere accident, I have made the following important discovery, namely, that the power of writing letters is regulated altogether by the writer's distance from the metropolis—that a person who lives within forty miles, for instance, possesses that power in the vast disproportion of eleven to two beyond one who lives two hundred and twenty miles from it, and so on; and that it of course follows that while I have been labouring under an intolerable burden of obligation to you for sending me two letters for one, you have, in fact, been under the highest obligation to my moderation in not insisting on receiving more than five to one. . . .

I am happy that you think with me about waltzing. Have you seen Sir H. Englefield's verses? They appear to me perfect as far as touching forcibly the proper points. They are supposed to be indignantly addressed to the man who is found waltzing with the poet's mistress :—

What! the girl I adore by another embraced!
What! the balm of her breath shall another man taste ?
What! pressed in the dance by another man's knee ?
What! panting recline on another than me !
Sir, she's yours; you have pressed from the grape its fine blue,
From the rosebud you've shaken the tremulous dew ;
What you've touched you may take. Pretty waltzer—adieu !

Is it not excellent? Before I had seen this I had written something to render the waltz odious, which I sent to a friend in town to get inserted in some newspaper, and if it should be printed, I'll refer you to it. Mine pretends to be a history of its origin (in prose), and I have endeavoured to give it an air of truth; with the exception of a few names of persons and places, the whole is sheer invention. I wish all good people would lift up their voices against the introduction of this dance. I am sure it will never be generally tolerated in this country, unless the moral feeling of the community has undergone a change, which I trust is not yet the case. Now adieu, my dear, for the present.

Now I am come to Wednesday the 29th, and have just a frank for Saturday the 1st; and so, in the first place, I beg leave to wish you, my dear and fair correspondent, and your papa and mamma a happy New Year, and many happy returns of the present season, etc., etc., which is, I believe, the proper form to be observed on such occasions.

I have not before, that is in the former part of this letter, observed on the epigram on your Scotch judge, which I like very much, although it is founded a little on puns, or at least, a certain degree on playing on words. I knew nothing of your humpback being a Welshman—why did you suppose I knew it? I will write out an epigram for you on a Mr. Wise, a Devonshire man lately appointed Consul-General in Sweden, who is anything but what his name imports, and who, I am informed, is about to return from his post under the sentence of incompetency.

> In pride of wealth and pomp of power arrayed,
> Caligula his horse a Consul made;
> More monstrous still, Lord Liverpool, alas!
> Confers that mighty honour on an ass.
> Indignant Rome the insult heard with sighs,
> But abject Britain calls her creature *Wise*.

If I was wise (worldly wise) I should leave this admirable *jeu d'esprit* unremarked on, in the hope that you might suppose by possibility that I had some hand in it; but I cannot, even for the high bribe of your good opinion, deck myself for a moment with another man's bays. I do not know the author, but I think it quite perfect.

What do you think about peace? I consider it as certain, and if you and I, your papa and mamma, and Lord Liverpool, and Mr. Fox, and Mr. Pitt were but now sitting down together, I could convince every one of you by incontrovertible arguments that the chances of a peace arising out of the present crisis are as a hundred to one in favour of it; and I intend, within a few days, to write down those reasons—to seal them up in the presence of credible witnesses, and if they are well founded, and demonstrate a proper insight and view of the different interests, objects, and motives of the various parties as they will be developed during the negotiation, I shall send them, duly attested, to the Prince Regent, and demand to be made Prime Minister out of hand—in which case, your papa being duly wigged, shall be immediately constituted Metropolitan of All England; your mamma be Chief Justice (you have heard that ' my mother's a justice of peace ') and you shall be Chancellor of the Exchequer and Poet Laureate. Don't say, therefore, when you see what I have done for you and yours, that men when they get into power forsake their friends.

Now I am going to bid you adieu, but not for ever (I mean for ever only till Saturday), as I hope my genius will be renovated sufficiently by that time to enable me to fill this page.

New Year's Day.—Last night was New Year's Day to me, and, if you can't make that out, you must know that I was forced to play a rubber of whist after twelve, after which there were two peremptory rubbers, which brought on the hour of one; when there being but four of us, and thinking it was not right to part just at that particular moment, we played our final peremptory, so that I did not get to bed till past two. All this happened at the 'Pope's Head' in Plymouth, from which I know you will infer that I am in favour of the Catholic claims.

I must finish my paper, and have room for very little more, but that little I cannot find. I remember in an epitaph written by a Dr. Greenwood on his deceased wife, after enumerating her various good qualities with much feeling and pathos, he proceeds thus :—

> ' Now, my grief for this dear woman is so very sore,
> That I really can write but four lines more.'

I have room only for two, which must be dedicated to wishing you all the joys of the present season, and assurances of affectionate regards from

W. ELFORD.

You owe me three letters

To WM. ELFORD.

One letter due on former account	1
For goods now sent	2
	3

P.S.—With W. E.'s humble respects to Miss Mitford—hopes no offence for sending in the bill, as is usual this Christmas time.

The following are specimens of Sir W. Elford's poetical productions :—

On hearing a young lady observe that ' kissing was a foolish thing,' who, on being asked how she could judge, replied that she had several brothers with whom she was a great favourite

> Never did love's tumultuous joys
>   That bosom yet inspire,
> If by a brother's mild embrace
>   You'd guess a lover's fire.
>
> Perhaps ere years, ere months are flown
>   Your radiant eyes may languish,
> Your beating heart, your trembling frame
>   May own the pleasing anguish.
>
> Then should the fond and favour'd youth,
>   As earnest of his bliss,
> Impart on his dear Laura's lips
>   A pure and ardent kiss,
>
> Would you those chilling words repeat?
>   Ah, no! I know too well,
> And tho' I guess'd your alter'd thoughts
>   You would not ' kiss and tell.'
>
> Then should you, Laura, dare to say
>   Your thoughts could never alter,
> Your conscious cheeks would tell the tale
>   Your trembling tongue would falter.
>
> But once at Hymen's altar bound,
>   You'd own all earthly bliss
> (If own you durst) was only found
>   In the pure nuptial kiss.

W. E.

October 16, 1803.

To Miss Treby *of* Goodamoor *on her desiring the author to write some lines on a scroll, on which others of her friends had written.*

> In ancient lore, we learn, Ithuriel's spear
> Made all, when touched, in their true form appear
> On kindred principles ; this magic scroll
> Draws forth the deepest secrets of the soul,
> The hand, whilst resting on this potent spell,
> E'en a poetic fiction dare not tell.
> Truth then must out, or else I would have told ye
> That young and old with apathy behold ye,
> That you have neither winning air, nor smiling eye,
> Nor dimpled cheek with hues of roseate dye—
> All this I would have told, and you believed,
> For thus might modest merit be deceived.

W. E.

February 13, 1808.

Occasioned by seeing Mrs. Siddons perform several characters on the stage at Plymouth.

> Far from the busy scenes of mirth and strife
> In listless indolence I passed my life,
> Felt neither pains nor pleasures in excess,
> And thought that apathy was happiness ;
> But Siddons came, and at her magic call
> The wildest passions fill'd my ravished soul,
> Sorrow and joy alternately prevail,
> Now pity melts, and terrors now assail.
> At her command, with jealousy 1 burn
> With her despair, and e'en to madness turn.
> When Love's the theme, her winning accents flow
> Soft as the sea, ere winds were taught to blow ;
> Her sighs I hear, her melting looks I view,
> And my fond heart allows the picture true.

Still as each varying passion she portrays,
The strong impression her whole frame betrays ;
Her looks, her voice, her gestures so agree,
Uniting all in such fine harmony,
That from her voice the blind her looks declare,
And in her sparkling eyes the deaf may hear.
To thee, oh! Siddons, now I call in vain,
Give me repose and calmer joys again :
In vain I call—these joys, alas! now fled
Have left tumultuous passions in their stead.
So o'er the heath at early dawn of day
The traveller winds his scarce distinguished way,
On either side beholds, with brow serene,
The dull, unvarying sameness of the scene,
Nor trees, nor hedges cross his languid eye,
And floating vapours still obscure the sky.
Soon from the hills in majesty sublime
The glorious orb of day begins to climb ;
At first he tries, with half averted sight,
The painful pleasure of the new-born light,
At every glance around new objects rise,
Fresh woods and rivers meet his ravished eyes ;
And as he eager contemplates the whole,
Ten thousand new ideas fill his soul.
What though alas! the sun's declining ray
Shall chase those charming objects far away,
Soon with another morn his rays again
Shall bless the traveller and illume the plain.
Oh! may'st thou, Siddons, like the sun return,
And with new ecstasies our bosoms burn,
Return and cheer us with thy genial ray,
Nor let a night too long succeed our happy day.

W. E.

Through Sir W. Elford Miss Mitford became acquainted with Haydon. The artist was a Plymouth man, and Sir William joined another Plymouth banker in purchasing his first important work, 'The Judgment of Solomon,' for three hundred guineas. Sir William told Miss Mitford to go and see the picture then on view in London. She went with a friend, but arriving late in the day was refused admission. A silver key, however, procured entrance to the room whence all had departed, except a bright, dapper, little man in a sailor's jacket and white trowsers. He pointed out to them the best position for seeing the picture. It was Haydon himself, who afterwards became one of Miss Mitford's most constant correspondents. The two Landseers and Eastlake were his pupils, but he was ambitious and persisted in painting immense historical pieces, for which there was little or no demand.

R. A. DAVENPORT *to* MISS MITFORD.

Perry Hill, Sydenham, January 29, 1815.

In spite, my dear friend, of your obstinate, detestable, and pernicious heresy with respect to the Spaniards—a heresy fit only for mad Edinburgh reviewers and mad 'Morning Chronicle' men—in spite of this, I should long ere now have done myself the pleasure of writing to you, had not various circumstances arrested my pen. Imprimis, I have been so exceedingly ill as to entertain hopes that I should be able to 'shuffle off this mortal coil;' as however I am fated to be always disappointed, I am still an inhabitant of this best of all possible worlds. In the

next place, the loss of time threw a heavy burden of
business upon my shoulders. Thirdly, I have en-
countered several severe vexations. I could go on
thus through a ream of paper, but if these reasons for
having been silent are not enough, I will sooner
appeal to your mercy than give any more.

But why do I talk of asking *you* for mercy, when I
feel so angry as to be hardly disposed to display any
myself? I protest that, were it not abominably in-
decorous to think of beating a lady, I should have
more than a month's mind to beat *you*. Yes, you are
a libeller—an inveterate, shameful libeller. Why,
Leigh Hunt has had two months' imprisonment for
an offence not a tithe of that which you have com-
mitted! Think of this and reform. Do you imagine
that I will allow my friends to be caricatured in the
most outrageous manner? You have with malice
prepense and aforethought, as the blessed lawyers
say, laboured to make me entertain an unfavourable
personal idea of a lady for whom I have the sincerest
esteem. But all your trouble is thrown away, for,
firstly, I do not believe a tittle of your description,
and, secondly, were every tittle of that description
true, I should still esteem and admire her. I flatter
myself that some day or other I shall have it in my
power to assure her of this *by spoken instead of written
words*. So pray leave off gnawing the file. To tease
you still more, I shall send you a sonnet to that lady
which I composed the other day :—

Sonnet to Mary Russell Mitford.

Mary, 'tis sweet from all the giddy throng
　Retired 'at eve, when all the woods are still,'
　To hear the lone and plaintive warbler trill,
By melody inspired, the liquid song.
'Tis sweet, reclined the woodland shades among,
　To list from Eol's lyre the tones that fill
　The breast with tenderness, or wildly thrill,
As zephyr breathes the magic chords along.
But sweeter than to hear the night-bird singing
　When peace reposes on the moon-lit plain,
Or tones from airy lyre of Eol ringing
　In bonds of harmony the soul that chain,
Oh, sweeter far, diviner pleasure bringing,
　To hear thee, Mary, pour thy heavenly strain!

R. A. D.

Now I will defy any living creature to say that there is not in the above sonnet at least four-fifths of a line which deserves to be praised. Should this be allowed, and it only be objected that all the rest is bad, I shall declare that the fault is not mine, that it belongs to the subject, and thus syllogistically will I prove it. The soul of poetry is fiction—there is no fiction in my sonnet—ergo, my sonnet, being denied a soul, *could not* be a good one. If I am not sufficiently entrenched here to set at defiance all the logical hair-splitters in Christendom, why the deuce must be in it!

How does your second volume go on? I hope that the genius of indolence does not still hold you in his fetters. We are all ready enough to put on those fetters—at least, I can answer for myself. But

Spenser says—speaking, however, on quite a different
subject—

> ' Folly it were in any being free,
>   To covert fetters, golden though they be.'

Positively I must insist that you do find or make a
story—not to excuse yourself, but to fill a second
volume.

Have you heard that I am to encounter a rival?
It is even so. There are certain persons at Edinburgh who, I know not for what reason, have *always*
regarded my work with an evil eye. Long ago
these gentry, of whose names even I am ignorant,
announced a volume, which, however, never appeared. They are now going to publish in good earnest.
The editor is Mr. Hogg, the Ettrick Shepherd, and I
am told that he has procured pieces from Walter
Scott and others of name in the poetical world. He
means to publish a volume half-yearly, and his plan
excludes, I am told, everything but original poetry.
I should never have dreamed that his book was meant
in direct hostility to mine had I not been apprised
of it by a gentleman of Edinburgh, who has a most
extensive knowledge of the Scottish *literati*. As
long as they do not personally attack me, I shall
neither strive to do nor even wish them ill. If they
think proper to cry me down, I hope to show them
that I have something of their own thistle about me.

I congratulate you sincerely on your deliverance
from the rhyming family—' farthest from *them* is best.'
It is to be hoped that they are not gone among people
who are subject to headache !

Present my kindest regards to your father and mother. Adieu, my dear madam. I am, with warmest esteem,

Your obliged and affectionate friend,

R. A. DAVENPORT.

The concluding letters of this chapter give us a last glimpse of Dr. Mitford's political connections. The first is from Mr. Perry,[1] the editor of the celebrated Whig 'Morning Chronicle.' From 1813 till his death in 1821, Miss Mitford spent a considerable portion of every year on a visit at his residence, Tavistock House, 'where they do the honours of London to great perfection.' She went to their box at the Opera, and met at their parties ' all that was greatest and highest in mind and accomplishment,' including Lord Erskine, Sir S. Romilly, Dr. Parr, Brougham, Moore, and Barnes the editor of the *Times.*

MR. PERRY *to* DR. MITFORD.

Strand, September 26, 1814.

MY DEAR SIR,

I am sure you and your dear ladies will be delighted to hear that at length I am relieved from the torture of suspense. I have a letter from Mrs. Perry, dated Gibraltar Bay, August 1. They were taken prisoners by an Algerine frigate on the very day they set sail, plundered of all provisions and water, reduced to absolute want, not suffered to land on reaching Algiers, not supplied with provisions, but ordered off

[1] The father of the late Sir Erskine Perry.

at an hour's notice. They sailed from there on the 17th of July, were becalmed for seven days in this exhausted state, and reached Gibraltar Bay on the 31st of July. There they are condemned to perform quarantine for forty-two days. My friend, Admiral Fleming, who commands at the station, gives them every comfort, and, I trust, will be able to send them home in a ship of war. My wife says they have passed through the calamity with fortitude, and that, under happier circumstances, the voyage would have been favourable to her health. She has suffered much from want of food, and they are all reduced by debility. Pardon my extreme brevity, as I have many letters to write to relieve our anxious friends; but there are none whose hearts will be more gladdened than your own, and my most dear and affectionate Miss Mitford's. Believe me all to be,

Your truly grateful friend,

J. PERRY.

Mr. Perry was a brother-in-law of Porson, and at his house Miss Mitford became intimate with the step-daughter of that celebrated scholar and wit. It was probably from her that she obtained the following lines, found among Miss Mitford's papers, and entitled,

CHARADE BY THE LATE PROFESSOR PORSON.

My first is the nymph I adore,
The sum of her charms is my second;
I was going to call it my third,
But I counted a million or more,
Till I found they could never be reckoned;
So I quickly discarded the word.[1]

[1] Several of Porson's charades may be found in Beloe's 'Sexagonorium.'

W. A. Madocks *to* Dr. Mitford.

Thursday ————— 1816.

My dear Sir,

1,000,000,000,000 thanks for your kind remembrance of me, and the valuable specimen of the swinish multitude, which, through your means, Mr. Haywood has favoured me with. How can I make him or you a suitable return? To send a copy of Bacon to me so well versed in the law as you are in your magisterial capacity, and so well grounded as you are in the principles of his liberal and enlightened philosophy would be superfluous. I must be content, therefore, to remain for the present, at least, your grateful debtor. My man starts to-morrow at four o'clock to be in Warwick Lane by half-past to await the arrival of his Boarship, and he will be conducted here to a breakfast of the freshest vegetables and purest milk. From him, no doubt, will spring a long line of illustrious successors, much to the gratification of the Christians and mortification of the Jews.

I have sadly regretted being prevented from attending poor Sheridan's funeral, by the obligation I was under to accept the invitation of my constituents to dine with them to celebrate my first election.

What a fame (monumentum ære perennius) has Sheridan left behind him!—that of having written the *best* comedy, and delivered the best oration that was ever produced in this eminent country. The last words he said to me at Cowes at parting after a delightful month last autumn, were, ' Do stop one day more. Upon my honour I'll set off to-morrow. My carriage is waiting at Portsmouth, and we will make two days' journey of it—we'll jog up together

> ' In gentle conversation, sweet and mild.'

My testimony to Sheridan's private character is that of his being a most amiable and full-hearted man. Glowing, generous, and friendly,

> ' If to his lot some human errors fall,
> Sit by his side, and you'll forget them all '—

most true of him while living; and now we shall never see him more, or his like again.

Most sincerely yours,
W. A. MADOCKS.

Sheridan's second wife, a Miss Ogle, was a sister of Lady Dacre and cousin of Miss Mitford.

CHAPTER IV.

ANOTHER of Miss Mitford's artistic friends, also
addicted, like Haydon, to covering yards of canvas
with sacred subjects 'whether people buy or not,'
was Mr. Hofland. He was a man of talent—'he
talks pictures and paints poems.' She introduced
him to Sir W. Elford; but his wife was her especial
favourite. This lady had great literary productive-
ness and ability, wrote seventy works, mostly
novels, and added descriptions to her husband's
engraved sketches. Miss Mitford tells her that 'the
pictures will get fame and money, the books money
and fame;' and observes, 'She is womanly to her
finger's ends, and as truth telling and independent
as a skylark.' She was a correspondent of Miss
Edgeworth, and of Miss Mitford from her early years,
and was with the latter in the 'deserted great house'
in 1818;[1] but the first letter we have from her is
dated May 25, 1820.

[1] Bertram House, which Dr. Mitford built, and had to part with
from pecuniary embarrassment.

May 25, 1820.

I made up my mind not to write even to dear you till I had with my own eyes seen Haydon's picture, and looked into it with all the powers of eye, mind, and heart I could muster. I have done so, and, after two full hours of gazing, shutting my eyes, thinking, and then gazing till the tears obscured 'em, I pronounce that 'The Christ' is admirable, sublime, affecting, and precisely what a Christian desires to own as his Lord and Master—the God he adores—the Friend he trusts—the despised One it is his pride to defend—the glorious One it is his honour to belong to—the Man who suffered on the cross—the Judge before whose eye the heavens shall roll away, and the sea give up her dead, yet whose benignant voice shall say to the trembling, lowly heart, 'Come, ye blessed of my Father.'

There were a great many people, but as I went alone, sat alone, and was alone with the picture so long a time considering it in every point, tracing through the written word all the succession of events, designs, and (so far as such a worm may presume) the feelings of that unfathomed and unfathomable ocean of goodness, the heart, which might be supposed to act upon the features, and impress them with character, so I conclude myself more mistress of this mighty object than many with whom it is a subject for criticism : and I have at least the satisfaction of *believing* that I know it as well as most of them, who have had far better opportunities of studying it; but mark, I gave my whole attention to *one* object. I saw much beauty in the whole, very much, but I was only fascinated by the great object, and that arose out of my determination of examining it—'having seen, I loved Him.' Now I apprehend this is a proof of excellence, for Raphael's pictures, I am told, have ever this effect—entre nous, Raphael never painted a head so full as this—yet I am mortal enough to wish it had not been so old, and that it had had a little more *positive* beauty in it; but I know myself to be wrong in this, for incessant thought must destroy mere beauty and ante-date age. There is a woman that will be seen in full front that I dislike much; it is ill-dressed, looks as if the posture (though natural) had been drawn from a lay figure, and the arms are so evidently a man's arms that to my eye they are quite offensive. They could be altered with the greatest ease—how I did long to do it! It is only putting flesh over that part just below the joint, which is always flat in a man, with evident muscular strength, but round in a woman, unless she is a char-woman. The whiteness, too, is that of a man's arm, which the sun has never visited—it is quite distinct from the lively delicacy of a woman's skin in the same part, and the wrists are those of a porter. What a pity he had not a lady to sit to him then.

Mr. Haydon had just left the place, which I was sorry for at the time, but I am not sorry now, for had he been there I could never have held such 'high converse' with his awful endearing picture as I did; nor have so saturated my memory and stamped it on my mind as I find I have. I must, however, go again to look at Wordsworth, &c., &c., for though indeed I saw a 'goodly company,' and they gave a magnificent impression as of a triumph, which called for my Alleluia, yet I have not acquaintance with any individual save the woman who teased me with her arms.[1]

I rejoice, my dear friend, that you are within reach of your old friends—the walks about Bertram House; for there is something to me inexpressibly dear in an *old* walk, and even the charm of novelty does not attract me so much in any scene as the delight of looking on that which I have looked on before, and loved before; flowers and shrubs so seen are friends re-visiting us, and claiming our wonted smiles; their beauty is friendship—it is more—it is the promise of immortality given us by their resurrection, when friends, still fairer and infinitely dearer, will bloom around us to part no more. So feeling, I am sorry to leave our walks, and maythorn, and nightingales, but, I believe, in about a month we shall go to Wells; *ad interim,* I shall have business to go through in my house, which you will be able to sympathise in after a removal. But mind, it will be at least three weeks before we go, so, if any gale of Arabia should blow you hitherward, *here* we are, proud and happy to welcome you, as a flower promised and delayed for three successive springs.

If my master were here, he would unite with me in every kind of respectful remembrance to Mrs.

---

[1] In her reply to this letter Miss Mitford says, 'I know the woman whose arms you dislike, the Canaanitish woman, the giantess in front of the picture which always seemed to me very unpleasant.

Mitford and the doctor, and all sorts and shapes of
good wishes to your darling self. Pray do not forget
me when you play nurse at Farley Hall, where I
envy your calling.   I hope Mrs. D. is quite well, and
all remains of Mr. D.'s accident forgotten.

My Fred[1] tells me he is well, but as he is very busy
reading, I have many fears for him. Mothers and
wives are trembling creatures at best. Happy are
the single !

I am at all events,

Yours most affectionately,

B. HOFLAND.

Between the time of writing the preceding letter
and the following, Mrs. Hofland's life was saved—by
a lawyer's bill ! Mr. Hofland had been engaged in a
Chancery suit, which, though gained, afforded no
pecuniary advantage, as the costs were to be taken
from the property. On Mrs. Hofland hearing of this
sad termination of their hopes she was greatly disappointed, and just as she was about mounting on
the Twickenham coach to return, remembered that
she might save sixpence in going by the Richmond
stage, and withdrew her foot. The coach was over-
turned on the journey, and the woman who took her
place was killed.

MRS. HOFLAND *to* MISS MITFORD.

December 23, 1821.

MY DEAR MISS MITFORD,

I have thought of *you* continually when the
terrible weight of my own affairs allowed me to

---

[1] Mrs. Hofland's adopted son.

think at all, but incessant occupation has prevented
my reading, and even seeking up the books necessary to be read. When I tell you that I have had
sickness in every branch of my little family at home,
and that he who is my *one* branch, fruit, and blossom
has been ill at Cambridge, and is coming home to be
nursed as soon as it is possible to remove him, you
will see at once how impracticable all efforts of mind
and imagination have been to me.

Yet this is not the worst. The person against
whom we got our suit in the spring was ordered to
pay the money into court November 1. He has *not*
paid, *will* not pay ; but will, by some of those nefari-
ous acts every day practised, contrive to turn bankrupt, go to prison, secrete his property, and not only
cheat us of the sum we sought, but throw the whole
costs on Frederick. So, just as he is straining every
nerve in attaining knowledge, he is suddenly cut
short, his efforts paralysed, his past expenses rendered nugatory, his health already injured, completely
destroyed, and—but I cannot go on—— I could
open my veins to save him, but it is not in my power
to help him. I am at times almost beside myself.

Mr. H. has been very poorly, which is no wonder,
for this unexpected stroke fell along with the difficulties of dark days and a large picture. It was on the
strength of having the means of payment fully in his
power that he ventured to engage in his exhibition
expenses, and took that ready cash which is now
called for a thousand ways, and which was Frederick's,
who wants it worst of all, and who, unused to grapple
with the world, shrinks into agony at the thought of

a creditor. Still the dear creature struggles to support me, and smiles in the storm. He will not smile long on earth, but, if there is a heaven, he will rejoice in it for ever.

When he comes I will try to think with him, for he is very likely to think of a character and story for you; for his reading is very extensive, and it will be well to wean him from his own oppressive state of feeling. Most thankful should I be if we could suggest anything that would give your exquisite powers a theme to work on. I assure you, uneasy as we are on our own account, both H. and I could think of nothing last night but your vexatious disappointment about ' Foscari.'

Give our best regards to those dear parents, who, I know, feel more for you than you do for yourself, and believe me, my very dear friend,

Most truly yours,

B. HOFLAND.

P.S.—Excuse all blunders. You are well aware what state my spirits are in, and how ill able I am to write at all. Rejoice, at all events, that you are not Haydon's wife.

We have now arrived at a time when, owing to the doctor's extravagance, money became very scarce in the Mitford cottage. As a writer of fugitive poems ' Missy Mitford ' had gained some little reputation, and the desirability of obtaining something more solid than praise now began to occupy her thoughts. The public owe much to her embarrassments, and

Mr. Harness often said that but for such pressure she would have published very little. On visiting London in 1820, she saw at one of the theatres an indifferent tragedy performed, the author of which, she was told, received three or four hundred pounds. This led to her entering a new and more ambitious field. The first play she wrote was 'Fiesco,' the dialogue of which 'put salt on Mr. Macready's tail,' but did not catch him, for she exclaims, in despair, 'Ah! I shall never have the good luck to be damned!'

But she continued to work, and was more successful in Julian, Foscari, and Rienzi.

Miss Mitford first met Miss Porden at Mrs. Vardill's house when staying in London in the summer of 1822. By a strange coincidence Mr. Whittaker had just sent her Miss Porden's 'Cœur de Lion' to review. Miss Mitford found her very pleasant, and her conversation earnest and natural, accompanied with a considerable amount of action. Truth compels her to add that she was plain, but this reflection she lightens by observing that she never saw a literary lady, except Jane Porter, who might not have served 'as a scarecrow to keep birds from cherries.'

ELEANOR ANNE PORDEN *to* MISS MITFORD.

Brighton, August 5, 1822.

MY DEAR MISS MITFORD,

I fear you have thought me very negligent and ungrateful in not replying sooner to so kind a letter as your last, but I have been induced to delay writing from day to day, first because I expected every week to see your sonnet in the Literary Gazette, and secondly because we were for nearly a fortnight on the eve of an excursion to White Knights, and I waited in the hope of telling you that we should intrude upon you for half an hour. But to show the vanity of all earthly expectations, the editor of the Literary Gazette has been so ungallant to us both as to keep the sonnet still imprisoned into his bureau; our journey to Berkshire vanished into smoke, and my letter remained unwritten. We are now at Brighton, in a state of similar uncertainty as to whether we shall again be attracted to the Norman coast or return to London, but I need hardly tell you that the vestiges of our ancestors on the opposite shore have strong charms for my father. It has been oddly remarked that England has been at the mercy of every invader, that she has acknowledged as conquerors the Romans, the Danes, the Saxons, and the Normans, and yet hers is the soil in which freedom has taken its firmest and healthiest root, and her sons are very apt to believe and boast her chalky cliffs inviolable. Shall I suppose that, as it was once fancifully believed of Ireland, not only is no noxious reptile native to her clime, but that those which are transported thither either perish or change their nature? or is it that the invaders, the Romans excepted, have found the conquered realm so fair that in making it their seat of empire they have adopted its interests as their own? At present her security is certainly in her seas and wooden walls, for if any enemy were once upon her shores, a fair and fruitful region is the easiest conquered. England would have no fastnesses, natural or artificial, and dreadful must be the waste of blood where there are no ramparts but those of flesh. However, I am not going to annoy you with a dissertation on a subject which, though hackneyed enough, has only arisen in my mind at this moment, suggested, I suppose, by the association between our Norman forefathers and the chalky cliffs we stand on.

A friend of mine scolds me frequently for my partiality to the rival coast, and professes himself a Saxon with almost as much pertinacity as Cedric in 'Ivanhoe.' He asserts that the Normans, cruel and despotic as they were, found the Saxon institutions so excellent that they durst not presume to alter them, and that we owe to them almost all the advantages of our boasted Constitution. This I will in a great degree admit, and yet, as far as regards myself, I would rather claim a Scandinavian than a Teutonic origin. I am inclined to trace to the Romans our patriotism and public spirit, perhaps also some of our democratic clamour. To the Saxons I allow our domestic character, with the coolness and intrepidity to which we have frequently owed so much; but I must claim for the Normans the spirit of chivalry and of mental activity which, exercised in one direction, has led to our superiority in arts and science, and in another has enabled us to combine in our literature the romantic and the classic. The military and the naval character we have equally inherited from all, and perhaps no three races could be selected better qualified to counteract the defects of each other, by which position I arrive at the conclusion that, if we are not super-excellent, it is our own fault, and we deserve a double punishment.

I have had a letter from Mrs. Niven, which breathes
all the happiness of the honeymoon, which, indeed,
ought to shine with peculiar brilliancy in the romantic scenery of Scotland. I wonder whether his
Majesty's visit to Scotland will tempt the bridal pair
again to Edinburgh?

Indeed you pay me a great many compliments
which I do not deserve. I have, I believe, a clear
head and tolerable memory, but I shall never rival
Mrs. Carter either in diligence or attainments. The
one is scarcely to be reached without the other, and
were I to attempt such application as hers, I should
lose health, and memory, and mind altogether. I
believe I must be content, like the sparrow, to pick
up what falls in my way, provided I can but retain
the power of digesting and assimilating it afterwards.

Our present correspondence reminds me of Miss
Edgeworth's tale, ' l'Amie Inconnue,' but our meeting
at Mrs. Vardill's has, I trust, precluded the possibility
of such a *dénouement,* and I speculate on many future
conversations with you, both in London and Berkshire. Should you write before my return to London,
your letter will either follow me or await me, according to our movements. This epistle, I am aware, is
very stupid, for it has met with so many interruptions
that the beginning of a sentence had to seek for its
conclusion among a herd of other fancies which had
been careering through my brain in the meantime.
My next will have a chance of being more amusing.
By-the-by, I think that *our* habit of employing the
plural pronoun to designate papa and me had nearly
made part of this page unintelligible to anyone not

accustomed to our regal style. Let me therefore say that my father begs a little corner in your mind till he can claim one in your memory, and that *we* would both express the same wish to your father. Does he never come to town, and do you scorn to make more than a flying visit?

Believe me, my dear Miss Mitford,

Yours very sincerely,

ELEANOR ANNE PORDEN.

P.S.—Are your labours nearly completed? I long to find that you have fairly beaten Lord Byron out of the field. I have not read his ' Foscari,' but perhaps yours may induce me to do so.

P. BAYLEY *to* MISS MITFORD.

Cumberland Place, September 21, 1822.

MY DEAR MADAM,

Accept my thankful acknowledgments for your very kind inquiries respecting my health, which, I am sorry to say, has rather declined since I had the pleasure of seeing you. But hope and resolution are strong in me, and though pain makes me occasionally break out into peevishness, I am on the whole resolved to bear what it pleases heaven to put upon me.

I cannot but regret that I had no opportunity of making inquiries relative to your tragedy, the success of which I hope speedily to hail. I confess I am somewhat anxious to know how you have been able to restrain the flow of your poetry, which appears to me copious and luxuriant, within dramatic bounds, and I cannot but suspect that some of your most favourite passages must be sacrificed to the call for 'Action, action, nothing but action.' This I understand to be the green-room language of the day—and I sometimes amuse myself with conjectures about the lopping and pruning that any one of our best dramatists would be obliged to submit to were he to appear in the present age. All that I have been able to learn from Mr. Kemble, whom my ill health has prevented me from seeing so often as I could wish, is, that he thinks very highly of your tragedy, and if I had never read a line of yours I should rest confident of your success on his opinion. I can also with sincerity approve all that you say of him and of Mrs. Kemble. It would be no easy task for me to point out in all my acquaintance two individuals of whom I think more highly. It was entirely owing to Mr. Kemble that I ever turned my thoughts to writing for the stage . . . .

I have by me a paper of yours, from which I wish to strike out a passage about hares, and I think to banish a portion of the poultry. I must also remark that however a *cat's foot* may be thought a perfection in a greyhound in Berkshire, my father, who was one of the keenest coursers in England, and celebrated in his part of the world for his matchless dogs, would never allow that a cat's foot was proper for anything but a cat or a cur. A long foot is surely more springy and elastic. You will, perhaps, think me very saucy, but I assure you I pique myself on my hereditary knowledge of the subject. And I ought to know all the good points of a greyhound, for I painted all my father's best dogs for him, and, poor as my performances were, they pleased him as well as if Snyders himself had executed them.

Very sincerely yours,
P. BAYLEY.

P. BAYLEY *to* MISS MITFORD.

Cumberland Place, Saturday.

MY DEAR MADAM,

I gladly avail myself of every opportunity that offers of writing to you, though at present I am about to teaze you. Your letters have afforded Mrs. Bayley and myself so much real pleasure that we seem to have lost something essential to our comfort now that we have been so long without hearing from you.

Mr. Valpy is absolutely *possessed* by a notion that whatever is done in the Literary Gazette must be imitated in the ‘Museum.’ When the papers called ‘Wine and Walnuts’ appeared in the gazette he cried out for a series of papers of the same kind, for which he is now tormenting one of our contributors. Then the poetry published under the signature L. E. L. caught him, and he could not rest for incessantly crying out, ‘We must get Miss Mitford to write us a series of poetry in the manner of L. E. L.’ It is in vain that I say, ‘Let Miss Mitford send us what she pleases, we shall be better than the gazette, our poetry on the whole *is* better than that of the gazette’; nothing but L. E. L. will go down with him.

Now, my dear madam, I beg you to send us just what you will, only send us something. I shall run no hazard of offending against truth in assuring him it is better than anything of L. E. L.’s, and you will see that I shall presently contrive to jerk that out of him. I have a very sincere regard for him, but really at times he tries my patience. It is 'in my office' to request that you will oblige us with something for the first week in February, when we are to do great things; but what they are to be I know not. For my poor self, I have always done as well as the great haste I am obliged to observe, from the quantity required from me, has allowed. And unless I have time to weigh what I write I see not how I am to furnish a less homely commodity.

Mr. C. Kemble is now so much engaged that it is next to an impossibility to find him at home, and my health does not allow me to make the experiment with the hazard of a disappointment . . . . Whatever may be the fate of 'Orestes,' I cannot but think myself extremely fortunate in having prevailed on Mrs. Kemble to substitute that play for the 'Charter of Seville,' since I must consider the chances of success are very much in favour of the former. It is resolved that the 'Furies' and 'Nemesis' shall be retained. I hope we shall have a fine overture and choruses from Mr. Bishop, who can do great things if he chooses to exert himself. I had an idea of getting a proposal for an overture, chorus, and songs of the 'Furies' sent to Beethoven. But Mr. C., though not dissentient, thought it needless . . . .

Believe me, my dear madam,
Always most sincerely yours,
P. BAYLEY.

In reply to the request in the above letter Miss

Mitford forwarded the following short poem, recording some pleasant social gathering :—

NEW YEAR'S EVE—*To a Friend.*

Banquet and song and dance and revelry!
   Auspicious year, born in so fair a light
   Of gaiety and beauty! Happy night,
Sacred to social pleasure, and to thee
Its dear dispenser, of festivity
   The festive Queen, the moving spirit bright;
   Of music and the dance and all delight,
The gentler mistress, beautiful and free!
   Oh, happy night! and oh, succeeding day,
Far happier! when 'mid converse and repose,
   Handel's sweet strains came sweetened, the lay
Divine of that old Florentine arose,
   Dante, and genius flung his torch-like ray
O'er the dark tale of Ugolino's woes.

MISS PORDEN *to* MISS MITFORD.

Mortlake, October 11, 1822.

I have been intending for some days to reply to my dear Miss Mitford's kind letter, but, having come to some good friends here for a little air and idleness, I have been so busy doing nothing that I could not find time even to write a letter. Had I been at home, where I have five hundred things to do every day, and that must be done lest the *house should stand still*, I should have had plenty of leisure; but I have often heard my dear papa remark that people in the country who have nothing to do, have never time to do anything, and I have certainly caught the infection. You, I suppose, will laugh at my speaking of the country within ten miles of London, but I feel that even this distance shuts me as completely out from all connection with home and its employments as a much greater would do, and if the smoke of the Metropolis be visible like a cloud in the eastern distance, the Thames, broad and blue, flows past the end of the garden in all its beauty, while boats and barges glide along its surface and glitter in the October sun. Have you ever noticed the different colour of sunlight at different times of the year and day? It seems to be as bright in one season as the other, yet the sun of autumn is not that of spring, and I think that a person waking up from a long trance would be able to distinguish them, even without looking to the landscape. Yesterday we were on the water, and I was enjoying at once the brilliancy and repose of the scene. At no other time could they have been thus united, with neither heat to oppress nor cold to annoy.

Next week will find me at home and hard at work after these my holidays; consequently, according to my former reasoning, both able and willing to find a spare hour for the perusal of your tragedy. I hope it is not very horrible, for I hate the horrors which have been so much in vogue, and have never read either 'Melmoth' or 'Frankenstein.' I believe I might have made myself much more popular if I could get over a certain dislike to write what I should dislike to read, and though it may be presumption to attack celebrated names and celebrated passages, I must own that Virgil's 'Envy' and Spenser's 'Cave of Error' are my aversion, as well as some other most exquisitely disgusting allegories. Our own Milton, I

think, always keeps clear of this fault, and I cannot
believe, in spite of Mr. Maturin, and Mr. Wilson, and
Lord Byron, that it is true taste which tolerates it.
Did you ever read the ‘City of the Plague’? If you
have, did you not regret that so many passages, such
pure poetry, tenderness, and sublimity are mixed with
descriptions that would almost prevent one from ever
re-opening the volume. Plague and famine are fine
subjects for the Muse, but she need not give one a
medical detail of their physical horrors. The French
have observed that there is one sense which poets
are never permitted to offend, that of smell. The
remark is of one, but I think that the other senses
also expect some degree of decorum to be observed
towards them, or why not give a description of the
cabbage-stalks and rotten apples, or the heads and
necks and other appurtenances of poultry which sometimes decorate a dunghill. I might almost be made
a companion for the dogs in the ‘Siege of Corinth.’
You will say that I am always catching hold of some
out of the way subject, and letting it run away
with me to the end of my paper. In truth I have
read nothing these three months but ‘Strathallan,’
which I heard much of when it came out, but feel
disappointed in now. The fact is that the time is
past for it. The best parts of it are those which
describe feelings that during the late war came home
to the bosoms of all. Since the peace, or, at least,
since her most precious majesty’s trial, all our political
and public feelings have been in a manner asleep, for
the interest taken in the distresses of the Sister Isle
was of a different kind, and, loyal as I am, I feel no

enthusiasm excited in me by the visit of our monarch to the rival capitals of Erin and Caledonia. Neither do I enter into the *housewifely* complaints of the new bread regulations, for I think they will be found an improvement when we get used to them. No, nor even at the maidenly sorrows of the alterations in the marriage act, and having got to this climax, which may as well be the termination of a letter as a novel, I will but express my good wishes for the health and happiness of you and those dear to you, and subscribe myself,

Yours affectionately,
ELEANOR ANNE PORDEN.

P. BAYLEY *to* MISS MITFORD.

Cumberland House, October 26, 1822.

MY DEAR MADAM,

Most assuredly I should have written sooner had not three days been entirely wrested from me by increased illness. And at this moment I am so weak from loss of blood, blisters, and from the plentiful use of that, to me, of all medicines the most lowering and distressing, digitalis, that I can just sit up in bed, pretty well backed up by pillows, while I write this letter. I hope it is not ungrateful in me to postpone my thanks for the service you have done me in your remarks on my tragedy until I have expressed the high gratification I have received from the perusal of 'Foscari.' I must frankly tell you that the play has very much surprised me. I gave you credit for a great deal, but not for what you are mistress of. The drama is your proper walk, and I pray you heartily henceforth to make the right use of your great talents, and to contribute something to the solid, permanent literature of your age . . . .

Will you be so indulgent to the invalid as to allow him to retain this treasure for a few days still? Tho' it might almost 'create a soul under the ribs of Death,' I have been reduced to such a state by digitalis that (what has never occurred to me before under the severest illness) for three days I have been almost senseless, and of course could not read. This very day, when, as I lay on a sofa, Mrs. Bayley played some of my most favourite pieces out of 'Mozart' for my amusement, I was so torpid that for a time I did not even know what was going on. I had always a horror of the medicine; its effects on me are so dreadful. I mean certainly to discontinue it for a time, and to-morrow I trust I shall be able to read the 'Foscari,' and to enjoy it. I cannot but laugh at my solemn remarks on your 'Agnes' when 'I look back. However, I cannot regret having made them, since they have been the means of my knowing the candour and goodness of your heart. How few are they who, without a hundredth part of your talent, would have refrained from exclaiming against the overweening insolence of the obscure editor of an upstart weekly paper.

Believe me ever, my dear madam,
Your much obliged,
P. BAYLEY.

The next letter was written three months later by Mrs. Bayley.

Cumberland Place, January 13, 1823.

MY DEAR MISS MITFORD,

You have doubtless heard of the dreadful event of last Saturday night, one that has for ever bereft me of a most tenderly beloved husband, whose loss I must incessantly deplore, and whose memory will be cherished by me with fondest remembrance. I venture to communicate with you, it relieves my overcharged heart, ready to burst with the violence of its emotion, but the hope of a re-union in another world gives me consolation, and, for the sake of my poor orphans, I will endeavour to bear up under this excessive weight of misery. Knowing the delight Mr. Bayley always experienced in the perusal of your letters, I had a melancholy pleasure in reading the one you last addressed to him. Your predictions, alas! how are they verified! When you wrote them the dear friend (you so kindly called him) was stretched on the bed of death. He often said 'Mary, Miss Mitford and you *must* meet; you would love and admire her; I should wish you to cultivate her acquaintance and friendship. I see her letters, her kind sympathy, and her affectionate wishes are as gratifying to you as to myself.'

(The next paragraph commences with some incoherent expressions of grief.) Amongst many kind friends, Mr. and Mrs. Kemble are foremost in their endeavours to serve me. Yesterday I had a visit from the latter with £50 from the Committee of Covent Garden Theatre as an earnest that 'Orestes' is received and will in due time be brought out. This will be a most anxious event to me, as its success will enable me to

publish with confidence his epic poem. Since his writings have hitherto appeared under a feigned name, Bayley (as a poet) would not excite the interest necessary to be obtained.

Let me thank you, my dear Miss Mitford, for your kind letters to my husband; they cheered him in the hours of pain and suffering, and may heaven bless and prosper you. My children fancy themselves acquainted with you.

Yours most truly and sincerely,

MARY BAYLEY.

CHAPTER V.

THE following letter from Miss Porden is interesting
for her allusion to Captain (afterwards Sir John)
Franklin, whom she shortly afterwards married.

Berners Street, November 22, 1822.

I am afraid my dear Miss Mitford will not think
that I manifest much regret at her having withheld
from me the expected pleasure of reading 'Foscari'
by the length of time I have allowed to elapse without expressing it. The truth is that I believe you
judged wisely in not sending it at this moment
(though it is no compliment to say I felt disappointed), for my head and hands have both been full of
employment, various in its nature, it is true, but most
unpoetical in every variety. I wish I could say that
my task was ended, or that I was out of this house.
It is the only home I have ever known, and I feel so
much attached to it as to be doubly anxious to quit
it. I know not whether you will understand this
feeling, but I could certainly have left it with much

less pain a month ago than now, and shall feel more in leaving it a month hence. However, it is not yet let, and I must await the consequence of two very picturesque *affiches* with which Mrs. Bates has decorated the dining-room windows. In the meantime my business seems rather to grow than diminish, for I could scarcely have imagined the quantity of papers which must be looked over and sorted by myself, besides a still greater portion appertaining to business, which come under the department of executors. I have, however, made much progress, and every day advances my preparations for flitting, notwithstanding that a bad cold has much delayed them.

I was half afraid that you might have misunderstood what I said about the prevailing taste for horrors; had I not been *certain* that you could not have fallen into it, I should assuredly not have hazarded my opinion. But now pray do let me have your tragedy when you can. I have the good habit of not flattering, of not expressing an interest I do *not* feel, but I have also the bad habit of often *not* expressing that which I do feel, and I believe that those who half know me are apt to be offended, because I cannot get my tongue to utter to their face what I can say glibly enough when they are not present. In the present case I can but muster two words. I am *proud* that you should wish me to read 'Foscari,' and I expect *pleasure* in reading it.

Mrs. N—— has been in town lately, but stayed a very short time. She appears much improved both in health and *embonpoint.* Pray do you know *him?* I was somewhat surprised to be welcomed at my first introduction by a shake of the hand (so long and powerful that I feared my arm would have deserted the socket), followed by half a dozen hearty slaps on the back. I have no doubt that he is a very worthy man, and that he thought it necessary to display some extra cordiality in the matter of his wife's friend, but I must own that I expected rather more polish from *her* husband.

We have lately been much interested in the return of our friend Captain Franklin from the Arctic Land Expedition. It was more than two years since any news had been received of it, and, as the newspapers will have informed you, those concerned have suffered quite sufficiently to justify any alarm of their friends. We have enjoyed the almost exclusive privilege of seeing the whole of the drawings. Those of poor Lieutenant Hood would do credit to *any* professional artist, and when we consider their number, the beauty and delicacy of finishing, combined with the extreme difficulties and privations under which they were executed, they become really wonderful and make him but an object of deeper regret. If he had died from the hardships which the expedition endured, or even if an earlier murder had spared him the miseries of famine, I think his death would be less painful. By-the-by, there is not a word of truth in the story of the *Elbe* and Dr. Richardson's tears. Compliments to your father. Write soon to

Yours sincerely,

ELEANOR ANNE PORDEN.

Joanna Baillie was one of those whose dramatic

power Miss Mitford especially admired. Writing in 1812, she says, 'Tragedy must now fly from her superb arena and take shelter in the pages of Shakespeare and the bosom of Miss Baillie.'[1]

JOANNA BAILLIE *to* MISS MITFORD.

Hampstead, October 7, 1822.

MY DEAR MADAM,

I was told some time since by Sir Archer Croft that you expressed a wish to have a copy of my verses on the death of Sir Walter Scott, which were printed, *not* published, not very long after that sad event, and I am quite pleased and flattered that you should desire it. I therefore beg you to accept the only two remaining copies, which, after searching everywhere, can at present be found. They are in bad condition, having been long in some dusty corner, and are not fit to be presented. The verses possess no poetical merit, but they give a. faithful picture of that amiable, extraordinary man, and for this you will read them with interest.

I am glad that our friend, Lady Croft, has had the good fortune to find herself in your neighbourhood, and that by her means I shall sometimes have the pleasure of hearing of you.

I hope, when you come to town, I shall have some opportunity of improving the acquaintance that I was so glad to make last spring by favour of our

---

[1] In another place Miss Mitford remarks that Miss Baillie's plays were not successful on the stage. Each of them was written to illustrate a single passion. 'Her writings are better as poems than as plays.'

mutual friend, Lady Dacre. It will make me very happy to do so.

Believe me, my dear madam,

    Your obliged and faithful servant,

        JOANNA BAILLIE.

ELEANOR ANNE PORDEN *to* MISS MITFORD.

      Hastings, December 18, 1822.

MY DEAR MISS MITFORD,

 I should not have detained your 'Foscari' so long, but that it reached me in the very moment when I was quitting London on a visit to some friends at this place, and I therefore brought it with me to peruse in the quiet of a *watering-place in the winter.* I know not whether you will feel it a compliment that I was much better pleased with it than I expected, though I can truly add that my expectations were somewhat highly raised. The interest begins at once, and continues throughout, and there are a thousand little touches of great beauty, although (and this in a drama is perhaps the best praise) there is no one passage on which I can fix as possessing a distinct and paramount superiority. I believe I am expressing myself very awkwardly, for my ideas are a little embarrassed by bad pens and bad ink; but I mean the charm of your imagery arises from its being appropriate to the speaker and the place. Lord Byron's brilliants are often so loosely set as to be taken out and replaced at pleasure, and frequently look better by themselves than where he had meant them to be. In your 'Foscari' I find also a much greater strength than is usual from a female pen, accompanied with many a lambent spark of genuine heartfelt feeling (what a phrase I have made of it!), which none but a woman could have given. With man it is frequently no less a duty than a habit to subdue the expression of feeling, and it is only in his most private moments that he can yield to it with propriety; and when writing for the public eye he is very apt to keep the same guard upon his pen as upon himself, and therefore I think it is that woman will often best draw a manly character, and that men certainly excel in their portraits of women. But really I am so stupid this morning that I cannot make anything of my own meaning, and must not expect it of you.

I have a bad cold, and have, besides, received a large packet of letters full of the most heterogeneous matter, and all requiring immediate answers, so that my head is a little bewildered. But in one word I like your tragedy very much, and can suppose your present conclusion to be superior to any of the six former ones. The only thing I could wish for would be a single word of mutual forgiveness between Francesco and Cosmo. Could you not put it in? I assure you I shall look impatiently for the moment of representation, and will do all that in me lies to promote its success. You may readily believe I am flattered about Rienzi, and shall at once pop down what occurs to me; you must not introduce him in his state of buffoonery, for it would be too like Brutus, and throws great difficulty in the way both of the author and actor, but the circumstance may be sufficiently shown, and the comparison made in the

first scenes, by the astonishment of the other personages at his change of character.

Petrarch, and the crowning in the Capitol, I would
certainly bring in, for it was one thing which made
me fix on the subject as dramatic. But I would by
no means introduce Laura. Her lover's passion was
too ideal in its nature to suit the stage, and besides,
what conversation could be imagined between them,
and who could *look* the character? To have given
that name even to Miss O'Neill would have been
robbing it of a certain sacred character of phantom
beauty with which the poet's fancy has invested it.
It would never do to show Laura cutting bread and
butter for her many children. But he may come in
fresh from a distant glimpse of her form, and, in short,
perhaps you will have little to do but to transpose
some of his sonnets. It is his high political character
which will give you most trouble to combine with
the sighs of his visionary passion. By-the-by, he did
not arrive at Avignon in the moment of her death or
funeral. That, perhaps, might make a fine scene, if
it would be kept from appearing an imitation of
'Hamlet,' which I think it might, especially as being
an historic fact. I think you have named all the
authors with which I am acquainted as likely to assist
you, but I am deplorably ignorant of Italy at that
time. Gibbon will go a great way, Sismondi, I believe, is very dull, but I dare to say contains a great
deal. I should think the first volume of his 'Literature
du Midi de l'Europe' would be of some use in colla-
teral information, and at any rate *that* is amusing. I
have an odd volume of 'Posies de Clotilde,' which

you shall also see. As for your friend with her ' sallow, sublime sort of Werter-faced man,' I know not whether to laugh or to cry. I have not time to enter into what I think of Englishwomen marrying foreigners, but the idea always makes me almost sick. I would even almost venture to say that either head or heart must have a fault in them, but, if you call on me do so, I will undertake to vindicate myself from the charge of uncharitableness in thinking so. Will you think me very old-fashioned for wishing you and all you love ' A merry Christmas and a happy New Year,' with many to follow them, or for adding the hope that something will soon bring you to London and your sincere friend,

ELEANOR ANNE PORDEN.

The letters of Macready to Miss Mitford are almost entirely upon business connected with the stage. It seems, however, desirable to publish them, as playwriting constituted no small part of Miss Mitford's literary work, and she even believed—with the usual blindness of authors about their own productions—that her principal talent lay in that direction. Mr. Talfourd introduced her plays to Macready's notice, and Mrs. Trollope carried on the negotiations, and so for a considerable time Miss Mitford only knew the great tragedian through correspondence. She afterwards says, ' They,' the Macreadys, brother and sister, ' are very fascinating people, of the most polished and delightful manners.'

W. C. Macready *to* Miss Mitford.

March 17, 1823.

My dear Madam,

Although you must expect from the greatness of your claim upon me some acknowledgment of the too kind, too flattering inscription on the first page of 'Julian,' I am compelled to disappoint you, for as I cannot say what I ought and desire from an inability to translate with truth my feelings from my heart to paper, I am obliged to request that you will permit me to be still further your debtor, and owe to your indulgence my pardon, as I am already so deeply indebted for my unmerited praise to your generosity.

Let me, however, assure you that my recompense is to me invaluable, and that I accept with gratitude the honour you have conferred on me, not as a remuneration for past services, but as an earnest for the security of my future exertions.

As our mutual good friend Talfourd is absent, will you permit me to instruct you in a few of the necessary *ruses* of dramatic authors? Lose no time in sending copies of your play with a note in each to the editors of the different principal papers—it will probably be the means of making them again recur to it, which is, of all things, most desirable.

Depend upon it, I shall neither be inactive in thought or effort until I see 'Julian' fairly established, which I am *confidently persuaded* it will be. Your method of rewarding your soldiers 'would make women fight' in all the secure anticipation of triumph.

I have the honour to subscribe myself, dear madam,

Your most obliged and faithful servant,

W. C. Macready.

P.S.—Pray urge the publisher to advertise the play almost constantly through this, and the next (Passion) week.

ELEANOR ANNE PORDEN *to* MISS MITFORD.

6, Upper Portland Place, July 31, 1823.

MY DEAR MISS MITFORD,

'Better late than never' is an old proverb, and so I will not allow my shame for not having written earlier to prevent my writing to you now. In simple truth I have often thought of you, but my convalescence, though in many respects rapid and steady, was for a long time not such as to allow me to write without great pain and fatigue from the posture it required— and even now a letter is a task which I put off from hour to hour, till perhaps some one comes in, and then it goes by till the morrow. I know not what is come to me, but since my illness I likewise read nothing, and have no pleasure in working. I hope the use of my faculties will return to me by-and-by, but now it is sometimes quite an effort to think—and yet I am well enough recovered in other respects. If you have heard what is about to happen to me, you perhaps smile, and ascribe my listlessness to that cause, but, I think, very falsely, and believe there has been no other part of my life in which a prospect of the same event would not have induced very different feelings.

When you next come to London I shall hope to introduce Captain Franklin to you. You will find him a man of sense and worth, but not a literary man —or, to speak more correctly, he reads and thinks much, but is not in the habit of communicating much of what he reads and thinks, except where he is very intimate : and neither his late journey of three years and a half, estranged from all civilised society, nor the being made a lion of, has contributed to wear off a natural crust of reserve. It will, however, I trust dissolve before your smiles. If not, you must be content to suppose, as others perhaps have done, that ' I love him for the dangers he has passed.'

Is it not curious, we are to reside in Devonshire Street, in the very house where I was born! I do not pretend to recollect it, having left it when nine months old, but I have always heard it spoken of as peculiarly comfortable and convenient; and I trust to find it so when we are settled in it, but that will not be yet, as we are off on a summer tour first. Not to the *lakes* though, albeit it that is the general course of a bridal excursion. Captain Franklin has certainly had enough of lakes, both frozen and unfrozen, and has perhaps even a bit of *hydrophobia*—that is, he prefers the *land* of his own country, much of which he has not seen, to the water, which he knows well enough : and surely we may find enough of romance in Dovedale and the Peak.

I suppose you think me in strange humour—but I am in and out of spirits twenty times an hour, emulating the moon my mistress; or the water his subject; or, if you like it better, emulating this strange weather, which jumbles March and April in the dog-days. St. Swithen should never have a candle from me, unless he would dry up some of his showers. He may be called the Jupiter Pluvius of England.

I have not seen ' Julian,' for I have not yet ventured to any public place ; but I read it, and with much pleasure. I doubt, however, whether I do not prefer your ' Foscari.' Are you at work on ' Rienzi ' yet? and does Ugo Foscolo help you with Petrarch? As I said before, I have read nothing, but I mean to read diligently next winter. In short, *we* both mean to do so much next winter that I suppose spring will find us stuck fast in the middle.

My sister has got a fine little girl, and is doing extremely well. Pray remember me very kindly to Dr. Mitford, and believe me,

Yours affectionately,
ELEANOR ANNE PORDEN.

In the next letter we find that Miss Porden has changed her name.

ELEANOR ANNE FRANKLIN to MISS MITFORD.

Devonshire Street, March 23, 1824.

MY DEAR MISS MITFORD,

Being at present relieved from part of my ailment, though still much of a prisoner, I am desirous of reminding my friends as frequently as may be, at once of my existence and regard for them, and so I will not pass by an opportunity of answering your letter. I am very sorry for the illness that has been in your house this winter, but if your mother has benefited by the late mild weather as much as I have, she has almost ceased to be an invalid. My cough has indeed flown off most agreeably, and were not I partly in Mrs. Niven's scrape, I might trip it gaily ; as

L 2

it is, my coming out will not be with the violets and butterflies, as you predict, though I may chance to pluck a few of the declining roses; and in the meantime am content to play the old woman. I have had too much to do with illness, during many years of my life, not to know how completely a sick charge absords one's time and intellect, and I congratulate you that, in spite of your complaint of stupidity, your own health does not appear to have suffered from nursing, and you have yet been able to snatch a few moments for composition. I shall have great pleasure in becoming acquainted with the inhabitants and economy of *your* village, particularly as you have sketched your portraits in the sunshine. ‘The short and simple annals of the poor,’ which have lately poured in such profusion from the Scottish press, I thought at first exquisitely beautiful and pathetic, and the tone of piety which pervaded them, at once appeared as a national characteristic, and was sublime in its simplicity. But after reading a succession of them I wearied of the beauty, the pathos, and even the piety, for they were brought forward too often, and betrayed too much of stage trick. Even the stage, which at first had been delightful, ceased to please, when its repetition proved it to be laboured and affected. Salutary as it may be to visit the house of mourning, or to read occasionally those works which make us acquainted with the sorrows and sufferings of our fellow-creatures, from which we ought to derive the double lesson of sympathy in their trials, and cheerfulness under our own, I have ever been of opinion that the brighter side of human

life is that upon which it benefits us to look most
frequently, and that we all of us need most constantly to be reminded of the blessings which we possess,
but too often neglect to enjoy. The ingratitude
which led to disobedience was the earliest failing of
our nature, and there is still in the gayest hearts a
chord of fretfulness and despondency but too ready
to vibrate at every trifle, while we are all of us deficient in what I consider the main duty of gratitude.

I was the more forcibly led into these reflections
from the periods at which two or three of the works
alluded to fell into my hands, and which convinced
me that they were no more beneficial reading for one
depressed either in body or mind than a sentimental
novel is for a girl of sixteen; in fact I would not take
them to the couch of an invalid, the place where
works of fiction are most resorted to, by those at
least whose general reading is not confined to trifling.
I think the public taste is not in any danger' of re-
lapsing into Arcadian pastorals, but I suspect these
Caledonian pastorals to be almost as ideal. Crabbe,
with his occasional coarseness and propensity to dwell
upon the disgusting 'where there is no need of such
vanity,' is almost the only one who has dared to be
correct, and he has given us some beautiful specimens of 'lights' as well as 'shadows.' Washington
Irving, too, has a few delightful fragments of equal
fidelity, rendered elegant by the elegance of his own
mind. You, I suspect, will remind me more of him
than any of the others, though your style is perhaps
very different. I am glad to hear that the 'Foscari'
are to make their appearance, and wish I could have

been of use to you respecting Mr. Young; but I have no one theatrical connection of any kind, and could desire for your sake that you had no need to trouble yourself about the caprices of a tribe proverbially fantastic and unmanageable. However, that and all your undertakings shall have my best wishes and support, little as I can do to help, for, shut up as I am, I not only cannot add my unit to the number of its friends at any critical moment, but I see too few persons to aid it with my tongue, as might have been at other times. By-the-by, have you read 'Alasco?' I have not, but mean to send for it. I do not know whether you are yet so disgusted with Lord Byron as to have lost all interest in his works, but I am informed that the 'Deformed Transformed' is absolutely a waste of time to those who peruse it, being without any of those redeeming flashes of genius, and touches of true poetry and feeling which so long beguiled the public into tolerating more than it ought. Pray do you know anything of Mr. Harness? Your account of his situation when you were in London made me feel a strong interest respecting him, but he has not called since my marriage, and I know not how he is now circumstanced. He was one of those whom I felt more of a friend than our degree of intercourse seemed to account for, and I should be sorry to lose his acquaintance; and, though he be a dandy parson, he is both a man of talent and sound thinking.

Pray say some pretty things to your father for me; and, with my husband's compliments, believe me,

Yours affectionately,   ELEANOR ANNE FRANKLIN.

W. C. MACREADY *to* MISS MITFORD.

Mornington Place, April 25, 1824.

MY DEAR MISS MITFORD,

Not knowing when our friend Talfourd may leave town, and being a most uncertain person as to my letters, I rather choose to send you this brief acknowledgment of 'Rienzi,' which I have received to read, than to wait to give a detailed opinion of 'Charles' as its companion. I think it extremely clever; some scenes are very powerful, and capable of being wrought into a most effective play. I have told Rignolds so, and have sent it to him, but though I am nearly certain his sentiments will not vary much from mine, yet I do not flatter you with the expectation that it will be produced this season at Drury Lane, nor indeed was it practicable, should I recommend the step. I shall have some conversation with Talfourd upon it when I see him, and I daresay we shall agree in our views. My sister desires me to say, with her love, that she has received your note, which in a day or two she will answer.

Believe me, my dear madam,
Yours most truly,
W. C. MACREADY.

MRS. FRANKLIN *to* MISS MITFORD, *Three Mile Cross, near Reading.*

Devonshire Street, May 19, 1824.

MY DEAR MISS MITFORD,

Your first note and your kind present reached me about the end of last week, and I did not acknowledge them immediately, because I wished first to read at least a part of the little book. I have since done so, and with as much pleasure as I can at present take in anything of the kind, but ever since my last year's illness reading has been so great a fatigue to me that my mind continually wanders from the sense. How much leisure should I otherwise have had this winter! whereas the whole amount of new ideas acquired since May last is not more than one moon should have furnished.

The first thing which struck me in your essays was the exact accordance between your printed and epistolary style. Are you aware how very little the idea of writing for the public changes your mode of expression? Some of your sketches I like very much. ‘Hannah’ I had read before, as well as the ‘Talking Lady,’ with whose portrait I was particularly struck, as she had left me about an hour previous to its falling into my hands. You have not done her justice in one or two particulars, for, by some means or other, she does contrive to read a good deal (aloud, I believe, always), and even writes very respectable verses. A friend of mine was greatly entertained at the change which once took place in her from a temporary loss of voice—a hint for your next edition. ‘Lucy’ also is no stranger to me, for she lived thirteen years with a near neighbour, but I believe her marriage did not turn out well. I also seem to remember your ‘Two Maiden Sisters,’ and wish I had been at the cricket match, though I prefer fair weather to foul on such occasions. And now I must tell you that I have a presentiment that you will be quizzed for some of your ‘Country Walks.’ I should have enjoyed them as much as yourself, but then I thought there did not exist another such grown-up baby for violets and primroses, hawthorns and wood-anemones, not to speak of the narcissus, with its beautiful pheasant's eye in the centre, and the lily of the valley. But half your readers, whose botanical excursions are limited by the conservatory, 'will but hear and smile.'

Your remarks on Lord Byron had peculiar force so soon after the news of his death, which could not have reached you. That intelligence came across me like a flash of lightning, or the shock of an earthquake. 'God forgive him all the mischief he has done,' was my first and involuntary exclamation. I wonder much in what tone and temper of mind he really died. He is a strong example of how much good or evil may be done in a very short life. His talents had raised him to a height from which no one but himself could have degraded him, yet more fallen than he has been lately he could scarcely be. I have heard many express the wish that he had lived to retrieve his character and change his opinions for his own sake, and for the example to society; but I had no hope that this would be the case. We have had many libertines, misanthropes, infidels, much of perverted reason and prostituted talent, but the deep and fiend-like spirit of revenge and hatred, mingling as it does with passages of the most exalted poetry and genuine feeling, with the noblest sentiments expressed with a sublimity that makes one feel proud of our species, have a character of insanity which renders me confident that, to whatever new objects he might have directed his energies, he never could have made a good or rational being. I have no more idea of moral responsibility as attached to his actions than to those of a maniac or an infant. One thing I am glad of. Murray has destroyed his memoirs, a sacrifice of nearly three thousand pounds, but I should think there is little doubt that the family will indemnify him. On inspection they were so disgraceful in every way that they could not be published, either on his account or that of the readers. A friend of mine who was at Naples when he gave them to Moore (a whole sackful of detached papers), and who read them in the carriage as they afterwards travelled through Italy together, told me at the time that, if ever they met the public eye, it must be with such changes and curtailments as would almost destroy their authenticity. No one whom he ever met, if but once and in the most casual manner, seems to have escaped vituperation in his black journal, and his pen was always dipped in the deepest gall when writing of those who were at the moment his greatest intimates—Hobhouse, for instance. That any man should be capable of so doing, and above all should contemplate the idea of so exhibiting himself to the public, is surely, as I said before, a strong evidence of insanity. The taint has been in his family for several generations; let us hope that it expires with him. I have still much to say, and have written a long letter without a word of my husband, or his expedition, or my little monkey that is to be. N'importe, you will say perchance, so farewell.—Yours affectionately,

ELEANOR ANNE FRANKLIN.

P.S.—I have seen no public notice of your book, except the advertisement a fortnight since. If I meet with any review of it I will let you know, though, in truth, I think you will hear of *me* first through the newspapers.

Mrs. Franklin *to* Miss Mitford.

Vale Cottage, Tunbridge Wells,
Monday, September 6, 1824.

My dear Miss Mitford,

I think you agreed to excuse apologies, and indeed I must tell so nearly the old tale over again that I am glad to commence with the assurance that the excellent air of this place, and the kind care of my husband and friends are beginning to restore me to my former self, and that I even venture to anticipate the time when I may once more write without pain. I am astonished at the change which has been wrought in me by a fortnight's stay at this most quiet of watering-places where, in spite of the rank and fashion with which it is crowded, the country is as rural and the denizens as independent as in your own village. Indeed I suspect the visitants who resort here are of too high a class to derive much pleasure from the ordinary routine of circulating libraries and public walks, and are too happy to escape from the gaieties of London, or their own country seats, to gain a stock of health against the winter by returning to the early hours of their fathers and enjoying their country rambles in perfect liberty. Of society there is plenty, but it is entirely without form, and an early dinner renders tea a welcome and substantial meal, towards which I feel certain longings at the present moment. As for us, we walk, ride, read novels, and nurse little Miss Nelly, who has now completed her third month, and, not having known either illness or drawback of any kind, is as fat and funny as possible. It would do your heart good to see her papa nurse her; he seems to enjoy it so completely . . . .

If I had not again given you some excuse by making the inquiry, I could quiz you heartily for having told me in three successive letters of Mr. Harness's chapel at Hampstead. I understand he now lives a very retired life, which makes me doubly anxious to meet with him and offer him a corner at our hearth or board whenever he may feel himself disposed to use the freedom of a friend. I always liked him, but while he was so much in high society should hardly have ventured to invite him thus familiarly, and in a party I never thought he appeared to advantage. I am sure my husband would be as ready to welcome him as I, and I can say the same of your father and yourself whenever you re-visit London. In the meantime I hope this fine weather has quite restored your mother's health, that your book prospers, and that you will write soon to

Yours very sincerely,
ELEANOR ANNE FRANKLIN.

CHAPTER VI.

IN 1822 Miss Mitford wrote that she was 'the least bit in love with Charles Kemble, because he was going to bring out her first play, "Julian."' It was performed successfully in 1823 at Covent Garden, with Macready as the principal character, and Miss Mitford was encouraged to persevere in the drama by Sir William Elford, Sergeant Talfourd, Mr. Harness, and by her own predilections. But notwithstanding the merits of her productions, she had great difficulty in obtaining their acceptance either at Drury Lane or Covent Garden. She was, as she says, thrown about like a cricket ball between Kemble and Macready, and an unpleasant misunderstanding arose with the latter about 'Rienzi.' He seems to have been anxious to oblige her, and wrote as follows :—

MR. MACREADY *to* MISS MITFORD.

10, Conduit Street, December 7.

Mr. Macready presents his compliments to Miss

Mitford ; begs to inform her that he has presented the play of ‘ Rienzi,’ with his own opinion of its merits—that Mr. Elliston thinks the play ‘ possesses great merit,’ and desiring a card of his terms to be sent to the author, has acquainted Mr. Macready that he will read it again, and wishes to have a personal interview with the author to give a final decision, or make an arrangement respecting it.

It appears, also, that Miss Mitford had already gone to London at Mr. Macready’s request to have an interview with him about altering some part of the play. Such negotiations might have led a less sanguine person than our authoress to suppose that the play was accepted. On finding that she was mistaken, her disappointment was great, and a friend wrote on the subject to ‘ Blackwood’s Magazine,’ using strong expressions, but doing good service to Miss Mitford and the public in bringing her case into notice.

No one appreciated Miss Mitford’s dramatic power more fully than Mrs. Trollope,[1] Fanny Milton, her friend from childhood, who in these days of embarrassment and despondency energetically advocated her cause. Mrs. Trollope had the happiness of being present when her anticipations were realised in the success of the ‘ Foscari,’ and, between joy for Miss Mitford’s triumph and sympathy with the play, ‘ cried herself half blind.’ Miss Mitford tells us that her

[1] See letter in the Introduction from Mrs. Mitford, dated November 14, 1802.

kind and warm-hearted friend had set her heart on securing the performance of 'Rienzi' either by Kean or Macready. Her interest in the matter is shown in the next letter.

MRS. TROLLOPE *to* MISS MITFORD.

Thursday.

One line, my dear Miss Mitford, I must write to thank you for the high, the *very* high, treat you have given me.

Your tragedy must neither lie on the shelf, nor must it be laid at the feet of 'dear William.' *If* Kean is about to return this year, I think I can see my way clearly. No, we will not intreat. Do not, however, be afraid of me. When I am talking to '*William*,' I always feel quite enough inclined to pet him, and, moreover, I know he would make a glorious 'RIENZI,' both strong against my offending him. But, by your leave, dear friend, he must not play out of 'charity.' Trust me, dear William would rather eat his heart than see Kean appear in 'Rienzi.'

Would you indulge Mr. Milman with a sight of the tragedy?

Should Colonna's wife be styled Lady Colonna?

May I write to you when I hear anything of the whereabouts of Kean?

And will you believe me, very sincerely and faithfully yours,

F. TROLLOPE.

The above seems to have been the first letter from Mrs. Trollope that Miss Mitford preserved. She calls her 'a lively, brilliant woman of the world, with a warm, blunt, cordial manner, and many accomplishments.'

MRS. TROLLOPE *to* MISS MITFORD.

Harrow, Monday, 15th.

Have you thought it very strange that you have not heard from me? I am sure you have, but it has not been my fault, believe me, my dear Miss Mitford. The first thing I did after my return was to see my Kean friend. I would have immediately written to you had I learnt from him anything *certain*, but I was only told that *nobody* knew what he intended to do, and that his wife was quite as ignorant of his intentions as the rest of the world. I then waited for the coming of Mr. Macready, and as soon as I heard that he was in town I wrote to him, asking him to come here to pass a day with us. He answered that he would do so, a day was fixed, but he could not come. Again and again he was prevented, but yesterday he came, and our dear Marianne with him.

And now, my dear friend, you will think me a sorry ambassador when I tell you that I have done *quasi nothing*. I never saw anything to equal the ice-case into which he retreats the instant a word is uttered relative to his profession, and I confess myself unable to pursue him into it. I got from him that his movements for *next* year (he leaves London on Monday next for *this*) depend entirely on Kean; if he acts in London, Mr. Macready will act in America, and *vice versâ*. Thus they cannot be *pitted*, as I had hoped, one against the other. Before he leaves town, however, he shall have a letter from me, which he must read, you know, and which I suppose he will answer. My object in writing shall be to obtain his final determination as to ' Rienzi,' and according to this answer we must look to Kean for next year or not. I think I can assure you with confidence that he *does not* know who wrote the offensive article ; the name of Mr. —— was mentioned incidentally, and he spoke of him with gentleness, and even with kindness, though he said, from what he had seen of him, he did not think him a man of first-rate intellect. Now our friend would not have stopped there had he known who wrote the letter to ' Blackwood.'

I was very unlucky yesterday in never being alone with Mr. M. for five minutes. I *would* have hazarded the putting him in a rage had no one been by to see it, but unhappily Mr. T. had brought down a young Oxonian with him, who never quitted us. *If* I hear from him, you shall hear again from me. Is there any chance of your coming to town ? I long to see you here.

I write in great haste to catch Mr. Partington, who will carry this to Reading. Let me hear from you, dear friend, and believe me,

Very sincerely yours,

F. TROLLOPE.

MRS. TROLLOPE *to* MISS MITFORD.

Harrow, Thursday, June 1, 1826.

I have just received a letter from Mr. Macready, my dear Miss Mitford, dated Bath. Had I the power of procuring a frank I would enclose it ; as it is, I will transcribe what he says upon the subject most interesting. He apologises very politely for not having answered my letter before he left town, but assures me that incessant occupation prevented it. He then says, ' I would not be ill-natured or ungenerous, but I must touch on things that are very painful to remember. All that I could do, and much more than prudence and my own interest suggested, I did ; and was prepared to do for Miss Mitford's play of " Rienzi." As a reward for all the friendship I could show her I was libelled in " Blackwood's Magazine " (and the *matter* could only directly or indirectly have been learned from Miss Mitford)—I should be ashamed if I bore her the least ill-will. I acknowledge and respect her very great talents. I think " Rienzi " an extraordinarily clever play. I should be *most* happy in an opportunity of serving her, and from my very soul I admire her excellent qualities of heart. But what is all this? I am wasting my paper and your time, and coming to no result. What does she wish me to do? I will do anything to serve her. I am not engaged in London; if I should be, which I do not think probable this year, the managers are so *economical,* I will present her tragedy again. If Mr. Young should be engaged, I will write to him about it. Is there anything else I can do? Instruct me how I can be of use to her, and how I can show you the esteem in which I hold your mediation in such a cause, and I will not be a sluggard in it.'

Now in this, my dear friend, there is nothing harsh or unreasonable. He *has* been wounded, and he has felt it ; but as far as I understand the business, he may yet bring forward your noble tragedy as it deserves to be brought forward. There is *nobody can* do it justice but himself. He says in another place that he should prefer the intervention or presence of a third person in any correspondence or conversation with you on this subject; and this is always right in matters any way connected with business. Could I be of any use in this way, you may most freely command me. Tell me how I shall answer this letter. I will say whatever you bid me; and you will I am sure agree with me that its gentlemanlike and conciliatory tone deserves an early reply.

Many, many thanks for your letter—it was very cheering to me, for truly I felt ashamed of the cowardice that made me shrink from entering upon the subject, which had occupied my mind the whole day; but I am now really glad I did not, because by transcribing his letter I can do more justice to his expressions than I could have done in repeating what he had said. I heartily hope he will not go to America. We may as well shut up our legitimate national theatre, if he does.

I am longing to get your new volume, and I am longing to see you. I hear in many directions of Mr. Milman's high admiration of 'Rienzi.' 'Said I not right?' You know Mrs. Milton and I differed on this subject—she did not do his taste justice.

It is midnight. I have been at the Harrow speeches, and afterwards dined in a very large party, but I was determined to write to-night. Adieu then, and

Believe me, truly and affectionately yours,

F. TROLLOPE.

MRS. TROLLOPE *to* MISS MITFORD.

Harrow, Sunday, [1826.]

I write, my dear friend, in all the haste of preparation for my departure, and as all my family are going somewhere or other, I have much to occupy me—so excuse a worse scrawl, if possible, than usual.

Our friend Mr. Macready is at Paris, and one of my first objects will be to write an invitation to him to meet *seul-à-seul* in the Bois de Boulogne. This is where the duels are generally fought—our meeting, I flatter myself, will be of a different kind. It strikes me that your letter is written so sweetly, so gently, so flatteringly, and so much to the purpose, that I cannot do better than to put it into his hands. And now let me give you, *en passant*, my ideas on this subject. I agree with you most completely as to the part's being fitter for Macready than for any other man that lives; it unquestionably is so, and if he would play it with all his heart and all his soul (as Young played the Doge) I know that it must do much both for you and for him. But, dear friend, if there be the slightest doubt, hesitation, or vacillation of any kind in him I would not, were I you, delay the appearance of this play. *Allez toujours* is what those who know the world best always say to the happy ones of the earth, who are sailing before the wind. *Allez toujours*, and you will reach a station which no woman has ever reached before. You will have possession of the stage.

It is hardly necessary for me to say that I would

choose Macready for your high priest, your prime minister, or what you will, and that nothing but his own *will* should prevent his being so. But, as you are no longer in a situation to rest solely on this, so neither must you. I am perfectly sure that in any case his noble nature and kind heart will lead him to wish the best success to the play. But suppose he does not take it, it will be because he thinks he cannot do so with advantage, but I do not anticipate this—*quite the contrary.* I only express what I think *in case* my expectations should be disappointed.

I go Wednesday, at 4 a.m., and hope to return the beginning or middle of October. You will see our dear Marianne before that time,—she will stay with me till I go. She will tell you of a scheme we have in which we think you may be able to help us, but remember *foi d'honnête femme.* You must betray us to no one. I daresay that you will laugh at our ambitious speculation—laugh, my dear friend—your arrows will be like Cobham's, tipped with good nature. Adieu! I *do* think you will come to me when the next play comes out. I charge you make ' Inez ' graceful, touching, and popular, that is all I ask ; am I not moderate ?

Ever affectionately yours,
F. Trollope.

Mrs. Trollope *to* Miss Mitford.

Harrow, July 2, 1826.

Your kind and gratifying letter, my dear friend, gave me very sincere satisfaction, as it proved to me most clearly that nothing like harshness could rest

upon your mind. I think Mr. Macready's faults have
been greatly exaggerated by those who have report-
ed him to you—at least, *I* have been able to discover
nothing but kindness in his mind towards you, and I
believe that this kind feeling has been more pained
than chilled by believing that you had ceased to feel
equal kindness towards him.

I have now to tell you that he is about to go to
America *immediately*, and he has commissioned me to
ask you if you would like that he should take your
tragedy with him. He desires me to say that he will
engage not to bring it forward unless he can do so in
such a manner as would *insure its being satisfactory to
you.* Let me have an early answer, dear friend, as he
is very soon to set forth, and in case you accept the
proposal, let us know what copy to send, and where
we are to get it. He has promised to come down
here one day before he goes, and I hope I shall have
your answer before that day.

Pray give my compliments to your father, and tell
him that though Mr. Trollope most cordially wished
success to the liberal candidates, he could not interfere with Burns, whom we now consider as Mrs.
Milton's *protégé* rather than ours.

I dined with Mr. and Mrs. Wilson at Mr. Randolph's
on Friday. They talked of you, and Mrs. Randolph
told me that she must invite herself to visit me whenever you were my guest, which I told her you had
more than half promised me. When will you redeem
this pledge ? Does this heat overwhelm you ? and
how do your flowers bear it ? My rose-tide (as Lord

Orford would call it) is almost over, but it has in every sense been a spring-tide.

Will you have the kindness to convey the enclosed notes for me, and will you believe me, what in truth I am,

Very affectionately yours,

F. TROLLOPE.

MRS. TROLLOPE to MISS MITFORD.

I will not leave the kingdom, my dear friend, only for a few weeks without saying adieu. I wish heartily that you were going too, as I shall be much with people that I know you would like, and who would like you. We shall pass the first fortnight of our stay at Lagrange, the residence of our valued friend, the venerable Lafayette. What a study would this admirable man be for such a pencil as yours! We shall then return to Paris, where we shall stay as long as Mr. Trollope's business will permit his absence, but this can only be to the end of October. I do hope and trust that nothing will prevent our having the happiness of seeing you here after our return—we shall have so much to talk of . . .

Perhaps you will hear that we have been amusing ourselves during the boys' holidays by acting plays. Do not, however, fancy that I have been representing the *Margravine in little.* Our theatre is made in our drawing-room, and the object of it was to improve the French pronunciation of our children by getting up scenes from 'Molière.' We have a French friend, who plays with us, and it is really astonishing how much they have got on by his aid.

Adieu, dear friend.   Present my compliments to Dr. and Mrs. Mitford, and believe me

Very affectionately yours,

F. TROLLOPE.

P.S.—We set off on Monday.

MRS. TROLLOPE *to* MISS MITFORD.

Harrow, April 22, 1827.

I was very sorry that Mr. Trollope missed seeing you.   It would have given him pleasure, and it would have given me news of you.   Moreover, he would have canvassed you for a favour, that I am now going to ask.   Among the many young Frenchmen who have been exiled for wishing for more freedom than the Bourbon fools and knaves allowed, is an artist, who first became known to us as a drawing-master.   If I have any knowledge of what is meant by the phrase, *a man of genius*, I conceive it to belong to him—but he is totally and entirely *alone*, and unknown.   His father, who was a colonel in the emperor's army, died in the retreat from Moscow, and left him no inherit-ance, but debts.   His only surviving relative is a rich priest—a jesuit—whom, as you may well imagine, he has utterly offended.   It would make your gentle heart ache if I were to tell you one quarter of what he has endured since he took refuge among us.   How he has contrived to live I know not, but he has now a few pupils, and this has enabled him (by sometimes going without his dinner to buy colours) to paint a picture, which has been received by the committee at

Somerset House. It is not *my* judgment alone that I give you, when I say that this picture is *most admirable*; but I well know its merits will never be felt without the aid of the public press. I know you have influence enough with Mr. Walter to get it spoken of in the *Times*, and perhaps in some other publications. All I would ask is to direct attention to it; for I am *quite* sure that, if it is hung where it can be seen, it cannot be looked at without admiration. The picture will be called in the catalogue, 'Love and Folly,' by A. J. J. Hervieu, No. 78, Newman Street. Will you then, dear friend, pardon all this long history, and try to aid by your influence a being who is worthy to call you friend—one day or other I shall hope to make him known to you.

Adieu! Give our kind compliments to your father, and believe me

Ever affectionately yours,
F. TROLLOPE.

P.S.—And so you would not come to do chief lion at Miss Landon's. It was really a very smart party, though *some of us* did look rather queer. You need not talk of our democratic friend to any of our dear good Tory ones. They would groan in spirit, and think that Trollope, his wife, and all his children were going to destruction. Adieu!

Towards the end of 1828 'Rienzi' was performed at Drury Lane, the hero being played by Young, and the scenery painted by Stanfield. The heroine, Miss Phillips, was then only a girl of sixteen. The success proved great, and there was a long run of crowded houses. Miss Mitford received £400 from the theatre, and sold eight thousand copies of the play. 'Rienzi' also became popular in America. It possessed considerable poetic beauty and dramatic power.

The following three letters relate to plays which Miss Mitford wrote: 'Cromwell' (or 'Charles I.') 'Inez de Castro,' and 'Otto of Wittelsbach.'

DR. MILMAN *to* MISS MITFORD.

My dear Miss Mitford,

I am quite ashamed of having kept your unread 'Cromwell' so long, but I have been intending to bring it myself. The weather, however, during part of last week, and latterly, I grieve to say, Mrs. Milman's indisposition, have been insuperable impediments. Thank you for it. It is a strange, clever, absurd, lively, queer, farcical, indescribable production. It is impossible not to be amused—impossible not occasionally to admire. On the other hand, the *Liston* farce of part of it—even exceeds my notion of the liberty of the *genre romantique*.

I heard from Harness. He is still unavoidably detained in town, but will really come as soon as he is at liberty.

Believe me, my dear Miss Mitford,

Ever very truly yours,

H. MILMAN.

Dr. Milman, afterwards Dean of St. Paul's, was vicar of St. Mary's, Reading. Miss Mitford spoke in high terms of his reading and preaching, and upon his leaving wrote, 'We have lost our neighbour, Dr. Milman, who has got a London living. I would rather have lost a hundred stupid acquaintances than one friend so entirely after my own fashion.'

C. KEMBLE *to* MISS MITFORD.

Theatre Royal, Covent Garden,
January 29, 1827.

MY DEAR MADAM,

On my return from Bristol, which will be in about eight days, I will rummage out what plays I have upon the subject of 'Inez.' My books being at present in utter confusion, it would take me more time than I can spare to find them before I leave town. The subject is very pathetic, and, I think, admits of strong and varied character. Has not Hayley, in one of his plays, drawn such a deformity as you propose for Mr. Warde? I am almost sure he has, and, if my conjecture be well founded, will it be prudent to follow an unsuccessful example? My wife and daughter send you their best compliments, and beg you to believe they will have great pleasure in seeing you on your next visit to London. With respects to the doctor, I must conclude this hasty scrawl. I am always, my dear madam,

Yours most faithfully,
C. KEMBLE.

C. M. Young *to* Miss Mitford.

November 21, 1828.

Dear Miss Mitford,

Your plot of 'Otto' is returned to me without remark, except to beg that you would go on with the writing it as fast as you can; and which of the many alterations (you offer obligingly to make in the melodrama) he will accept I know not, but I think the part will fall to Miss Love, and 'tis time enough to settle about alterations when the period of producing the piece shall approach. At present we are up to our necks (that is, not I, but they) with the 'Blind Beggar of Bethnal Green' and the Christmas pantomime. I'm playing ill, or I'd run down to Three Mile Cross. I've no comfort but 'Our Village,' which I eat like an epicure, bit by bit, to prolong the meal—beautiful, quite beautiful, dear madam.

Yours faithfully,

C. M. Young.[1]

The following is interesting as showing the manner in which Mrs. Hemans first became acquainted with Miss Mitford. 'Our Village' had been published in 1824 :—

[1] The biography of this celebrated actor has been written by his son, the Rev. Julian Young. Fanny Kemble writes: 'Young had handsome, regular features, of the Roman cast, and a deep, melodious voice, but no tragic mental element whatever, but great comic power of mimicry. He was a cultivated musician, and very popuar in the best society. He made £4,000 per annum.'

Mrs. Hemans *to* Miss Mitford.

Rhyllon, St. Asaph, June 6, 1827.

Madam,

I can hardly feel that I am addressing an entire stranger in the author of 'Our Village,' and yet I know it is right and proper that I should apologize for the liberty I am taking. But really, after having accompanied you, as I have done again and again, in 'violeting,' and seeking for wood-sorrel—after having been with you to call upon Mrs. Allen in 'the dell,' and becoming thoroughly acquainted with May and Lizzie, I cannot but hope that you will kindly pardon my obtrusion, and that my name may be sufficiently known to you to plead my cause. There are writers whose works we cannot read without feeling as if we really *had* looked with them upon the scenes they bring before us, and as if such communion had almost given us a claim to something more than the mere intercourse between authors and 'gentle readers.' Will you allow me to say that *your* writings have this effect upon me, and that you have taught me, in making me know and love your 'Village' so well, to wish for further knowledge also of *her* who has so vividly impressed its dingles and copses upon my imagination. and peopled them so cheerily with healthful and happy beings? I believe, if I could be personally introduced to you, that I should in less than five minutes begin to inquire about Lucy, and the lilies of the valley, and whether you had succeeded in peopling that 'shady border' in your own territories with those shy flowers.

My boys, the constant companions of my walks about *our* village, and along our two pretty rivers, the Elwy and the Clwyd, are not less interested in your gipsies, young and old, your heroes of the cricket-ground, and, above all, Jack Hatch. Woeful and amazed did they all look when it was found out at last that Jack Hatch could die!

But I really must come to the aim and object of this letter, which I fear you may almost look upon as 'prose run mad.' I daresay you laugh sometimes, as I am inclined to do myself, at the prevailing mania for autographs, but a very kind friend of mine in a distant county does no such thing, and I am making a collection for him, which I should think (and he too, I am sure) very much enriched by your name. If you do me the favour to comply with this request, it will give me great pleasure to hear from you under cover to the Bishop of St. Asaph, 78, Gloucester Place, Portman Square, to whom I should have sent this letter to be franked, but that, being ignorant of your address, I am obliged to entrust it to a bookseller in town.

With sincere esteem, I beg you to believe me, madam,

Your faithful servant,

F. HEMANS.[1]

Miss Mitford writes in 1836: 'On her dying bed Mrs. Hemans used to recur to my descriptions of

---

[1] By a curious coincidence the signature to this letter has been cut off for an autograph.

natural scenery, and meant, if she lived, to have inscribed a volume to me. She was a charming woman, and so is my friend, Mary Howitt.' Mrs. Hemans
wrote several letters to Miss Mitford, some of which
were published in Mrs. Hemans' 'Life,' by Mr. Chorley.

CHAPTER VII.

THE remark has often been made that we meet with no romance in Miss Mitford's history—no trace of even a passing predilection or an unfortunate attachment. In her earlier years she was sometimes twitted about partialities for her cousin, Bertram Mitford and others, but no impression seems to have been made. That she was so far heart-whole was evident, for she could be jocose on the subject. She says that General Donkin[1] wanted his son to marry her, and speaks in 1818 of an American 'who was a sort of lover of mine some seven or eight years ago'—when she was about twenty-three—'but who had the good luck to be drowned instead of married.' When the family were turned out of Bertram House by Mr. Elliott, she writes: 'But for the ill-luck of his having a wife, I need not move at all, since he says,

[1] Perhaps Sir William Elford alludes to this in asking about the 'Quartermaster' in his letter of April 9, 1812.

had it not been for that misfortune, he would have married me himself. He is a little, mean-looking Bond Street shopkeeper of sixty-five, with a Methodist face, all bile, and wrinkles, and sadness, and a spruce wig in fine curls, shining like a horse-chestnut. I would certainly have married him, though.'

There were afterwards great difficulties in the way of any matrimonial settlement. The family had sunk from opulence until her parents had become in a great measure dependent upon her, and nothing would have induced her to leave them. Suitors would have had before them the prospect of supporting a penniless old man with extravagant ideas, to whom his daughter was blindly devoted. Miss Mitford possessed the attractions of worth and genius, but a lover is not guided by such advantages, and would perhaps have required stronger attractions than a stout figure and a pleasant intellectual countenance. From those who knew her circumstances no offers seem to have come, but the following letter of admiration from a stranger, raised to enthusiasm by her literary talent, is too characteristic to be omitted :—

Govan, December 31, 1827.

DEAR MADAM,

I remember quite well sending you a letter long ago, but nothing more; for, to tell you the truth, it was written under an hallucination. You cannot believe how much pain the reflection cost me, having no recollection of what I said, and fearing I may have spoken indecorously to you. But as this is our

Hogmanay,[1] I have got somewhat elevated in spirit, and feel disposed to write to you again, without fashing myself at all about what I said before.

Dear madam, excuse my freedom, but I love you with all my soul. Since I was fifteen, I had a vast number of loves, that is, I have at no time been destitute of a dreaming passion for some one or other, without going farther; but *you*, for more than this year back, have been my beau-ideal, and are likely to continue so, because my love for you is founded on realities, and not on imaginings, as the others were. I have never seen you, to see you might make me love you more, but could not possibly make me love you less, for it is your heart, feelings, thoughts, genius, that I love—they accord so beautifully with my own. I sometimes think you are me. I mean—though I could no more write like you than fly—that if I could write, I would write exactly the same. Now what puzzles me is this: I wonder how you can possibly be a woman. I never saw a celebrated female writer in my life. Of how you look, and how you conduct yourself in private and among friends, I cannot form the slightest conception. Male authors one has some idea of—I have seen two, that is all, Sir Walter Scott, and Mr. Jeffreys in the Court of Sessions once three years ago—but you go beyond my grasp. There is Miss Baillie, and Mrs. Hemans, and Miss Landon, and yourself—these are all I remember. I am not *very* anxious to see Miss Baillie; I suppose she's a sort of nun; nor Mrs. H.; I take her to go swimming like a fine, tragic queen; nor Miss L. Yes, I would like

[1] The last day of the year.

very well to see her, though I care little for her poetry. But you, above all things in the world, I would like to see—and next to that I would like to know the particulars of your life. There is nobody in this village can tell me anything about you. The minister himself is grossly ignorant. We have not now got a circulating library. It was too near Glasgow to thrive, and I am no ways acquainted in Glasgow. I am, therefore, famishing for the want of books. I have to pick up all my news of literature from the newspapers. I saw a delightful piece of yours quoted there lately from a book called 'The Coronet, or Literary and Christian Remembrancer.' It was entitled 'Fanny's Fairings,' and how I did 'Ho! ho!' with Tommy Stokes! My mother thought I was getting crazed. I wish you knew my mother. A better woman does not breathe, but I doubt I have broke her heart. It was all her wish and ambition to see me wag my pow in a pulpit, but to be a minister dressed in black all the days of my life, and obliged to preach and pray whether I felt disposed or not, I could not think of it. I would rather have taken the red coat. So here I am with my mother in our own little house, attempting to learn the weaving, with a view of commencing manufacturing by-and-by in the famous city of Glasgow. It is well I don't need to depend upon it, for I am singularly lazy, especially in fine weather, and vastly prefer a loiter by Cruikstane Castle, or a danner[1] by Kelvin-side to anything else. Were you ever in Scotland? It is a foolish notion—but could anything be more beautiful than the thought of you (a fine,

---

[1] A saunter.

English lady) asking your way to our house, and I
putting you on your right path, knowing you afterwards to be Miss Mitford. Or what is better. Suppose you storm-stead, and obliged to seek shelter with
us. Oh, delicious! To see you sitting at the fireside, cracking with my mother, while I would be ran-
sacking the presses for everything drinkable and
eatable. In such dreams I am for ever indulging. I
have bought a copy at last of 'Our Village,' and am
never done reading it. I read it aloud, every word,
to my mother; but I will not tell what she said of it.
She thinks it her duty to discountenance all novels,
but when she begins one she is as bad as myself.
'Pamela' is her delight. Now I must not hide what
she said of 'Our Village,' for I know you cannot be
offended at an old woman's prejudices. She said
it was unco clever—just extraordinar clever, but she
thought you was a wee glaiket. She could not see
how you could set up your face in the clachan[1] after
exposing so many characters. I said that much of it
might be fanciful, and that the characters were probably disguised. 'Then it's no true,' said she, 'I canna
believe that, for I ha'e seen the like o' Hannah mysel',
and that hempie[2] Cousin Mary, everybody maun ken
her.'

You must think me impertinent, and so I am, on
paper. To-morrow is New Year's Day. I will drink
your health for the hundredth time. Excuse me. If
I were sure this letter would reach you, I would have
taken pains, but I have gone on rum-strum, and find
myself at the bottom. I am, with deep admiration

[1] Village.   [2] Roguish.

and attachment, your humble servant till death.

C. G.[1]

P.S.—The minister thinks you must be a daughter of Mr. Mitford who wrote the 'History of Greece.'

[Writing ten years later Miss Mitford says—'It is most certain that I shall never marry, at my age it would be most foolish, even if anyone were simple enough to desire so old and ugly a wife. There is no sight so melancholy as a wedding, and when there is no money the thing is worse.'

Towards the end of her life Miss Mitford's fondness for the drama brought her into connection with some gifted actors, and there was one for whom she certainly expressed great admiration. In her letters to Miss Jephson forwarded to me that lady has invariably erased several lines where that gentleman is mentioned. But it has been stated on good authority, and I believe correctly, that she merely appreciated his professional talent.]

ALEXANDER DYCE to MISS MITFORD.

London, 72, Welbeck Street, Cavendish Square.
October 20, 1828.

DEAR MADAM,

Accept my best thanks for the copy of 'Rienzi,' and allow me to assure you that it has not been thrown away, for, as Harness can bear witness, I can repeat long passages of it by heart. I have now the pleasure of forwarding to you the volumes I mentioned. If you were a mere poetical antiquary, and

---

[1] The name of this letter has been torn off, perhaps by Miss Mitford.

valued what was rare more than what was excellent, I should expect that Peele would find great favour in your sight, for of some of his pieces (now for the first time repeated) not more than two copies exist. Still I think that whoever reads his works with the hope of finding poetry in them will not be utterly disappointed. Recollect that he wrote at a time when there was no English drama worth copying ; and you will surely be forced to allow that he possessed considerable genius.

'The Old Wives' Tale' (which everybody had heard of, but nobody had seen till my reprint appeared) is very interesting, as having most probably furnished hints to Milton for his 'Comus.' I take the liberty of sending with 'Peele' another small volume, which I published some time ago. You will not, I trust, be very angry with me when you find that it contains some of your own verses; but I must account to you for having selected what you perhaps think an unfavourable specimen of your poetry. Though the volume bears date 1827, it was printed several years earlier, and lay in sheets at the printers, owing to the pecuniary difficulties of my publisher, till my patience was almost exhausted. At the time I put its contents together you had not written, at least not published, those smaller poems, some of which would have suited my purpose so well.

Believe me, dear madam, very faithfully,

Your most obedient servant,

ALEXANDER DYCE.

The Rev. Alexander Dyce was the well-known

editor of 'Shakespeare,' and of the elder dramatists.[1]
The allusion at the end of the above letter is to some
specimens of our 'English Female Poets,' published
by him. Mr. Harness introduced him to Miss Mitford,
who said she felt highly honoured by his approval of
' Rienzi.'

ALLAN CUNNINGHAM *to* MISS MITFORD.

27, Belgrave Place, November 21, 1828.

MY DEAR MISS MITFORD,

I thank you for your kind and candid letter. I
shall be silent, you may be assured of that—and am
indeed glad that you think as I do respecting the
Annuals. I beg you will be mine exclusively next
year—we shall not disagree about the terms. I shall
want something like a couple of stories and a little
dramatic scene; but of this we can talk when the
time comes. My scheme is to secure the constant
and exclusive help of four or five authors of fame and
name, pay them well, obtain a certain quantity in their
best manner from them, and then make out the book
with my own hand and the help of a few other friends.

I shall not hurry you for the tale for volume second.
I cannot begin to print before April or May. The
book will be out on Tuesday; but before then a copy
will be on its way to you; a copy also goes to the
king. Our friend the Scotsman speaks highly of
your communication to me. I have to send him your
address, that he may send you a paper whenever he
praises you. I think, from his admiration of your
writings, you will see many of his papers. He feels

[1] He left his valuable library to the South Kensington Museum.

the right-hearted, straightforward English character
of your compositions, and that you never write for
words but for ideas.

My wife unites with me in love and esteem, and in
assurance of lending tongue and voice to the further-
ance of your new play when it is represented. Nothing indeed could be more successful than 'Rienzi,'
and it reads better than it acts.

I am, my dear Miss Mitford,

　　　　　　　　　Yours very faithfully,

　　　　　　　　　　ALLAN CUNNINGHAM.

Allan Cunningham, a native of Scotland, was a poet,
novelist, and sculptor. He published a 'History of
British Painters,' &c.

C. M. YOUNG *to* MISS MITFORD.

December 20, 1828.

MY DEAR MADAM,

'Rienzi's' twentieth night went off to an admirable audience, and was extremely applauded. Your
difficulties about 'Otto' I feel. I think he must not
be Brunswick, I think he must not be killed *on the
stage*, because he is an emperor, and because we have
a licenser—mum! I wish you were not forty miles
off; so many things come into one's head to say
when one is absent which will not from pure perverse-
ness 'come to your call' when most needful. One
thing I'll mention—with all we can do, cutting and
clipping, speaking fast and with energy, speaking
slow and with pathos, however it may be, the devil a
bit can we help the last scene of Claudia dragging,
dragging, DRAGGING! I think it is because *the Event*

(a small matter of Execution) is in process, as well
the audience know; whilst Claudia is talk, *talk*,
TALKING! Now, when the audience is in the scent
of any incident, I don't think they like suspense! Am
I wrong? I only mention, be it right or wrong, that
you may think of it whilst composing fresh matter.
If you agree with me, you'll avoid it again; if you
don't, why then you'll do it again. 'Words *is* no
blows, and speaking don't break no bones!' as an
erudite farmer once told me.

The postman rings! The bell, the bell, the mighty
bell! Adieu, dear madam. Success to your pen.

Your faithful servant,

C. M. YOUNG.

Through the Hoflands Miss Mitford had become
acquainted with Mr. and Mrs. S. C. Hall about the
year 1826. Mrs. Hall was now writing her celebrated
'Sketches of Irish Character.' She dedicated this
work to Miss Mitford, and observes, 'My first dear
book was inspired by a desire to describe my native
place as Miss Mitford had "Our Village."' The
following letter, written at this time, has been kindly
contributed by Mr. S. C. Hall.[1]

MRS. HOFLAND *to* MRS. S. C. HALL.

23, Newman Street, March 3, ⌈1829⌉.

Och! to be shure, my dear honey, and it's your own
swate self that is quite ignorant of the most wonder-

[1] Between 1829 and 1832 Miss Mitford frequently wrote for
Mrs. Hall's 'Juvenile Forget-me-not,' her fellow contributors
being Mrs. Hemans, Miss Strickland, Mary Howitt, Mrs. Opie,
Hannah More, &c.

fullest, astonishing surprise that is just come upon a body, and that has done a body's heart good to think about—an' nivver a word the spalpeen rascals i' the *Times* has tould us about it, becase, you see, she commanded her nibours (the faather and thim) to hould their black and white tongues, and never mintion the particklar case. But as to not tellin' o' you, my dare, all as I jist happen to know why, it's out o' the question, honey—so hear goes. Miss Mary Mitford is married, honestly married to one of her own kith and kin, a true Mitford of Northumberland, tho' his relationship is a mighty way off. An' he have taken her down to his own fine estate, a noble ould mansion, an' made her, who was a rale lady, jist asy for the rest of her days, an' her parents asy too, an' if that isn't good news, what is, honey dear?

My dear Mrs. Hall, in plain English, this is the fact, not communicated to me by her, for she has not told any living creature, for what reason I do not know, but I conjecture that it may not interfere with arrangements respecting her forthcoming tragedy. I have no doubt that the song[1] printed in your excellent magazine (for it is, so far as I have seen, as good as the first) was written in reference to this gentleman, who was attached to her in early life, but could not then marry, and whom she had not seen for many years till within a very few weeks. The marriage and all the arrangements have been kept

[1] The song begins:—

> And art thou come back safe again
> From over the salt sea?

a profound secret, and they are gone to his seat in Northumberland. The friend who told me mentioned it a fortnight ago in confidence. We had it from Mr. Mitford's brother, an officer, who, I believe, is sorry it takes place, because people don't like bachelor brothers who are wealthy to marry, otherwise he has all respect for the lady's talents and character. They are perfectly suited in age. He is a man of great ability, and proud of her fame, so that there is every prospect of happiness. It will surprise many—people concluded that at her age, and with her genius, the men would have

> ' Left her alone in her glory.'

I am glad there was one found who knew better. No woman wanted a friend more, or deserved one better, and I sincerely thank God she has found such a friend, and knowing your heart and mine beat alike on the subject, I could not forbear telling you the news hot and hot.

Mr. Hall's true tale[1] does him honour for its selection and its telling, and it will do good, I am confident, which is what he most desires—yours is as good as Miss Edgeworth's best. I shall be most happy to see you. I have been poorly, but am better. The house is like a fair, with pictures going in to the Suffolk Street Gallery, and the business of secretaryship, and I am writing, when I can write, no less

---

[1] 'A Scene of Every-day Occurrence,' which, together with one of Mrs. Hall's 'Sketches of Irish Character,' appeared in Mr. Hall's Magazine, the 'Spirit and Manners of the Age,' for March, 1829.

a thing than a novel of three vols., an undertaking
I wonder I have courage for. Give my kind regards
to Mr. Hall and Mrs. Fielding, and believe me very
truly and with every good wish

Your faithful,

B. HOFLAND.

MRS. HOFLAND *to* MISS MITFORD.

[1829.]

MY DEAR FRIEND,

Mr. Ackerman has just sent me this parcel to
forward to you, and as I was on the point of writing
to the Doctor to inquire after you, I think it better to
send with the parcel that inquiry, which I can no
longer withhold. I have loved you too long and too
well to sustain the solitude which belongs to uncertainty any longer—are you married or not ?

A month ago, I was told as *a secret* that you were
on the point of marriage with a gentleman of your
own family whom you had not seen for many years,
but who had loved you all this time ; he was a man
of great literary taste, landed property, excellent
character, and, in short, all one's heart could ask for.
Then I was told ' to look in the papers for three
successive days, and I should be sure to see it.' I did
not find it, and I saw my informer, and said so. The
answer was, ' But the marriage *has taken place*, and
Miss Mitford, now Mrs. Mitford, has gone down to
Northumberland. I had it from the gentleman's own
brother, who is Captain Mitford. My first informer
was young Taylor, who is, I believe, very distantly
related to Miss Mitford, but naturally proud of the

alliance with her cousin; and I now tell you *positively* she is married, and gone to the mansion house of her husband, which is a very pretty place, and you may rest satisfied she is in every sense of the word *well married*, for the gentleman complied with every wish of her heart as to settlements and all that. All the world will know it soon, but they have been particularly private.'

This was Mr. Lane's news. Well, whilst I was for the first time rejoicing in the '*certainty* of wakening bliss' on this account, cómes a magazine from Mrs. Hall, in which I found a song from Miss Mitford, which formed the best possible comment on the news; so down I sat, and wrote to Mrs. Hall, telling *her* that she might be happy too; and at home we talked of nothing else for two or three days, but on the fourth came Frederick with a grave face, saying 'the whole matter must be a mistake, that a Captain Mitford had married a Miss Frances Mitford, and taken her to his seat in Northumberland, was *certain*, but it was utterly unlikely two gentlemen should have *both* married wives of their names and journeyed northward the same week, and that he was fully persuaded, in short, *our* Miss Mitford was still the wise woman he believed her to be.' Well, this plagued me all day yesterday after I heard it, and this morning comes Mrs. Hall, who says her husband spoke last night to Mr. Martin, whom he saw in the House, on the subject. Mr. M. said, 'Miss Mitford is not yet married, but she is engaged, and it will take place soon,'—he heard no more.

Mrs. Hall will write you, for she wishes to dedicate

her new book to you. Mr. Ackerman desires I will
try to persuade you to send a good budget for both
his annuals, but if you are really going to take him,
' who is come home with a kind heart and free,' I fear
you will do but little in that way.

' Rienzi ' is performing to-night (by special desire).
I was so ill of a cold and hoarseness, which confined
me, I think, for five weeks, that I had no chance of
getting to see your picture within *the . time*, which
vexed me much, and disappointed Mrs. Hawkins, who
was to have gone with me to Kensington.

Well, now, I don't ask for any particulars—indeed,
it seems Mr. M. must know, and that you are not
married, but, it seems, will be soon. God grant you
may be most happy, as I have no doubt you will be.
Perhaps Mr. M. may not know after all. People are
so occupied with this awful question—all else seems
forgotten.

Mr. H. is perpetually engaged at this vile gallery,
which never did him any good, nor ever will. We
are all better in health. I trust you all keep well. I
am aware it is a time of great trial to you all; it
must be so even with the happiest prospects. My
prayers and every affection go with you.

B. Hofland.

Mrs. Hofland seems to have had a feminine weakness for marrying her friends, for she wrote to Miss
Mitford on another occasion that Miss Edgeworth
was going to be married to her (Miss Edgeworth's)
step-mother's father!

MRS. TROLLOPE to MISS MITFORD.

Cincinnati, January 20, 1829.

I believe, my dear friend, that you were once among the short-sighted mortals who deemed me in the worst stage of lunacy when I left the Old World to pay a visit to the New; but as the wreath of bays you wear has never, as I think, impeded one glance of kindness from your friendly eye towards the ordinary working-day mortals who surround you, so neither have your many and absorbing occupations been able to make you forget those you have honoured by the name of friend. Let me, then, repass in fancy the Atlantic to greet you—let me tell you that I never see a paper professing to give literary news from England without anxiously looking for your name. I have read whole pages of extracts from the Annuals and 'Our Village'—so well do the savages know how to make their papers sell--but I have not seen, what I chiefly sought, any account of the appearance of the noble tragedy, three acts of which you read to me when I last saw you. Our dear little Marianne writes me word that she believes Young is going to play 'Rienzi.' I know there *is* great power in that man, when he is warmed sufficiently to put it forth. Write to me, dear friend, I entreat you, in this remote but very pretty nest, where I am sitting to hatch golden eggs for my son Henry. A letter from you would be like the first warm bright sunbeam after a long dreary winter; yet is the country beautiful, and wonderful in its rapid progress towards the wealth and the wisdom, the finery and the folly, of the Old World ; and I like it well—the better, certainly, that while Henry is making money I am saving it; but, alas! there are no Mary Mitfords, no Marianne Skerretts here, and I do sometimes languish for that fine full flow of London talk which Johnson describes.

We are not, however, without our lions. Miss Wright, to visit whose residence was one of my inducements to cross the Atlantic, has abandoned for the present (and as I think for ever) her scheme of forming an Eden in the wilderness, and cultivating African negroes till they produced accomplished ladies and gentlemen. She is now devoting all the energy of her extraordinary mind to the giving of public lectures through all the cities of the Union. Her subject is *Just Knowledge*, and in strains of the highest eloquence she assures the assembled multitudes that throng to hear her that man was made for happiness, and enjoyed it till religion snatched it from him, leaving him fantastic hopes and substantial fears instead. I am told that she means to repeat her lectures through England and France. Wild, and often mischievous, as her doctrines are, she is a thing to wonder at, and you must hear her, if you can.

Henry's prospects here are, I think, very good; but eighteen is too young to be left, too young to be judged of fixedly. I believe him to be very steady, but I must watch by him for a year or two longer. I think Mr. Trollope returns to us next year, and I shall then be able to decide whether it will be advisable to continue here or not. My girls have very good masters, and I know that they are not losing their time. *Nothing* shall keep me here after my eldest girl is sixteen—at least, nothing that I can possibly foresee or imagine, as I think I owe it to her to let her see young ladies' daylight in a civilized country.

Oh! my dear friend, had I but the tenth of an inch of the nib of your pen, what pictures might I draw of the people here!—so very queer, so very unlike any other thing in heaven above or earth below!—but it may not be. I can look, and I can laugh, but the power of describing is not given to above half a dozen in a century.

Will you accept, during my absence, of my eldest son *as a friend and enthusiastic admirer?* I pray you do. I cannot describe to you the earnestness with which he desires this. He is immediately to be entered as a student at Lincoln's Inn—and, poor fellow, he means to be a good boy and a lawyer—but his heart and soul are literary, and all the consolation he can receive under his enforced studies will, and must be, derived from letters. Will you, dear friend, receive him among your *friends?*—let him be your slave and servant for all and any of your London affairs, and, if you find him a faithful and useful servant, pay him by a chat or a line, when your leisure serves. I *think* there is some soul in him, but I remember that I am a Nemo, and will not rest too firmly on my own judgment. Pray remember me very kindly to Dr. and Mrs. Mitford, and believe me very affectionately yours,

F. TROLLOPE.

ARCHDEACON WRANGHAM *to* MISS MITFORD.

Chester, February 21, 1829.

DEAR MISS MITFORD,

Mr. Goodlake, in reply to a suggestion of mine, informs me that he has already sent you one of the copies of the book to which in every sense you are so abundantly entitled. I trust you will think it, to use the technical phrase, 'well got up.' Mr. Goodlake's generous purpose to transmit the net produce to Mrs. Barnard, who with her three tender orphans is but ill provided for, deserves and has our warmest gratitude.

If I were an official man, with the butterflies I should enclose my letter to my clergy of the arch-deaconry of the East Riding of Yorkshire on the Catholic subject, as I declined calling them together, and have since *ostensibly*—for I was in the minority *of one* in the Chapter—concerned in an anti-Catholic petition. I thought it due not only to myself but to them to explain both what was the real state of the case, and upon what views my conduct had for thirty years been uniformly in favour of the claims. However, as I possess no privilege of the franking kind, I fear my donation and your curiosity (if you feel any upon this head) must undergo a little suspension.

I shall not, I fear, get to town this spring, though invited both by my old friend and constant host, Basil Montague, to Bedford Square, and by my gay statesman and his wife to Wilton Crescent. But new furnishing a drawing-room at this place, and taking possession (at a great expense) of a new and almost incomeless archdeaconry, besides a heavy subscription toward repairing the woeful calamity of York Minster, will make me too poor for London ; or I should consider it one of my first pleasures there to find out Mr. Lucas. Your character of him as an artist, and also as a man, would entitle him, independently of my wish to see your *very self*,[1] to my earliest attention. But *I* too must wait for more auspicious circumstances.

I remain, however, dear Miss Mitford,

Ever yours most truly,

F. WRANGHAM.

Mrs. Hall *to* Miss Mitford, *Three Miles Cross, Reading.*

April 28, 1829.

My dear Miss Mitford,

I trust you will find nothing in my ' Sketches of Irish Character' to offend your political feelings. I can love a Catholic as well as a Protestant, although I think we ought to have kept the upper hand with them. However, I care naught about the matter, except as far as it vexes my much respected friend Mr. Sadler, who unites fine mental qualities to one of the most noble and yet simple hearts in the world.

Miss Smyth's album is quite safe, but the fact is we wished to enlarge it by the addition of some very pretty pictures. I found I could not paste them neatly in, so I took the liberty of placing them properly, and then getting all *re*-bound together, which is much the best way. I know she will not be angry at this, if *you* make a pretty speech about it for me,

---

[1] Referring to Lucas's portrait of Miss Mitford.

and I assure you every portion of the book is preserved with the greatest care. Westley says I shall have it back in ten days, and then it shall be left in Printing House Square, as you directed.

Dear Mrs. Hofland spent an evening with us lately. I wish you had been of the party. I am going to spend a few days with our friends the Carnes, at Blackheath. I suppose you know his 'Tales from the West.' They are very hospitable, nice people, and you meet *everybody* (literary) at his house.

I have not time to enlarge my epistle, but conclude, requesting you to accept 'lots' of love from us all. I finished my last tale, 'Peter the Prophet,' last night.

Most affectionately, my dear Miss Mitford,
Your sincere
Anna Maria Hall.

Miss Strickland *to* Miss Mitford.

Reydon Hall, near Wangfield, Suffolk,
June 2, 1829.

To Miss Mary Russell Mitford.

Thy ' sister poetess,' thou gifted one !
Never for me will lyre like thine be strung :
Never to me will Nature teach the art
To sketch the living portrait on the heart ;
With her own magic pencil to portray
The storms and sunshine of life's varied day,
The fond anticipations, hopes, and fears
That gladden youth, or shade our riper years ;
With Nature's untaught eloquence to trace
The joys and sorrows of a fallen race,
Till the heart's fountains at thy page run o'er ;
We know the author, and the scene adore

From infancy my steps have wandered far
Through flowery fields, beneath Eve's dewy star,
And I have flung me on the earth's green breast,
Till my heart heaved against the sod I press'd,
And tears of rapture blinded fast the sight
Of eyes that ached with fulness of delight.
In this our souls are kindred, for I love
The flowing corn-field and the shady grove,
The balmy meadow and the blossom'd thorn,
The cool fresh breezes of the early morn,
The crimson banner of the glowing west
Flung o'er the day-god, as he sinks to rest;
The witching beauty of the twilight hour
In hazel copse, green dell, or woodland bower;
The plaintive music of the wind-stirr'd trees,
The song of birds, the melody of bees;
The kine deep lowing on the marshy mere,
The sheep-bell tinkling on the common near;
The reaper's shout, the sound of busy flail,
The milk-maid singing o'er her flowing pail;
The voice of ocean heaving in my view,
Reveal'd through waving boughs in robe of blue.
Or when the moon has risen high and bright,
Girdling the east with belt of living light.
'Mid Nature's solitude my days have pass'd;
Here would I live—here breathe in peace my last!
Fame is a dream! the praise of man as brief
As morning dew upon the folded leaf;
The summer sun exhales the sparkling tear,
And leaves no trace of its existence here—
That world I once admired I now would flee,
And to win heaven would court obscurity.

SUSANNA STRICKLAND.[1]

This Miss Strickland, a sister of the celebrated authoress, married eventually a Mr. Moodie, author of

[1] There are references to this poem in pages 206-7.

'Ten Years in South Africa,' and emigrated to Canada. In her work, 'Roughing it in the Bush,' she gives a most discouraging account of the miseries to be endured in colonial life by those who have been accustomed to the refinements of civilization. She wrote songs which became very popular in Canada.

MR. BARNES *to* MISS MITFORD.

Tuesday, July 14, 1829.
48, Nelson Square,

MY DEAR MADAM,

I am very sorry that you have had the trouble of writing an explanatory letter, though I must always be pleased to receive any communication from you. Dr. Mitford has misunderstood my meaning. Having heard that you had finished two tragedies, I asked, with an interest which it is impossible for anyone who has seen and read 'Rienzi' not to feel, when either of them was likely to appear. Dr. Mitford then told me of the impediments which had been offered to the representation of 'Charles I.' I observed that such an opposition was the more absurd as there was already a tragedy with that title, which had been acted without scruple above fifty years ago. Dr. Mitford then proposed to favour me with a perusal of your tragedy, which, of course, I was happy to accept, though, at the same time, I expressed considerable apprehension for the safety of the manuscript, should it have to travel backwards and forwards from Berkshire to London.

This, as well as I can recollect, is the substance of the conversation to which your letter refers. I will add that I fully appreciate the justice of the reasons which you urge against any public allusion (at least at present) to the conduct of the licenser. I need not say how proud I should be to express publicly as well as privately my great admiration of your extraordinary talents—allow me to add, not even yet developed to the full extent of which they are capable; but I know well, what you accurately describe, the necessity of 'bending to the various difficulties that beset a dramatic writer.' I think, too, that there is some loss of the dignity of a superior writer in appealing to the public for sympathy. Miss Mitford is in a condition to demand public admiration, not to solicit public compassion.

Mrs. Barnes, as well as myself, regretted greatly your absence last Saturday; she is very grateful for your kind remembrance, and very proud of your good opinion.

I am, with great esteem,
Your faithful servant,
F. BARNES.

Mr. Barnes was editor of the *Times*. Miss Mitford seems to have met him at Mr. Perry's.

The following is written in a round schoolboy hand, and undated. It is, however, interesting, and Miss Mitford's reference to it is quoted by Dean Stanley in the 'Life of George Cotton, Bishop of Calcutta.' She wanted for one of her plays 'The Ban of the Empire,' and after having fruitlessly enquired among her literary friends, German historians, and law professors, obtained it from a boy in these words:—

G. E. LYNCH COTTON *to* MISS MITFORD.

St. Peter's College, Westminster, July 20.

MADAM,

Having understood from a friend that you wished to obtain the words of 'The Bann of the Church of the German Empire,' I take the liberty of sending them to you, and I hope you will find them correct. It is one of the earliest examples of this mode of proscription, and was launched against the Duke of Suabia : 'We declare thy wife a widow, thy children orphans, and discard thee, in the devil's name, to the four corners of the earth!'

You will find it in 'Les Anecdotes Germaniques,' page 151, and as I have experienced so much pleasure from the perusal and representation of your beautiful tragedies, I shall have great satisfaction in being of the smallest use to you, and hope, as I have no other mode of conveyance, that you will not think me an intrusive schoolboy.

Allow me to remain, madam,

Your obedient servant,

GEORGE EDWARD LYNCH COTTON.

The above was written in 1829. Miss Mitford informed him in her reply that she wanted the actual German words, and those he shortly afterwards sent her. 'We shall hear of that youth himself in literature some day or other,' she observes.

CHAPTER VIII.

LETTERS FROM MRS. HOFLAND, MISS STRICKLAND, DOUGLAS JERROLD, MISS SEDGWICK, AND MRS. TROLLOPE.

Mrs. Hofland *to* Miss Mitford.

' WHO can write to me on *pink* paper, scented? Bless me, how it is perfumed!'

' Some magnificent *blue*, of course,' said Hofland.

The letter was opened, your hand, my dear friend, was seen, and I said, ' How could Miss Mitford think of sending such a *fine* lady as this must be here?'

' I don't see why she should not. She pays us the compliment of considering us a lion and lioness in one cage.'

Thus stands the matter—Mrs. Morgan says ' she will be here to-morrow at twelve,' and will take charge of a letter to you, so I, at twelve at night (or after) write this note to be ready for her. My master goes off a-fishing[1] at six in the morning, and will, of course, not be seen, which is a sad reverse of the order of things, for he's quite a man to be exhibited

[1] He wrote a work on angling, a sport of which he was very fond.

to ladies who write on pink paper; and to all intents and purposes his wife is a thing to be hidden in any hole or corner, where all women are thrown. Certes, one less likely to please the fashionable and reward the fastidious could not be selected from the many who may now be found.

I grieve that you have been all ill, and I can well sympathize with you, though my *grand*, my *unceasing* object is for the present in a state of relief; but Tom, my dear little Tom, whom I love with such pity and such peculiar, and, I fear, excessive feeling as few people can conceive, is in a deplorable state. He has got a white swelling in the knee, and it is an equal thing whether he *can* or *cannot* weather it. I am going to the sea with him soon;—we are under the care of Scott, of Bromley, a successful kind of half-quack, of whom you will have heard. The child sleeps with me—leans on me for all his comfort. He can move a little on crutches, and his patience and cheerfulness, his delicacy and meekness, make him altogether the most affecting creature in the world. Indeed, there is an interest in his manners, and his talents too, which renders one inevitably superstitious. I feel sure he will be taken, but it may be long, very long, first.

I hear from Mrs. Hall you are getting on with the tragedy, but hindered by the annuals, which are, in fact, 'plagues of the land.' Nobody knows the miseries of writing to prints but those who do it, and my master cannot see this for a moment, and thinks I ought to do whatever is asked.

I think Mrs. Hall's book beautiful, but am not in love with her dedicatory letter; it is meagre.

In London all is misery, unmixed misery. There has been no such time in my life, though I remember much that was alarming. I think the misery may in a great measure be traced to the avarice and ambition of the trading world, who, in their *haste to be rich*, have drawn the poor to become manufacturers, who ought to have been agriculturists; worked too hard, overstocked the markets, and then thrown their tools out of employment, and, of course, into extreme misery. People may reason as they will, but *this* is the *true source* of the mischief. Had they gone on *moderately*, masters and men would alike have prospered, but, as the Bible says, ' they made haste to be rich, and pierced themselves through with many sorrows;' this, and marrying soon, and getting children without end, has ruined the country, yet Thirlwall two years since told me ' population was failing.' What a fool, we are eaten up by multitudes.

I went to the Academy to look at you, and was vexed to see you stuck up at the top of the room, and so feebly <u>painted</u>, the whole was lost. The figure is well managed, but the hat badly fixed ; the likeness is unquestionably well preserved, and very agreeably given, but in its position, the painter, poor young man, received a great blow, which even the *Times'* praise cannot soften. The Academy folks are sad folks—cruel ones to many a clever young man.

With a thousand good wishes and kind regards,
Believe me, your truly affectionate

B. HOFLAND.[1]

P.S.—What a monstrous advantage those 'Irish' writers have in their brogue.

The picture above mentioned was by Lucas, who was introduced to Miss Mitford by Mr. Milton, Mrs. Trollope's brother, one of his early patrons.

Miss Strickland *to* Miss Mitford, *Three Mile Cross, Reading.*

Reydon Hall, July 31, 1829.

My dear Miss Mitford,

Your kind and generous letter, while it afforded me the deepest pleasure, affected me almost to tears, so totally undeserving do I feel myself to be of so great and distinguished a favour. I can scarcely believe that it is to one so little known and who has such slight claims to literary merit that Miss Mitford has addressed herself in such friendly and liberal terms. I fancy you mistake me for my second sister, Agnes Strickland, the authoress of 'Worcester Field,' and the 'Seven Ages of Woman,' and many other minor poems that have appeared in the 'New Monthly Magazine' and the annuals, and who is a very talented and accomplished woman, quite the reverse of the plain, matter-of-fact country girl, her youngest sister, who is now writing to you.

---

[1] This letter was marked on the back 'Honoured by Mrs. Morgan,' but that lady has crossed out the word 'honoured,' and substituted 'forgotten.'

My name is almost unknown to the world. A solitary piece of poetry in the 'Pledge of Friendship' for 1828, a few stanzas in 'Friendship's Offering' for this year, entitled 'There's Joy,' and some sketches from the country both in prose and verse, that have from time to time been inserted by my friend, Mr. Harral in 'La Belle,' are all the articles of mine that ever came before the public with my name or initials appended to them. I candidly confess that I consider *none* of these worthy of notice, and they were written more with the view of serving several dear friends to whom I was tenderly attached, than with any idea of establishing my reputation as an authoress. I cannot, therefore, appropriate to myself your flattering opinion of my merit, though I am not less gratified with the kindness and benevolence which induced you to give such encouragement to a young and nameless authoress to pursue her literary career.

You have written to me as a friend, and I shall reply to your kind queries with the same frankness with which I should answer an old and valued correspondent. I have been one of Fancy's spoiled and wayward children, and from the age of twelve years have roamed through the beautiful but delusive regions of Romance, entirely to gratify my restless imagination, to cull all that was bright and lovely, and to strew with flowers the desert path of life. I have studied no other volume than Nature, have followed no other dictates but those of my own heart, and at the age of womanhood I find myself totally unfitted to mingle with the world. I perceive with regret that I must hereafter render an account to my Creator for those precious hours and talents that were wasted in forming those vain theories, those fanciful dreams of happiness that have faded in my grasp. Experience has traced upon the tablets of my soul, with many tears, that

'There's nothing true but heaven.'

A desire for fame appears to me almost inseparable from an author, especially if that author is a poet. I was painfully convinced that this was one of my besetting sins. You would have pitied my weakness could you have read my heart at the moment of receiving your sweet verses, directed in your own hand to me. I had always ranked Miss Mitford as one of the first of our female writers, and though my knowledge of your writing was entirely confined to the sketches in the annuals, and to some extracts from the 'Foscari,' these were sufficient to make me feel the deepest interest in your name, and even to rejoice in the success that ever attended the publication of your works. But when you condescended to place me in the rank with yourself, all my ambitious feelings rose up in arms against me, till, ashamed of my vanity and presumption, I stood abashed in my own eyes, and felt truly ashamed of being so deeply enamoured with a title I did not deserve, and I felt that that insatiable thirst for fame was not only a weak but a criminal passion, which, if indulged, might waken in my breast those feelings of envy and emulation which I abhor, and which never fail to debase a generous mind; conscious, too, that I had employed those abilities with which heaven had endowed me, doubtless for a wise and useful purpose, entirely for my own amusement, without any wish to benefit or improve my fellow-creatures, I resolved to give up my pursuit of fame, withdraw entirely from the scene of action, and, under another name, devote my talents to the service of my God.

It was this determination which induced me to conclude the few lines I ventured to address to you in the manner I did; and could you read my mind, and enter fully into my motives for seeking to withdraw from all notoriety, I feel confident that I should gain from you, my dear Miss Mitford, an approving smile.

Mrs. Hemans is indeed a child of song—a complete mistress of the lyre. She possesses at all times the key of my heart. It will require another age to give birth to another Felicia Hemans!

Should I ever again visit London, I should indeed consider it a privilege to be allowed a friendly interchange of hands with Miss Mitford, an honour which a few months ago I should not have imagined it possible for me to expect, and which I do not deserve from any individual merit of my own, but owe entirely to your generosity.

I have pictured to myself your little cottage, and your poor lame maid Olive—‘is it not Olive Hathaway?’—who is a great favourite of mine. And now, I almost fancy I see your surprise, but I cannot tell you now how I came to know your maid Olive. Should you ever visit the eastern coast of Suffolk, my mother, my sister, and myself would feel ourselves highly honoured by Miss Mitford becoming an inmate of our old-fashioned mansion. The country is well wooded, but flat, and is not remarkable for its picturesque scenery, though it abounds with such sweet woodland lanes as you so inimitably describe. Sometimes I think that you have rambled down all my dear old lanes, about which I could preach for an hour. Our coast is interesting, from the many beautiful and venerable relics of antiquity which form the chief attraction to strangers. The ruins of Dunwich, Covehythe, Walberswick, Blythburgh (which still contains the tomb of Ina, king of East Anglia), and Leiston Abbey, would not fail to excite your attention. But I must not dwell upon my favourite spots —spots endeared to me from infancy—but hasten to conclude this unceremonious epistle, which I hope my dear friend and yours, Mr. Pringle, will obtain a frank for, and with sincere wishes for your mother's health and your own,

Believe me, dear Miss Mitford,
With a grateful sense of your kindness,
Your truly obliged friend.
SUSANNA STRICKLAND.

MR. WILLS *to* MISS MITFORD.

5, Great Queen Street, Lincoln's Inn.
October 12, 1829.

MY DEAR MISS MITFORD,

I availed myself of the very first opportunity after my indisposition to witness the Juliet of Miss Fanny Kemble, in order that I might judge for myself whether all the good and civil things that were said and written of her were founded in fact, and although I cannot go the lengths of some of her admirers, yet I have no scruple in affording her the rank of the very best actress since Miss O'Neil. Her peculiar forte to me seems to be a thorough legitimate downright thick and thin *dash* sort of style—a fearful experiment, but perhaps justified by the vast capabilities of the aspirant. She has all the right points about her, or, as our emerald friends would say, she has the makings of an actress. In short, she is in the Siddonic school (an excellent one, certainly), but that is all. In person she is infinitely inferior to Miss Phillips, though both have bad *arms*—the former round, red, and milk-maidish; the latter lean, long, and—but no matter for the other 'and'—I am getting ungallant. Contrasting the two, the summary is this: Miss K. has grandeur of expression and action, Miss P. delicacy and softness, which will ever render her superior in the more pathetic walks of the drama. Had Miss P. the other's *power*, and the other Miss P.'s pathos, each and the other would be tremendous creatures, but at present Miss K. stands a very good chance of obtaining the highest rewards in theatrical ambition. This surely will make for you—for from what I have seen I should not hesitate to trust Inez to her keeping.

I intended last night to have witnessed the new tragedy of 'Epicurus,' by Mr. Leslie—do you know him ?—but in consequence of the dying state of Mr. Wallack's eldest son, he is in such a distracted state of mind that at five o'clock the piece was obliged to be changed. Only think of the state of mind of the author. God be praised 'twas not your piece!

I saw 'Rienzi' on Thursday, to which there was the best house (though not too good) of the season, excepting the opening night. Some of the business is advantageously altered. Miss P.'s action is improved, and Mr. Young as good and bad as usual.

There has been a Miss Forrest roaring through Ophelia like a town bull in a thunder-storm. I need not say I should like an opportunity of reading 'Otto' as well as 'Inez.' Can you indulge me with convenience?

I am greatly obliged by the doctor's present. What about Cumberland? he says you have had fifty or sixty copies. I have just heard there is a new tragedy in Covent Garden ready for Miss K.—surely it can't be yours. Mrs. W.'s love and remembrances to all.

Believe me, most sincerely yours,
—— WILLS.[1]

Mr. S. C. HALL to MISS MITFORD.

2, East Place, [1830?].

MY DEAR MISS MITFORD,

I am 'perplexed in the extreme,' and now know not what to do. When your first two sheets came, I sent them to the printer, and had them *set*. When the last arrived, I felt that I should incur much danger in publishing it, because of its want of moral, or, rather, its prejudicial effect—which I knew *well* my readers would charge upon it. I, of course, allude to the conclusion, which describes a young couple as

---

[1] The initials of the Christian name are illegible.

having deceived their parents, privately married, and pursued a course of deception. Now you will believe me, I know, when I state how deeply it distresses me to write thus—I am more vexed and grieved than I can tell you—but I have a very *peculiar* class to cater for, and this year there is a rival religious annual. I am, therefore, bound to be especially careful, and if you knew the tales in my former volumes that have been cavilled at, you would laugh at the cavillers and pity me. I must not, however—I dare not—run any *risk*.

Do not think ill of me; do not be much annoyed with me, for, in truth, I cannot help myself. Of course, my trouble does not arise from any fear of *inconveniencing* you, because you have too many, and not too few, sources by which your writing can be disposed of.

Now, to another matter. I shall be greatly disappointed, indeed, if my volume has nothing from your pen—for many *weighty* reasons. Can you, then, within ten days give me half a dozen pages of a village sketch?

I must leave this matter with you, but pray write me by the next post, for, in truth, I feel more vexed than I hope you can do.

With my wife's affectionate regards, believe me,

Ever faithfully and sincerely yours,

S. C. HALL.

Mr. S. C. Hall was at this time editor of the 'Amulet,' a religious annual, which flourished from 1826 to 1836. Miss Mitford generally wrote for it,

and among the other contributors were Bulwer,
L. E. L., Lady Blessington, Mary Howitt, ' Barry Cornwall,' Mrs. Hofland, and Emma Roberts.

The next fragment refers to the stories of gipsies
and of Grace Neville in ' Our Village.' The latter
had a ragged boy who carried love-letters for her.

MISS STRICKLAND to MISS MITFORD.

There is another very interesting gipsy family of
the name of Chilcot—ditto Barwell ; perhaps you
may have met them in their peregrinations. In your
delightful sketch of Grace Nugent I was much
amused by the donkey messengers. Such mercuries
are common in Suffolk, and I greeted your boys as
old acquaintances. My eldest brother, who is settled
in Upper Canada, was a famous cricket-player, and I
used often by his earnest solicitations to walk across
Southwold Common, to witness his dexterity, and I
felt no small degree of interest in his *éclat.* He was
a fine, handsome fellow, and promises to do something for himself in the country to which he has
emigrated, and to which I often feel strongly induced
to follow him, having many dear friends in that land
' of the mountain and the flood.' He gives me such
superb descriptions of Canadian scenery that I often
long to accept his invitation to join him, and to
traverse the country with him in his journeys for
Government. But I fear my heart would fail me
when the moment of separation came, and my native
land would appear more beautiful than any other
spot in the world, when I was called upon to leave
it. Yes, I do agree with you that a woman would

miss the smile of affection more than all the applause of the world. I know I would rather give up the *pen* than lose the affection of my beloved sister Catherine, who is dearer to me than all the world— my monitress, my dear and faithful friend. She is the author of several popular works for children : 'The Step-brothers,' ' Young Emigrants,' ' Juvenile Forget-me-not ' (the first series), and many other works of the same nature. But it is not for her talents that I love my Kate, it is for herself. She is absent now for a few days, and I feel lost and lonely without her ; she is the youngest of the six girls, next to me. We are all authoresses but Sarah, the third ; but then she is a beauty, and such a sweet girl withal, that everybody loves her, and I often think she is the best off, for she has elegant tastes and pursuits, and no clashing interests interfere with the love her sisters bear to her. I am writing you a sad, egotistical letter ; my tongue and my pen never know when to lie still, and I quite forget your dignity as a celebrated writer when I am scribbling to you as a friend. Mr. Pringle will, I know, kindly enclose this in the next packet he transmits to you. In the meantime, believe me, dear Miss Mitford, to remain,

Your grateful and sincere friend,

SUSANNA STRICKLAND.

The following letter is interesting as having been written by Douglas Jerrold when he was a young and struggling author, shortly after the appearance of his successful drama, ' Black Eye'd Susan.'

Douglas Jerrold *to* Miss Mitford.

4, Augustus Square, Regent's Park, [1830].

My dear Madam,

May I be allowed to offer my sincere expressions of condolence for the loss you have so recently sustained, and to venture a hope of your timely recovery from the effects of so afflicting a visitation.[1]

That the dramas, which I have taken the liberty of intruding upon your notice, receive your commendation, is to me a subject of pride and pleasure : for wanting the suffrages of the few, popular success is as empty as it is frequently unmerited.

Long before I could hope that any effort of mine would receive the attention of Mr. Talfourd, I had admired the acute, liberal, and dispassionate tone of that gentleman's criticisms ; consequently I felt additional gratification from his praise in this month's ' New Monthly.'[2] At the present ebb of dramatic criticism, when *ipse dixit*, not analysis, decides on the faults or merits of writers, it is most encouraging, especially to the young beginner, to know there is at least *one* publication where he may meet with fair and gentlemanly treatment. There is, too, another satisfaction to the dramatist, who, at the outset, encounters the prejudice and ignorance of what is termed, ' daily and weekly criticism.' He has but to make two or three

---

[1] The death of Mrs. Mitford.

[2] Mr. Talfourd says in this review, ' We are quite sure that the gentleman who wrote this piece, " Black-eyed Susan," though he seems to have been unfortunate in his " Witchfinder" at Drury Lane, will one day rank high among dramatists.'

fortunate hits—no matter whether borrowed from Messrs. Scribe or Mr. Colburn—to change unthinking abuse into equally ignorant encomium. With such critics, how short the pause from a hiss to a huzza!

My 'Witchfinder' at Drury Lane was a decided failure. The subject was ill-chosen; for few who condemned it were aware that they were judging an attempted representation of historical character, but condemned it as a monstrous fiction. Neither had the piece one intrinsic advantage. Mr. Farren first injured it by his extravagant praise, and then made the mischief complete by his utter misconception of the part. Then came the learning, the intelligence, and the liberality of the newspapers. In the present day a moderately gifted dramatist has a pretty time of it: if he succeed, his piece has the immortality of a month—if he fail, his name is gibbeted in every journal as a dullard and a coxcomb. French melo-dramas have ruined us.

I have, madam, to apologise for inflicting so long a letter on your patience, and again repeating my wishes for your convalescence, and my acknowledg-ments of the honour which you have done me in the notice taken of my dramas (which, unless they be followed by much worthier things, I had rather had never been),

I remain, my dear madam,
Ever truly and obliged,
DOUGLAS JERROLD.

The acquaintance between Miss Mitford and Miss Sedgwick commenced in the following manner:—

MISS SEDGWICK *to* MISS MITFORD.

New York, June 7, 1830.

MY DEAR MISS MITFORD,

I cannot employ the formal address of a stranger towards one who has inspired the vivid feeling of intimate acquaintance, a deep and affectionate interest in her occupations and happiness. You cannot be ignorant that your books are re-printed and widely circulated on this side of the Atlantic, but we all have dim impressions of the actual existence of those that are unknown and distant, and it is probably difficult for you to realise that your name has penetrated beyond our maritime cities, and is familiar and honoured, and loved through many a village circle, and to the borders of the lonely depths of unpierced woods—that we eagerly gather the intimations of your character and history that we fancy are dispersed through your productions—that we venerate 'Mrs. Mosse,' are lovers of 'Sweet Cousin Mary,' and have wept, and almost worn mourning for dear, bright little 'Lizzie,' that, in short, such is your power over the imagination that your pictures have wrought on our affections like realities. I have long been restrained only by fear of intrusion from expressing to you my admiration and gratitude, not merely my selfish gratitude for my own individual pleasure, but for the great good you have done to our race by elevating the humbler members of the human family above the mere subjects of our condescension and charity, and showing that they have abundant sources of independent, home, heartfelt happiness, which asks nothing of their superiors, and will receive nothing, unless it be such generous sympathy as yours. As the humblest artizan may in all humility offer a specimen of his wares, I have requested Mrs. Miller to send you a copy of ‘Clarence,’ a work which I have just published. It is not professedly a delineation of our scenery or manners, but, wherever they are incidentally introduced, I have endeavoured to make the portrait accurate, neither exaggerating beauties nor veiling defects. My niece, a child nine years old, who is sitting by me, not satisfied with requesting that her *love* may be sent to Miss Mitford, has boldly aspired to the honour of addressing a postscript to her, and I, like any other doating aunt, and not forgetting who has allowed us a precedent for spoiling children, have consented to her wishes. Forgive us both, my dear Miss Mitford, and believe me sincerely

Your friend,
CATHERINE M. SEDGWICK.

The following is the ‘postscript:’—My dear Miss Mitford, I cannot miss the opportunity my aunt allows me of writing to the author of ‘Our Village,’ to express my interest in her, and in the perusal of her charming book, one of the most valuable in my library, which I have read several times, and at each repetition have experienced increased delight. How is ‘May Flower?’ the dog of whom you relate so many little anecdotes, or is she a mere chimera, a child of fancy. I do not particularly admire shadows, and, to tell the truth, I have some apprehensions of the celebrated hound's actual exist-ence. And has Joel Brent's marriage turned out happily after all Harriet's coquetry? And sweet Dora Creswell, what has become of her? And where is Fanny, the pretty gipsy girl, with her husband, her old grandmother, and her two brothers? And where is Thomas Clere, the man whose wife died in his arms, in her excess of joy at his arrival? And where are Grace Neville, the old barber, and all the other interesting personages mentioned in your book? I think I hear you say, 'This little girl asks too many questions,' but I will put an end to them, and only add that I remain, my dear Miss Mitford,

Your devoted admirer,
C. M. SEDGWICK, JUN.

PP.S.—I would have corrected this young lady's language, but I wished her postscript to have at least the merit of being the genuine offspring of her own mind, neither dictated nor retouched by an older hand.

Miss Mitford, in replying to Miss Sedgwick, September 6, 1830, sent also an answer to her little niece's questions—

MY DEAR YOUNG FRIEND,

I am very much obliged to you for your kind inquiries respecting the people in my book. It is much to be asked about by a little lady on the other side of the Atlantic, and we are very proud of it accordingly. 'May' was a real greyhound, and everything told of her was literally true; but, alas! she is no more; she died in the hard frost of last winter. 'Lizzy' was also true, and is also dead. 'Harriet' and 'Joel' are not married yet; you shall have the very latest intelligence of her; I am expecting two or three friends to dinner, and she is making an apple-tart and custards—which I wish with all my heart that you and your dear aunt were coming to partake of. The rest of the people are doing well in their several ways, and I am always, my dear little girl,

Most sincerely yours,
M. R. MITFORD.

MRS. TROLLOPE to MISS MITFORD.

Stonington Park, Washington City,
July 28, 1830.

It is but a few days, my very dear friend, since I learned the death of your beloved mother. The remembrance of all you have been to her in life must be to you the sweetest consolation, now you have lost her. I trust that many months will not elapse after you receive this before I shall again be within the possibility and the hope of seeing you. I have nothing now to detain me but the waiting to know Mr. Trollope's final decision as to the necessity of his once more crossing the Atlantic to arrange himself the final settlement of our untoward speculation at Cincinnati, and my wish to see a few more of the wonders of this wonderful country.

I, too, am writing a book, my dear Miss Mitford, which, let its success among others be what it may, has helped to amuse me at many mo-

ments that would have passed heavily without it.
Captain Hall's book (and himself too, by the way)
has put the Union in a blaze from one end to the
other. I never on any occasion heard so general an
expression of contempt and detestation as that which
follows his name. This hubbub made me very desirous
of seeing his book, but I am glad to say I did not
succeed till after my first volume was finished, and
most of the notes for the second collected. I thus
escaped influence of any kind from the perusal. A
few days ago, however, I was at Philadelphia, and
there I got his very strange work. I had one or two
long and interesting conversations with Lee (the
publisher), who knew him well, and from one or two
anecdotes he gave me, it appears that the ' agreeable
captain ' was under writing orders as surely as he
ever was, or hopes to be again, under sailing orders.
He would have done quite enough service to the
cause he intends to support if he had painted things
exactly as they are, without seeking to give his own
eternal orange-tawny colour to every object. His
blunders are such as clearly to prove he never, or
very rarely, listened to the answers he received—for
we must not suppose that he knew one thing and
printed another. Do not suppose, however, that I
am coming home fraught with the Quixotic intention
of running a tilt with Captain Hall. My little book
will not be of him, but of all I have seen, and of much
that he did not.

I long ago determined that my American letters
should not ruin my European friends; it is therefore
that I have not written before, but, now I am within

reach of the minister's bag, I may venture to recall myself to the memory of my distant friends. Do ask that very dear, very capricious little pet of ours, Marianne Skerritt, why she has given up writing to me. I have had, during the early part of my residence here, one or two of her delightful, glowing, affectionate letters—but for more than a year I have not had a line. *Trollope senior* is a most kind and constant correspondent, but *Trollope junior* (your admirer) is a most idle personage, and rarely does more than give me a scrap in one of his father's sheets of foolscap. Miss Gabell has been a faithful recorder of all that was literary, and Lady Dyer of all that was droll among [*torn*], these have been my constant and unfailing correspondents. I have had one or two very agreeable letters from Mrs. Milton, and you may tell her I should like to have another; your one delightful letter was a *legion*. I will not attempt to tell you how I rejoiced in the splendour of your success. Since then, I doubt not, other successes have followed, and so it will be as long as you wield a pen.

Henry's miserable health, my own narrow escape from death, the failure of our hopes of placing him advantageously, and my peculiar disappointment in not benefiting him, as I had hoped to do, by this expedition, all tended (together with backwoods' disagreeabilities) to make me dislike Western America; but there is much to like and admire on this side the Alleghany Mountains, many very estimable and well-informed people, and an almost endless variety of objects and of circumstances in the highest degree interesting ; yet would I not pass the remnant of my days here, even if I could have all my family around me. America is a glorious country for Americans, but a very so so one for Europeans.

I shall long to show you my dear girls. I think the expedition has done them good in many ways, if it has produced no other advantage. They are very dear creatures, I assure you. Adieu, dear friend ; remember me kindly to your father, and do not forget that if you could find half an hour to scribble a few lines to me, *Washington City*, you would give me great, very great pleasure.

Ever affectionately yours,

F. TROLLOPE.

P.S.—I am staying, and have been for the last three months, with the oldest friend I have in the world, Mrs. Stow, the eldest sister of the Julia Gunnell you have heard of. She has a charming family.

MISS STRICKLAND *to* MISS MITFORD.

Reydon Hall, August 12, 1830.

It was with regret, my dear Miss Mitford, that I quitted London without seeing you. It was not so much on account of the literary fame you have so justly earned that I was anxious for a personal interview, but for the sake of those kindly and benevolent feelings towards all of woman born which are so naturally and touchingly scattered through those pages we admire and read with such pleasure. All probability of a personal acquaintance, I fear, is at an end, as it is very likely I shall bid adieu to my native land in the course of a few months for ever. I am yet selfish enough to be unwilling to resign the privilege of addressing you, and I am perhaps too proud of the kindness you have shown to me. I have at length seen and been domesticated with my dear adopted father, Mr. Pringle, who more than realized my most sanguine expectations by his worth and genius. To me he has ever shown himself a kind and disinterested friend, and I think the faculty of memory must be extinguished in my breast when I cease to recall with gratitude the obligations he has conferred upon me. I came to town in very poor health for change of air, and joined Mr. and Mrs. P. at Hampstead. The few weeks I spent in this delightful village restored me to my former strength, and I greatly enjoyed our long morning and evening rambles upon the heath. We wanted Miss Mitford's pen to describe the picturesque groups of Irish haymakers bivouacking upon the heath. Every little declivity had its human tenants, and presented a scene of mirth or misery, of pastoral simplicity, or extreme distress and wretchedness; some of these poor people were laughing care in the face, while their haggard and wasted features told of sorrows which belied their affected gaiety. Poor Ireland! How my heart aches when I think of her degraded state, of the sufferings of her rash but warm-hearted children !

My stay in London was greatly saddened by the loss of a very dear young friend .... I saw but few of the literary lions. Most of them had retreated into the country to enjoy air and liberty. Mrs. Lee (the Mrs. Bowdich of the annuals) was the most charming specimen of the female *literati* to whom I had the honour to be introduced. She is so perfectly the lady that we forget that she is a blue-stocking. Will you excuse the liberty I am taking, dear Miss Mitford, in enclosing the prospectus of a small volume of poems which a friend of mine has undertaken to publish for me by private subscription? I should feel greatly obliged to you if you would circulate them among any of your wealthy friends who are *unfashionable* enough to be lovers of poetry. The high opinion which my friend has of their merit makes him anxious to bring them before the public. But the method he has taken to give them publicity is most repugnant to my feelings. With every kind wish for your health and happiness, believe me, my dear Miss Mitford,

Yours most sincerely,
SUSANNA STRICKLAND.

CHAPTER IX.

MISS MITFORD was unable to obtain a license for the performance of 'Charles I.,' and the refusal, repeated by the Duke of Devonshire, appeared the more unfair as John Kemble had already taken the principal part in a play on the same subject and with the same name. All political allusions were carefully avoided by Miss Mitford, and both Charles and Cromwell were represented as greater than they were. But owing to this adverse decision the play was only performed on the other side of the Thames.

DUKE OF DEVONSHIRE *to* MISS MITFORD.

London, March 25, 1831.

MADAM,

The very sincere admiration and respect I feel for your talents, and the pleasure I have derived from your works, make me feel much regret in not answering your letter as you would wish. But I have made a rule not to reverse the decisions of my predecessor, the Duke of Montrose, with regard to any play which he prohibited.

Mr. Coleman is now, I trust, so much disposed to enter into my views on the subject of the drama that I should be sorry to compel him to the alternative of retracting or of losing his situation, which my making any departure from the rule I have mentioned would have the effect of doing.

I hope that you will not be subjected to any inconvenience by my decision, or think me unreasonable in making the following request, which is that you will allow me to retain the copy of your play, to add it to my dramatic library. That collection consists of nearly six thousand plays, some of which are of the greatest rarity, and if ever you should wish to refer to any of the early dramatic authors, it would give me the greatest pleasure to show you the works of any of them.

I have the honour to be, madam,

Your sincere humble servant,

DEVONSHIRE.

MRS. TROLLOPE *to* MISS MITFORD.

New York, May 29, 1831.

I write to you, my dear friend, almost on the eve of departure, and would rather have done so on the eve of my arrival in my own dear land, were it not that I wish to propitiate your assistance in the business that must occupy me immediately on my arrival. I ask for it frankly, and frankly must you refuse should granting it include any inconvenience which my ignorance prevents my foreseeing—of this yourself only can be the judge. You know, I believe, that I have looked and listened since I have been here with a view to publication, and you know also, dear friend—for how can you help it?—that I am as utterly unknown in the world of letters as your dog May was before you immortalized him. What I would ask is such a letter of introduction to your publisher as would enable me to present myself before him without feeling as if I had dropped upon him from the moon.

My book is gossiping, and without pretension most faithfully true to the evidence of my senses, and written without a shadow of (previous) feeling for or against the things described. I have about thirty outline sketches by Hervieu,[1] not of scenery, but of manners, which I think will help the book greatly. I am well aware that it is difficult to bring a first effort to the light, but I think your powerful name will help me much.

I am delighted with New York—it is the only place where I have found the society really good for anything; the locality is unequalled in beauty and convenience as a mercantile city. It is here, and here only, that I have had an opportunity of seeing 'Rienzi'; it is a noble tragedy, and not even the bad acting of the Chatham Theatre could spoil it. I never witnessed such a triumph of powerful poetry over weak acting as in the magnificent scene where Rienzi refuses pardon to an Orsini; the narrative of the mother and her babes drew tears from American eyes, albeit unused (God knows) to any mood of deep feeling.

[1] An account of him has been given in pages 168-9.

A letter from M. A. Skerritt followed me yesterday into the state of New Jersey, where we have been passing a few days with a friend. She speaks of 'Inez' as *about to be produced.* I have been long expecting to hear that it was out. Do you remember reading it to me (excepting the fourth act, which was not then born) just before I left England? Marianne says something very unintelligible about Miss Fanny Kemble not liking her part. I fear this *young* and highly supported actress must have too entire possession of the first parts to leave any opening for an admirable woman, who has one or two theatres in the west, but who sometimes talks as if she would leave them all for the glory of appearing in 'Claudia' on the London boards. She is a charming actress, but she writes me word that she is quite sure she never played anything so well as the last scenes of 'Rienzi.'

We are just about to start for Niagara, and shall leave New York for London immediately on our return thence.

With best remembrances to your father, believe me,

Ever affectionately yours,

F. TROLLOPE.

MRS. TROLLOPE *to* MISS MITFORD.

Harrow, September 16, 1831.

Have you not thought me the most ungrateful of women, my dear kind friend, for being thus long before I thanked you for your compliance with my request, and still more for the very kind manner of it ? I have, however, not been ungrateful, but, as I can get no frank at Harrow, I would not write till my letter might contain the result of your kind service, as well as my thanks for it.

You will not be surprised to hear that Mr. Whittaker received graciously a communication from *you*. He was very civil, and desired me to leave the MS., saying he would get a literary friend to read it, and that in a fortnight he should be ready to give me an answer. Tom called on him after this time had expired, and was told that the MS. was with Captain Basil Hall, who had not yet returned it. I was rather alarmed at this, as he was almost *too* good a judge of the subject. A few days afterwards, however, I received a very flattering letter from him, accompanied by several pages of remarks, all very much calculated to give me confidence in my new enterprise. This was very kind, as I am quite a stranger to him. He says that 'he has strongly advised Mr. Whittaker to lose no time in publishing the work, which he is sure will interest the public greatly.' Whether he said more than this to Whittaker, I know not; to me he said considerably more. However, Whittaker only told me that 'Captain Hall spoke rather favourably of the work, and that he was willing to print it, dividing the profits with me.'

I suppose, however, that this is as favourable an offer as a person so utterly unknown can expect. *But*, as we have been losing money on both sides of the Atlantic, a little money *in esse* would have been more agreeable than the hopes he gives *in posse*.

Miss Milman tells me that this Miss Fanny has

actually written and published *a very fine tragedy.*
To me this appears like a joke—a girl of nineteen
write a fine tragedy! Do you believe this possible?
I do not.

I was told at New York that this young lady was
expected there with her father. If this be true, it
does not look as if she were very successful here, as
she will be the first actress of any distinction who
has condescended to cross the Atlantic.

How delightfully English everything looks! I
cannot describe to you the pleasure of returning to
Europe after an absence of nearly four years.

I know your good father (to whom present my
kind remembrances) is a bit of a radical—so I was,
too, once, but the United States offer a *radical* cure
for this. Adieu.

Ever affectionately and gratefully yours,

F. TROLLOPE.

MRS. TROLLOPE *to* MISS MITFORD.

Will you, my dear and kind friend, accept my little
volumes, though their politics may not quite agree
with yours? They owe their birth to you, so be
tender and pitiful to them. Had you been four years
among the people I have described, I do sincerely
believe you would not have described them as more
amiable. I write in great haste. Would you had
time to tell me something of yourself and your
concerns. I hear of an opera. What does it mean?

Ever gratefully and affectionately yours,

F. TROLLOPE.

MISS ROBERTS *to* MISS MITFORD.

MY DEAR MISS MITFORD,

May I be permitted to address thus familiarly a
lady with whom, though not personally acquainted, I
have long been upon terms of intimacy, and for whom
I have felt the most lively sentiments of regard and
esteem. Ever since I had the pleasure of being a
fellow contributor of yours in the Ladies' Magazine,[1] I
have most anxiously wished for an introduction to
you, but was deterred from seeking an opportunity
of making myself known by the consciousness of my
own obscurity, and the impossibility of founding any
claim upon those literary compositions which were
always at so immeasurable a distance from yours.
When, however, I became an inhabitant of the house
in Hans Place, which I knew to be the scene of your
juvenile days, from the description given in the
'Boarding School Recollections,' and began to entertain a hope that my intimacy with Miss Landon and
the acquaintance of Miss Skerritt would sanction my
long-cherished wish, I ventured to add my invitation to that of L. E. L., that you would give us the
great pleasure of your company at our ball, and the
very kind and flattering message addressed to me
in your reply, has emboldened me to trouble Miss
Skerritt with a note, which would have been written

---

[1] 'Our Village' first appeared in this little known periodical,
which also contained many exquisite sketches of country life and
scenery by M. R. M. The editor of the magazine finally ab-
sconded £40 in Miss Mitford's debt. 'The only comfort is that
the magazine cannot go on without me.' Her contributions had
increased the sale from 250 to 2,000.

long ago, had I not feared you might think me intrusive.

It is impossible for me to say how very much delighted I should be if I could hope for the opportunity of cultivating your acquaintance. If you would condescend to employ your pen upon the reminiscences of others it would be in my power to offer you subjects so admirably adapted to your exquisite talents that I, despairing of doing anything like justice to them, have suffered them to remain dormant in my mind, content with fancying the pleasure I should derive from the delineation by so masterly a hand as yours. My friends are envying the privilege I enjoy in writing to you, and the occupation is so fascinating that, had I not taken the precaution of choosing a half sheet of paper, I fear I should inflict more of my tediousness upon you than you could by any possibility pardon. In the hope that you will not think me too encroaching by this tax upon your patience,

I remain, with the sincerest regard,
Yours,
EMMA ROBERTS.

Miss Emma Roberts, during her travels in India, wrote ' Scenes and Characteristics of Hindostan,' and ' Oriental Scenes and Sketches.' The latter, a poetical work, she dedicated to her friend, Miss Landon, of whom she published a biography, saying that the year spent under the same roof with her was one of the happiest in her life. The above letter seems to have been written during this period, and when she

and Miss Mitford were contributing to the 'Amulet.'
Mr. S. C. Hall, who edited this periodical, and is, perhaps, the best authority living on such subjects, tells
me that about this time Miss E. Roberts and L. E. L.
were staying at No. 22, Hans Place, at a finishing
establishment, kept by a Mrs. Lance. In the St.
Quintins' time L. E. L. had been at school in this
house, and it stood but three doors below that in
which L. E. L. was born. Miss Roberts returned to
India, where, owing to severe literary labour for
periodicals, and the heat of the climate, she died in
1840, in the forty-seventh year of her age.

Mrs. Trollope to Miss Mitford.

Harrow, April 23, 1832.

My dear Friend,

Whittaker told me the other day that he had
agreed for your fifth volume—trust me, I long for it.
Whittaker must have made a great thing of you,
dear friend. He told me some time ago that your
name would sell anything. I think he is a *little* inclined
to make the most of one. Had it not been for the
friendly exertions of Captain Hall, I should hardly
get on so well as I have done. £250 is what he has
paid me for the first edition, and I am to have £200
more next week, when the second will be out. The
first was one thousand two hundred and fifty, the
second one thousand copies. This must pay him well,
but I suppose it is all right.

How *very* wise you have been to keep yourself
above the fulsome nonsense which I find it is the
fashion to shower upon people 'what makes books.'

I cannot express to you how heartily I dislike it. I hope and trust that you never mistook my earnest wish to be acquainted with you, for a wish to *lionize*. I liked and I loved you, and it is very possible I may have told you so, but indeed and indeed it was not because you were *the* Miss Mitford. How much I admire you for keeping out of London!

I never felt less in good humour with people in my life than I have done since I have been so be-puffed and be-praised. I am, however, thankful for the *money* I have gained by it; it has been very useful to us. My dear Henry (whom you do not know, but whom I hope you some day will) is to be immediately entered at the Temple by means of it—so *vive la plume!*

What does one do to get business with the mags and annuals? Does one say, as at playing ecarté, 'I propose,' or must one wait to be asked? Remember, dear, that I have five children.

I was not lucky enough to see Miss Sedgwick, but I will transcribe for you a passage from the journal of a lady, which has just been lent me. I *may* not name her name as I quote her. 'Miss Sedgwick's novel of "Hope Leslie" had prepared us to think well of its author, nor were we disappointed in spite of the extraordinary portion of drawl she has to contend with. Her countenance is pleasing, and her conversation so infinitely superior to that of the ladies we generally have met in America that it was quite refreshing. The Sedgwick family is that of the greatest importance in Stockbridge, and both the males and females are more cultivated than most families.'

Ever affectionately yours,
F. TROLLOPE.

MISS SEDGWICK *to* MISS MITFORD.

New York, May 14, 1832.

Your letters, my dear Miss Mitford, are destined to be to me what an exquisite dessert is to a man whose keen and wholesome appetite would fain have been regaled with the first course—the dessert is delicious, but it only appeases the cravings of hunger without satisfying them. 'Mr. Jones' is my Petruchio. His very name has a *knell* in it, and if your kind heart should prompt you again to write to me, I entreat you to eschew my countryman Mr. Jones. I am not surprised (revolted I think I could not be at anything from you) at your *feudal* tastes. Old institutions and usages, under which you have been educated, and which have formed your mind, naturally inspire respect and affection. They are endeared by habit, embellished by romance and poetry, and consecrated by history ; they must be inwrought with your thoughts and affections, and cannot be touched without jarring the whole fabric. There is, no doubt, a dignified tranquillity in living as you of the aristocracy do, within barriers that cannot be passed 'without permission.' We, on the contrary, are on the world's wide common, where everyone is entitled (to borrow the words Dr. Franklin put into the mouth of St. Peter

in addressing a heterodox saint) to take the best place
he can find.   This occasions much loss of the picturesque, and some jostlings and hard rubs, no doubt;
but the lines of demarcation here, though impercepti-
ble to a stranger's eye, are understood and felt among
us.   I doubt if the born and bred gentry of England
could *relish* the state of things here; and yet believe
me, my dear Miss Mitford, there is much to delight a
spirit so benevolently interested as yours in the happiness of humanity.   The million have now their just
weight in the scale, and for their sakes you would
renounce old prejudices.—Forgive me!   This dis-
courteous *Americanism* dropped from my pen unwit-
tingly.   We are such a new modelling and re-modelling
people that we are apt to condemn all 'forms and
pressures past' as prejudices; with us everything is
in a state of fusion to be cast in the best (and sometimes for best read *newest*) mould.   I was reading
your letter to one of my nieces—a girl of eleven.   I
said I suspect our dear Miss Mitford is an anti-reform-
ist.   'Oh,' she exclaimed, 'I wish that everybody we
love in England would not be against the reform!'
'Who do you mean by everybody, Jane?'   'Why, Sir
Walter Scott and Miss Mitford.'

The mention of the little girl reminds me that I
have yet a great deal more to say than you would
have patience to read, and the limits of my paper
whisper brevity.   My condition is strikingly unlike
yours in one respect.   I have brothers who, I think
(and as we think of our friends so they are to us),
have no superiors; one beloved sister, and four sisters
as true and devoted as if they were born flesh of my

flesh, though 'in law' has to be written after the title by which I am allied to them. Besides, I have a little community of nephews and nieces, including my adopted child—the little girl who is honoured by your regard. Am I boasting of this wealth? God forbid! A friend of mine once said to me, 'You touch the world at too many points.' Events that have made heaven nearer and dearer to me have taught me that the keenest suffering is the price to be paid for the greatest blessings. My brother Robert, with whom I live in New York, is your devoted admirer. I wish I could describe to you the unaffected enthusiasm with which he kissed your signature. I have this moment open before me a letter just received from one of my sisters, Mrs. Theodore Sedgwick. I am tempted to make an extract from it. 'I was delighted with Miss M.'s letter; its frankness, cordiality, and spirit show how much of her character is infused into her village sketches, and make them doubly valuable. I beg you will let her know the admiration your sister entertains for her. I am entitled to this introduction, as, without my urging you, you would never have written her.'

My heart urged too, my dear Miss Mitford, but I shrank from obtruding.

I write by Mr. Ashburner, who is going out for his daughter, to return the 1st of August. He will bring a letter to me addressed to the care of Miss Sharp, 14, New Ormond St., London. Shall he not bear the precious freight? Tell me anything of yourself—anything of your noble father (long may he live!) whom I have loved ever since you took that ride with

him in a one-horse chaise of a misty morning. Do
you remember?

My Kate begs her grateful and affectionate remembrances may be sent to you. She would not be
satisfied without writing, but she is just now sick in
bed—a rare occurrence for her. She has been with
me in the City all winter, and her progress has satisfied my most ardent desires for her. May I send my
affectionate regards to your father? Believe me,

Yours truly and affectionately,
C. M. SEDGWICK.

MRS. TROLLOPE *to* MISS MITFORD.

Julian Hill, November 13, 1832.

I would not write, my dear friend, to thank you for
your letter till I could thank you for your book too.
Now, I am happy to say, I can do both. But I was
put in a fright for fear I should miss the letter, for
when my son called at *our man's* to ask for it, Mr.
Howe told him that all the gift copies were already
sent. I was in a bit of a rage, because Whittaker
knew that you intended one for me long ago. However, I took wisdom in my wrath, and determined to
be refused by the master as well as by the man before
I cried out. The instant I mentioned the circumstance to Whittaker, he said, 'Most certainly there is
a copy ready for you;' so all is well, and I thank you
much, and will thank you more still when you come
to see me (as you have so often promised to do), and
will write my name in it. It has made me extravagant, for I have ordered the four other volumes. The
work is perfectly *unique.* I know nothing like it in

any language, and it is among the few to which one can turn again and again with even new pleasure. The 'Farewell' is one of the sweetest bits of writing that I know. I should have paid you (not in *kind*, God knows! but) in *produce* by sending my three big volumes.—By-the-way, I think you rather extravagant for giving such extra good measure ; why, there is matter enough in your volume to make two of the novel genus. But the reason I have not sent them is that Whittaker, to my great satisfaction, told me that he expected there must be another edition directly, and that he should be glad if I would delay sending *my six copies* till then. So I shall wait upon you then, if you will condescend to be at home to it.

When shall you come to town? Mrs. Bentley writes me word that Covent Garden is *beautiful.* She tells me of some American actor who has come over to perform here, whose name, however, I cannot read in her MS., that says, 'Every word in Mrs. Trollope's book is true without the slightest exaggeration.'

The Kembles, she tells me, are doing wonders— poor Charles will be rich at last. I hear Macready is quite out of fashion—he had better have played 'Rienzi,' dear. It is long since he has made a hit— his benefit brought nothing.

You can form no idea of the pleasure your Bramshill scene gave me. That part was the favourite, and in summer often the daily haunt of my youthful days. There was one particular spot under a high oak, where I have sat alone for hours. It was within hearing of the great clock, and but for that I should often have been benighted there. I wish I knew Sir

John Cope. I would give a joint of my little finger to visit Bramshill again. Adieu.

Ever affectionately yours,

F. TROLLOPE.

MISS SEDGWICK *to* MISS MITFORD.

New York, December 12, 1832.

MY DEAR MISS MITFORD,

Do not discard me as an over-punctual correspondent. I am writing thus promptly after the receipt of your kind letter in the hope of procuring for my nephew, Mr. George Pomeroy, the happiness of an introduction to you. He is now in England on the business of a large commercial house of this city, of which he is a partner. He is in some sort entitled to the pleasure of seeing you, being among your most enthusiastic admirers, and may I not hope that he has some claim, or, more modestly speaking, chance, as my friend as well as kinsman, of your acquaintance. Lord Bacon commends the Italians for making little difference between their children and nephews. I certainly have found the sweetest fountains of my affections and happiness opened by the children of my brothers and sisters.

That was a fortunate clause in Mrs. Trollope's book, in which she speaks of her 'friend, Miss Mitford'—to borrow a cant phrase of our business city, it was a 'heavy name,' a 'Baring' or a 'Rothschild' on doubtful paper. Mrs. Trollope must have been very unfortunate in her associations in this country. There is undoubtedly a very crude state of society in the new towns of our western states; and in every part of our country, in our best circles there are persons to be met who have not been able to throw off the coarse habits as they rose above the fortunes of their early years. But Mrs. Trollope, though she has told some disagreeable truths, has for the most part caricatured till the resemblance is lost. Wherever she has attempted a characteristic conversation she has given a slang unknown, even among our domestics, and mingled with a dialect that is anything but American. It is difficult, almost impossible, for a foreigner to comprehend this country, and I am not surprised that those accustomed to the thorny and almost impassable barriers of England should be shocked at finding themselves in an open field, where they seem to be turned in with all sorts of cattle. But the case is not quite so bad. Distinctions are felt, though not seen, and there is as little real danger to any personal rights or individual dignity as there was (do not think me presuming in the comparison) to Adam and Eve moving in Paradise amidst its races subjected by the inviolable laws of Providence.

In your own kind language, my dear Miss Mitford, I am certain *you* would like America, but I am aware that in order to your liking it your very superior heart as well as mind must operate. No benevolent being can help liking a country where happiness is so attainable and so diffused, and where there is so rapid a progress in all the arts, comforts, and enjoyments of life. And as to *my liking England*, I love and honour it now, as a dutiful child loves and honours a parent. Sir Walter Scott's death has been mourned through our land, as we mourn for our personal benefactors. We had a little family *fête* in honour of him at my eldest brother's in Berkshire a few evenings since. We were all required to produce some tribute to his memory.

The seeds were a most delightful little gift. We had the flower in one of the gardens of our valley for the first time last summer—but this is from *your* garden, and there is nothing about which that wonderful electric chain is so wound as a plant from the garden of a friend.

Do I love flowers! Better than anything but friends, who can speak or *write* to me. If ever I have an opportunity I will send you some of our indigenous plants. Have you the orchis? Any of our aralias, or calmias? Is our fringed gentian,

> ' Whose sweet and quiet eye
> Looks thro' its fringes to the sky,'

a stranger to you?

Fanny Kemble is here, witching the young, and making even old eyes weep. She is much courted and admired in society—at least, among the ultra-fashionable. The sages say she is an actress, and therefore disqualified for society.

I am truly obliged to you for saving me from the mortification of inflicting postage on you. I made an unsuccessful effort to avoid it when I last wrote to you. When you write again, do tell me more of yourself. When do you appear again in public? So great a favourite ought not to be so long behind the scenes—these busy scenes that somebody will tread.

What is the state of your father's health?   God bless him and you, my dear Miss Mitford!

Yours truly and affectionately,

C. M. SEDGWICK.

MRS. TROLLOPE *to* MISS MITFORD.

Julian Hill, December 27, 1832.

MY DEAR FRIEND,

Not knowing where to get a frank, I have delayed answering your letter till I could get a copy of the book I wished to send you from Whittaker. Not that I have suffered the interval to pass in idleness. I have (without using names) been obtaining all the information within reach on the subject of your last letter. For myself, I can truly say that there is no literary enterprise I should set about with so true a relish as that of reviewing 'Our Village,' and I think I could write an interesting article on it. But I am assured from the best authority that *no woman* has ever written for the Quarterly.

Respecting Captain H——, I was assured by the most intimate friend he has, to whom I applied (not now, but respecting the domestic manners of the American) that the surest way to prevent his writing any review at all would be to mention the subject to him, and many anecdotes were told me to prove the truth of the statement. This being the case, I fear that not all my good will can avail. Could *you*, by your literary connection, obtain insertion for such an article in any review or magazine? I would joyfully write it *gratis*, and to the very top of my power. It

R 2

has occurred to me that Mr. Harness is an intimate friend of yours; he, I know, writes for the Quarterly, for he reviewed Fanny Kemble's play. Could not he be made useful? I cannot tell you how heartily I wish I could be so, and how mortifying is the consciousness of my want of power.

How I wish you would set about a novel! It is *impossible* that it should not have been a brilliant success. Your manner of writing, your knowledge of character, your pathos, and your rich vein of quiet humour, to say nothing of your previous reputation, must infallibly insure it. I do not believe that there is one left who could compete with you in this walk.

Is your member in? I hope so. The elections have passed off very quietly, which has certainly been a great comfort; but some of them have been very queer—Gully, for instance—a prizefighter making laws! It is new.

I will not give up the hope of seeing you here this spring. You *must* have business in London, I am quite sure. Adieu, dear friend. Tell me that you believe in my zeal, though you perceive my impotence, and accept the very affectionate best wishes of

Yours most truly,

F. Trollope.

CHAPTER X.

LETTERS FROM MISS SEDGWICK AND MRS. HOWITT.

MISS SEDGWICK *to* MISS MITFORD.

New York, May 17, 1833.

I THANK you most heartily, my dear Miss Mitford, for
your last kind letter, which seemed to me more
charming than any of its forerunners; but, on inves-
tigation, I believe its superiority consisted in its being
a little longer.   Gold is always gold, but a little more
of it is always acceptable.   I grieve to know that
you are feeling the leaden weight of mortality; there
are no doubt uses in every mode of affliction, but
that particular form of it which makes the body
press upon the mind, which substitutes weariness and
imbecility and nothingness for the joy of exercise
and the fine fruits of exertion—in short, that horrid
state of things called ill-health, which subjugates the
mind to its mere vehicle and instrument, is to me one
of the most puzzling articles in our probation.   Do
you not think that some such change as crossing the
Atlantic would renovate you?   You suggest it yourself, and therefore I am emboldened to urge it; you

cannot leave your father, nor would I ask you, for I feel a sort of filial interest in whatever touches him. But is it impossible that he should accompany you? Last year an English gentleman of seventy-five came to this country in May, visited Niagara, more than four hundred miles from this city, and recrossed the ocean in September. The facilities for travelling here (notwithstanding the horrors recorded against us) are very great. We have steamboats and canal navigation to Niagara. A friend of ours took tea with us last Friday evening who left Richmond, Virginia, a distance of nearly five hundred miles, on Tuesday morning, and accomplished the journey without excessive fatigue. Now I would not certainly travel at this rate, but where such travelling is possible a passage through the country cannot be very formidable, even to a person of advanced years. Apart from all the delight I should expect from seeing you, I am sure you would find much to like and to enjoy here, and for once our country would be painted by an accomplished artist, who at least was willing to give it its best expression. I am rejoiced to hear that your father is friendly to us, for though I think it absurd to be sensitive about the opinion of foreigners, yet the kind dispositions of those I think of as friends is highly gratifying. It must be confessed that we are nationally ridiculously sensitive on this matter of opinion. It is a kind of new-small-town-ish feeling, an anxiety to be known, and a determination to be admired when known.

There is undoubtedly a crude state of things among us, Mrs. Trollope (by the way, I am exceedingly obliged to you for your very fine account of her, which has very much raised her in our good opinion) has not much misstated, though she has grossly caricatured, us. You may imagine in a country where everybody travels, and where there are no acknowledged distinction of classes, no barriers obvious to the senses, that in such places as steamboats, canal-boats, and stage-coaches, the respect with which any individual is treated must greatly depend upon circumstances. It is not very easy for a person educated in a different condition of society to adapt themselves to the peculiarities of a new aspect of society, but from my own experience I am sure your father is right in saying that a lady may travel from Georgia to Maine without meeting any impertinence. Try it, only try it, my dear friend, and if I am not right I will turn traitor.

Bryant, who is living in a cottage at Hoboken, a place separated from the most dense part of the city only by the waters of the Hudson, and peaceful and beautiful as Paradise, a fit residence for a poet, has just brought me a bouquet of wild flowers, tied with a knot of Seneca grass. Would that I could send it to you! Its fragrant breath would speak for me more expressively than my pen can.

A neighbour of ours, who is not rich enough to keep a coach, but has sense enough to keep a sociable and enjoy it daily, took me a few days since a little drive into the country, and, avoiding the thronged, broad avenues, selected an obscure road that, but for occasional glimpses of the Hudson, whitened with the tokens of commerce, sails and steamboats, would have cheated us into the feeling that we were a thousand miles from the city. We came to a sudden turn that led into a deeply shaded, nooked lane. ' Ah, turn here, Sydney,' said my companion, ' into Miss Mitford's lane, as you call it.' This, as you may suppose, made my heart beat quicker. Is it not something to have given a name and a heightened charm to Nature three thousand miles away? The mother and the son proceeded to tell me of their exquisite pleasure from your works, of *the boy's* familiar acquaintance with May and Dash, &c.

I was reading your inimitable description of Dora Creswell the other day to a friend of mine who was confined to his bed by illness. He laughed and cried by turns, and averred there could not be a word changed for the better, except that of reaper applied to Dora. Being a practical farmer, and not very familiar with the licence that would allow you to call her a reaper though she did not actually cut down the grain, he was, as we say, *exercised* about that word. My good friend is a philanthropist, too, and would hardly let me off without promising to interest you in the cause of the Peace Society. I had to tell him that all our sex were born members of it. There is here, as I presume there is in England, great activity in all the modifications of the cause of humanity. New York would remind you of the Oriental faces on the 'Anniversary week,' as the week is called when the benevolent societies from all parts of this great continent meet in this city. Alas! Kate asks for a scrap of paper, and I am too much in the habit of saying yes to her. I have not, nor can

I, my dear Miss Mitford, express the pleasure your letters give me. I am truly concerned that you have had any disappointments, and could pray for protection from every evil for you, but I have much faith in clouds, and must not ask for all sunshine, even for you.

My very best regards to your father. Tell him sixty and upwards in England is not more than fifty here. Oh, that I had space to write all I would deduce from this. I have another nephew who is travelling in Europe, and will present himself to you within a year. We think him a clever and accomplished young man. I hope, if he has the happiness to see you, he will not appear to you a North American savage.

Well, my dear Miss Mitford, allow me once more after so long a time the pleasure of telling her how much pleasure I have had in poring over her letters, and re-reading 'Our Village,' and how much delighted and how grateful I am of her kind remembrance of me. I am enchanted at having before me the prospect of meeting more of the inhabitants of 'Our Village.' Is it not natural that, with such fresh, vivid and agreeable recollections of Sally, of Lucy, of Harriet and Joel, of the Loddon, of the copse and the straw, I should wish to see the children of the swing breathing creatures, and the perpetual beauty of the river, the fields, and woods. Alas! I have only room left to tell you with what true and hearty affection I am yours. I cannot but smile that the construction of my sentence imputes *advanced years* to you, my dear Miss Mitford, and I find, as I before conjectured

by your last letter, that, as to distance, we are equal
travellers in this 'vale of tears.' I am sure that you
have made a portion of it to me a vale of smiles;
but does not this bond draw us closer? God bless
you!

Yours,

E. M. SEDGWICK.

MISS SEDGWICK *to* MISS MITFORD.

New York, April 6, 1834.

I hoped, my dearest Miss Mitford, to have heard
again from you or of you before I wrote. We have
heard newspaper reports of your being very ill. This
is a cruel way of hearing from one in whose welfare
and happiness I take a real and deep interest, and
whose departure from this world, even though we
must always dwell three thousand miles apart, would
materially circumscribe the sphere of my enjoyments.
Should this letter find you recovered, as I trust in
heaven it will do, write to me immediately, and tell
me in good, *womanly phrase* your *complaints*, and
whether you have not reason for expecting better
health for the future. Write as you would write to
one who cares for all your maladies great and small.
Your life is such a public blessing and such a necessity, as it seems to me, to that dear father (of whom
you have so often made such affectionate mention
that I feel as if he were very near of kin to me) that
I tremble when I think by how frail a tenure you
may hold it. Thank you for introducing your friend
or your friend's husband to us; we have found him a
most amusing and original person, and he has laid

me under everlasting obligations to him by present-
ing me with a charming bust of you, looking just so
intellectual, sweet-tempered, and kind-hearted as
does the dear Miss Mitford of my imagination. The
little figure is regularly presented to all our friends
and visitors, and the sagacious and *likeness*-seeing
among them pronounce it a striking resemblance.
Mr. W. has, I believe, decided not to transfer his
residence to America. I think he is right; it is wisest
to let the young bees swarm for themselves, the old
ones remain in the old hives. America is not the
place for an eminent artist. We are a nation of
workers, and have not leisure or fortune for an extended cultivation and patronage of the fine arts.
We have no society or association for artists. Irving
said to me this winter, in relation to Leslie's experiment of a residence here, 'We have plucked a star
from the firmament.' Poor Leslie! after passing the
winter in complete seclusion amidst the snows of our
Highlands, he has decided to return to England. It
is said the government institution by which he was
employed has not kept faith with him; his brother-in-
law told me Leslie had lived too long in England,
and that his English wife had come resolved to be
dissatisfied. She is said to be a weak woman, full of
prejudice and inflexible in her English habits. I do
not blame her; it demands rare sense and temper to
get the better of all the prejudice of education, to
divest ourselves of habit and association. We are
accustomed to the inconveniences that result from
our condition, and we can remove or submit to them.
An Englishwoman finds an American servant intoler-

able; we know and humour their peculiarities, and thus get on comfortably with them. Our own artists who have not been long enough abroad to acquire new tastes and habits are happy and successful among us. Grant we have some who would, I believe, be distinguished anywhere. Alston's name must be known to you, and Cole paints Nature so truly and beautifully that, dearly as I love our misty mornings, dewy hills, and ever-varying sunsets in Berkshire, I think I could exist through a summer in New York, if I had his landscapes to look at. I regret that we shall not see your friend Mrs. Westmacott here. Her husband half promised he would bring the old lady, as he calls her, across the water. I hope she will not quarrel with me for being the fortunate subject of Mr. W.'s bounty; she must forgive me while she has the advantage of seeing the original.

I had a great deal to say to you, but I have been prosing on here confused by half a dozen of my petted nephews and nieces, who would not be driven out of my room. I dare not begin upon another sheet, as Mrs. W. tells me that Mr. Palmer is no longer M.P., and I am too sure my letter would not pay its own way. Have you any other *franking* friends? And will you not come to us? I know that such spirits as yours and your father's would find much to love and commend, and you should love merry England best, and I *think it best* too if you would.

Kate says I promised her a space. How kind of you always to remember her!

Truly and affectionately yours,
E. M. Sedgwick.

P.S.—Aunt Kitty never knows when to stop when she writes to you, dear Miss Mitford, and she has cut me off with this mite of a corner to tell you how much I love and admire you, and how I wish to see you, and with what pleasure I look upon the little bust which Mr. Westmacott has given my aunt, discovering that nothing would so effectually establish him in her good graces as this image of one so dear to her. Thank you again and again for your kind remembrance of me. I am so proud of a place in Miss Mitford's affections.

Believe me to be,
Ever yours affectionately,
KATE SEDGWICK.

PP.S.—I see a great deal of Fanny Kemble when she is in the city. I admire and love her. She is to be in New York in a few days to bid us professionally farewell, and is soon after to be married. Butler is a gentlemanly man, with good sense and amiable disposition, infinitely her inferior. Poor girl, she makes a dangerous experiment; I have a thousand fears of the result. My affectionate respect to your father. Your letter written in July remained with Mrs. Griffiths album in the Custom House, and did not get into my hands till March.

The publication of ' Our Village,' and Miss Mitford's success in the drama, led to her becoming acquainted with Mrs. Howitt, who sent her in 1834 a copy of her ' Seven Temptations.' [1]

---

[1] A volume of dramas, in which the personification of the evil principle attempted through various trials to ruin mankind.

Nottingham, February 27.

DEAR MISS MITFORD,

I rejoice in finding an occasion to address you, that I may express the very great pleasure both my husband and myself have always derived from your writing. We know your ' village,' and all its crofts, and lanes, and people, and we wish we had the happiness of personally knowing you.

May I beg your acceptance of the volume I send herewith. You are a worshipper of the Drama like myself, and I hope you may find something in it to like.

My husband begs to present his kind regards to you, and hoping by some good chance or other we may shake hands before long.

I am, dear Miss Mitford,
Yours very truly,
MARY HOWITT.

MISS SEDGWICK *to* MISS MITFORD.

Stockbridge, September 26, 1834.

Your introductory note by Miss Martineau, my dear Miss Mitford, was forwarded to me from New York a few days since. I am delighted to owe to you the right to ask this distinguished lady to visit us in Berkshire. This is a new bond between us, and though those that already exist are sufficient to bind me to you for life, and all beyond, yet I care not how much they are multiplied. I have participated in your dramatic success; it is an exalted sphere, and one worthy of you. How happy you are in having such an infusion of pure disinterested feeling in the pleasure of your triumph—to attach a fellow-conqueror instead of a captive to your car. Your association with your father always seems to consecrate your literary labours, to give you such a sacred pleasure in success that you must be saved from all the littlenesses of literary vanity, to satisfy the cravings of a generous nature to some object beyond self. Is it not so? Dear Miss Mitford, may this high motive and reward long be continued to you!

Miss Martineau has been received at New York with a cordiality befitting her claims; to tell the truth, our good people have been so roughly handled by some of our English friends that they are now a little shy of them, and an individual must have especial merit to counteract the general prejudice. There is a foundation of truth in all censure, even calumny, and I do not in the least doubt that members of refined European society must be often shocked at the coarseness and occasional vulgarities to be met with in the motley crowds of our steam-boats, lodging-houses, and even *sometimes* in our drawing-rooms : but the philosophy of our sagacious visitors should penetrate below the surface. In a country absolutely without castes, where the childhood of those who fill our first offices was passed in the family of the mechanic or the farmer, the habits of early life *will out.* How much should I have, if we were together, to say on this and kindred subjects, all which I should finish with the humble confession that we are over-sensitive to foreign opinion, and betray thereby a want of a fixed and independent self-respect. Miss Martineau is coming this week to Stockbridge, and I would defer writing to you till after that great event, but I am induced to send this letter by my nephew, Mr. George Pomeroy, who deserves the honour he covets of an introduction to you. He missed seeing you when he was in England before, but I trust he will now be more fortunate. Thank you, my dear friend, for your great kindness to and flattering mention of Theodore Sedgwick. He was charmed with his visit to you. Our girls were quite annoyed that you should have attributed his gentlemanly air to his visit to Paris. I mention this as a pretty fair specimen of our national nervousness on certain subjects. Since Theodore's return he has made his fortune by an engagement to a charming creature whose wealth is in stores of fine qualities, embodied in a beautiful form. Their mutual attachment has been growing from the time they first met in Stockbridge, when my brother removed from his residence in New York to my father's place in Stockbridge, and Sarah Ashburner came from Bombay, *viâ* England, to live in our village. What wonderful means are used to bring about the matches made in heaven!

You ask news of Fanny Kemble; I have not seen her since June, but I had a letter from her last week written in most delightful spirits; she is in Philadelphia, her husband's residence, and they are shortly going into their own house, where she invites me to come and see the little Englishwoman manage her Republican independent dependents. She is publishing her journal, and, after scolding me for confessing that I had some 'flutterings' about it, she says that every sheet, as it goes to the press, is submitted to the soberer judgment of her husband, in which she says, 'You have justly more confidence than in mine.' Butler, though inferior in genius and in all that gives charm to the character, has very good common sense, is a true American, and has an American *ear*, which is as important in this case as a musical ear to a composer. I must cut myself off and give you a little extract from her letter; it is so agreeable, so characteristic :—

'The beginning of your letter was dated Niagara, and full of the inspirations of your whereabout; now I have a great mind to treat you to the very perfection of contrast and reply in the same spirit of my "whatabout," viz., *book-keeping*, a whole four pages of day-books, journals, invoices, commissions, bills of exchange, per centage, and all the jargon of a thorough double entry desk. Now, pray exclaim aloud, as I have done internally a thousand times since I began to learn this most matter of fact of sciences, "Great is the power of love."'

So you see what she is about, a loving wife.

We expect Miss M. this week; would it were you, dear Miss Mitford. Shall I confess to you I have some dread of this wonderful lady like that I have seen in some *very* simple people for me who, forsooth, have thought me a lion, me 'an innocent beast of a good conscience.' I agree with a good, simple lady of my acquaintance that 'political economy is an *excellent thing*,' but, alas! when I read Miss M.'s books, I slip the political economy as a friend of mine did the *muscles* when he studied *anatomy*. But again, would it were you, and *because you are you.*

I have not yet thanked you for the nice present of the books, nor for your kind intention of sending the flowers—oh, they shall bloom in our sweetest of all valleys, and you shall some day come and see them! Will you not? I have so many dear, and, I think, charming friends who already love and honour you.

I walked from my brother Charles', Kate's father, to our valley, eleven miles, yesterday. Can you do more, my dear lady?

Mrs. Butler is under another engagement to perform another year for her father, should he require her, but, as he went off in a pet with Butler, his pride may save her that misery.

[My aunt, dear Miss Mitford, says that her letter is very particularly dull, and this melancholy circumstance is owing to poor me. Can you forgive me for such an offence? Thank you a thousand times for your kind remembrance of me, it is one of the many pleasures, and one of the greatest, for which I have to thank my dear aunt. Believe me, my dear Miss Mitford, ever very affectionately (if you will allow me to quote your own words), your own

KATE.]

How I wish I could show you our own Kate— 'Euphrosyne,' Fanny Butler calls her,—and she is no goddess, but the very spirit of cheerfulness. My letter is already so full, but I must add my very affectionate regards to your father and my earnest prayers for you both.

Yours most truly,
E. M. SEDGWICK.

MISS HOWITT *to* MISS MITFORD.

Nottingham February 1, 1835.

MY DEAR MISS MITFORD,

The most truly *English* sketches in the language are your country volumes. Well, through these volumes we have been wending this winter. We had read them before, and many of the stories were as familiar to us as household words; but they have been read this time principally that William might trace out their localities, and a great additional charm has his knowledge of your part of the country given them. But, dear Miss Mitford, you are a bold woman —nay, you are the most imprudent woman I ever knew. I always thought so, if it should turn out, as it does, that 'Our Village' is Three Mile Cross. Did not your neighbours tell you so—'The man would have been better had he not drank so much,' 'The woman, whose fat, dirty children were the picture of vulgarity,' 'The man who was incorrigibly lazy and good-for-nothing,' 'The touchy lady,' and so on. I should have expected the people to mob you, for I take it for granted that all these people live where you have placed them. Nobody can doubt for a moment but that they are all sketched from the life. We are here divided into two parties touching that same touchy lady; one party stated that she could

s 2

not have passed through a courtship without ascertaining what the initial B of her husband's name stood for, the other says you are right. I do not tell you to which faction I belong.

Your letter was brought to me by a very sweet, gentle girl, Fanny Cartledge, who is staying with her friends in Nottingham. She has not the pleasure of a personal acquaintance with you, but looks forward to it. I think you will like her much; she will make a very pretty sketch for you, and must accompany you and poor Mayflower's successor to the copse, or the dingle, or violeting, or on a visit to Lucy.

I wish you would come and see our great flower-show next month—no, this month, February. The vernal crocuses in our meadows—and beautiful meadows they are too on the banks of the Trent—but these flowers surpass belief, and I always despair of making one comprehend how beautiful they are. They are seen to many miles distance—spaces of twenty acres or so in the green flats of the meadows of one intense lilac-colour, as clearly and vividly lilac as the grass around is green. But when you walk among them the effect is inconceivable, the petals, of transparent, tender hue, contrasting so beautifully with the yellow of the inside. The expanse is so unlike the common covering of the earth that for one moment it seems a sin to tread them down. They look almost spiritual, and you think of the flowers of heaven. Then, again, they are so lavishly spread, so thick, springing up by millions, that one longs to grasp them by handfuls, to lie down among them, as the children do. But their most beautiful attribute is the joy they diffuse over the hearts of thousands. They make the paradise of the poor. Here come the poor, pale children, who have sat scaming stockings, or running lace thirteen or fourteen hours a day for a few pence—here they come in the half hour they can steal from their meals and gather up flowers by thousands, and no low alley shall you enter at this season but in its poorest dwelling you shall find the little cup of crocuses, brought by some little child or old man. I wish you could see them, dear Miss Mitford —what a glorious paper would you write about them !

William admonishes me to make an end that the parcel may go to-night.

I am, my dear friend,

Yours affectionately,

MARY HOWITT.

CHAPTER XI.

NATHANIEL PARKER WILLIS was a most popular writer both in America and in this country. He was the originator of the American Monthly Magazine, and the author of 'Pencillings by the Way.' The following is the first letter he wrote to Miss Mitford:—

MR. WILLIS *to* MISS MITFORD.

Thursday Evening.

DEAR MADAM,

I regret more than I can well express my disappointment on arriving last night at the Victoria too late to have the pleasure of seeing you. I dined out, and was not able to get away in time, and to-day I have an engagement to dine with Lady Blessington at eight, which deprives me again of one of the chief pleasures I had promised myself in coming to England. Mr. Rand (who waits kindly for this note) tells me it is possible you do not leave town to-morrow. I have taken your address, and shall call to-morrow at twelve in the hope of finding you. My literary countrymen would never forgive me for leaving England without seeing one of the most unexceptionably popular authors in the United States, and as a matter of popular feeling it would be to me a serious disappointment. I hope you will excuse the extreme hurry of this note, and believe me, dear madam,

Most respectfully and truly yours,

N. P. WILLIS.

The first letter of Miss Martineau to Miss Mitford was to thank her for one of her tragedies which she had sent, and to hope that they would become personally acquainted. The next letter was the subjoined :—

MISS MARTINEAU *to* MISS MITFORD.

17, Pludyer Street, Thursday Morning.

MY DEAR MADAM,

Mr. Hayward tells me that we are to consider ourselves already acquainted, and your kind intention of calling on me removes from me all scruple in doing so. I wish I could come to you, but my time is parcelled out so that I cannot get even as far as the Strand without breaking a previous engagement. I should be most happy to see you this afternoon, if you would not mind the risk of having to pass a few minutes with my mother while my banker and I are settling a little business. He comes at five, and at half-past six, or a little earlier, a friend calls for me to visit Mrs. Somerville at Chelsea. I am ashamed to ask you to visit me thus, but it is my only chance; and you will pardon my freedom, I trust, if you cannot give me the privilege of seeing you—a privilege I have long desired, for I owe more to you than you can possibly be aware of, though you may have discovered traces of the influence which the spirit of your writings has had over me.

Believe me, with much respect,
Your obliged,
HARRIET MARTINEAU.

The following letter from Miss Mitford is here published, as it contains an interesting account of her meeting Miss Martineau and Mr. Willis :—

MISS MITFORD *to* MISS JEPHSON.

July 23, 1834.

At last, my dearest Emily, I have returned home. My spoiling place was not the theatre, but the world. Every day we had from sixty to seventy visitors, and three times more parties made for me than I could have attended, even if I had refused all exhibiting show parties, and gone only to friends, dining with what they called quiet parties of twenty or thirty, and thirty or forty more arriving to tea. At last, however, I was forced to break off this, or I should have returned to the country without seeing any public place whatever, and my last week or ten days were spent in seeing all to be seen in London in the morning, and attending operas and plays every evening—the artists all writing to show me their galleries, and the very best private boxes everywhere

being reserved for my accommodation—no queen
could have been more deferentially received. Even
my maid was shown everywhere as a part of me. I
have not yet recovered the fatigue; but most certainly nothing could be more gratifying. I formed
many valuable friendships, renewed old acquaintances, and made many new. The woman whom I
like best is Harriet Martineau, who is cheerful, frank,
cordial, and right-minded in a very high degree—
and my favourite amongst the men is decidedly that
most accomplished and delightful person, Mr. Hayward (the translator of 'Faust'), a very young man,
but decidedly the leader of the best London Society.
I also liked much Mr. Willis, an American author,
whose unwritten poetry and unwritten philosophy
you may remember in my American book, and who is
now understood to be here to publish his account of
England. He is a very elegant young man, and
more like one of the best of our peers' sons than a
rough republican.

MR. W. HOWITT *to* MISS MITFORD.

Nottingham, January 30, 1835.

DEAR MISS MITFORD,

I herewith beg to introduce to you the ancient
and venerable sage, Pantika. I do not imagine that
he will very much please you, as you are so much
more interested in modern and living characters than
in such legends as he has to relate. But I introduce
him principally for a good excuse for renewing that
acquaintance I much wish to make again with you
when in your pleasant country. We have been

reading your volumes a second time just lately, and I now see the whereabouts of your situations, and even your characters (whereof my charioteer, Ben Therly, is not the least), far better than I did. With two things I have, however, been much struck. One is that you never mention, as a characteristic of your landscapes, those grave herds of black and white Berkshire hogs, which are seen as steadily grazing in the fields as sheep. You, I daresay, do not see anything strange in this, but it struck me as a peculiar feature of Berkshire and Hampshire. In the Midland Counties you never see anything of the kind. The other *wonderful thing* is that, in your very graphic descriptions of your woody lanes and copses, you never, as I perceive, deign to notice that species of clematis which hangs in such rich masses on the bushes and along the upland thickets all across the south of England, and is everywhere dignified with the name of ‘Old Man’s Beard.’ Have you taken a spite against this, in my opinion, very ornamental plant? If you have, I wish you would, by pure legerdemain, transfer it to our hedges, for it does not grow wild in this part of the world.

I am right thankful to see that you have got in your eloquent friend, Sergeant Talfourd, for Reading. I can imagine you very much occupied and interested during the progress of that election—ay, even canvassing mightily. For my part, I feel quite easy as to the course of political events. I have now just as much fear of the progress of reform being arrested as I have of the stream of the Thames being stopped. To attempt such a thing is to be sure of getting swept away by it, though perhaps not without some damage to the country.

Mrs. Howitt will write with this to thank you for your welcome present of your tragedy, and as welcome letter. After I left you I had a most delightful ramble of a walk. Such weather at such a season surely never was before sent out of Heaven. I strolled through the New Forest, chatted with Miss Bowles in her sweet cottage near Lymington, went on through Winchester, Salisbury—traversed its great plain, and wondered at Stonehenge. Then on into the beautiful county of Devon; into Dartmoor to Plymouth, across the water to Falmouth, St. Michael's Mount, Penzance, Land's End. A glorious wild scene! Amongst the Cornish mines to Tintagel—the very birthplace of King Arthur—only think of that! And I have some pieces of his old castle, too. I traversed Cornwall on foot, from the Land's End to its northern boundary, and saw as many glow-worms one night as would stock all your Berkshire lanes. I also dined one day, on a certain moor, upon a *turnip-pie* fit in *size* to set on Arthur's own round table. I found also in that luxurious land fish-pies, squab-pies, sweet-giblet-pies, and pies such as neither Adam nor his sons ever knew, except his Cornish ones. You cannot imagine what a self-indulgent race is congregated on that western promontory. It is enough to spoil me for the rest of England! Well, I must forget turnip-pies, and tell you that I crossed from Ilfracombe to Swansea, and spent a week most delightfully in the vale of Neath. If you have not seen the gardens and orangery at Margam, you have not seen what would charm all England through the medium of your pen. Thence I progressed to the banks of the Wye, Tintern, Bristol, and home—where three merry faces were looking out for me, and were, I thought, after all, the prettiest sight I had seen.

When does Bentley mean to let 'Our Market Town'[1] be heard of? He ought to fix on an early market-day. I send this parcel to his care, and trust he will not detain it very long.

Wishing you every blessing and prosperity, believe me to be,

Yours very truly,
W. HOWITT.

MR. WILLIS *to* MISS MITFORD.

Travellers' Club, February 22, 1835.

MY DEAR MISS MITFORD,

Nothing has prevented my acknowledging sooner your last most delightful and kind letter but the fear of inflicting a correspondence on you, which I know too well the value of your time to take upon my conscience. It has lain on my memory, however, with a continual feeling of gratification and pleasure, and now that some weeks have elapsed, perhaps you will permit me to 'supplant the geraniums' in your mind while a letter may be read.

Thank you most sincerely for the confidence with which you write to me of your literary projects. Your instinct has not failed you in selecting ears that are open to everything that concerns you, either as

[1] Belford Regis?

an authoress or a woman. They are hardly separable indeed in your case—for you are as distinguished in the world as the 'gentlewoman' among authoresses, as you are for your rank merely in literature. I have often thought you were very enviable for the universality of that opinion respecting you. You share it with Sir Philip Sydney, who was in his day, in the same way, the *gentleman* among authors.

I look with great interest for your new tragedy. I think your mind is esentially dramatic; and in that, in our time, you are alone. I know no one else who could have written 'Rienzi,' and I felt 'Charles I.' to my fingers' ends, as one feels no other modern play. If I were to 'farm out' your mind (*sui generis* as your village sketches are), I would have a tragedy every year.

You very kindly suggest a book to me on England. I cannot do it, and I will convince you of it in a moment. I have been overwhelmed with kindness from the first step on the shores of this country, and I have seen everything *en beau*. Not falsely, but quite seriously, I could not with truth express myself except in superlative admiration of everything in England; and this, though a true view, would seem in a book like a picture without shade—insipid. Besides, my countrymen would tear me in pieces if I were to say in print a tenth part of what I feel on the subject. And then my whole experience has been in a vein of magnificent, but still *private* hospitality, and I could not make a book interesting without trenching on what is sacred. I have a great reverance for household gods. Still I am writing constantly for an

American periodical (the *New York Mirror*) sketches of distinguished people, &c., &c., and these will convey to my countrymen the most of what I feel and see, and in a shape which will never reach England. I am flattered all the same by your suggestion, *à même temps.*

I met Jane Porter and Miss Aiken and Tom Moore, and a troop more of *beaux esprits*, yesterday at dinner. What an intoxicating life it is! I never shall be content elsewhere. Any other country now would unsphere me.

I hope to see you in town, and really feel a strong disposition to flatter myself that I might secure your lasting friendship. If the sincerest admiration and the most kindly leaning of heart towards you are at all provocative of return, I may already write myself, dear Miss Mitford,

Faithfully your friend,
N. P. WILLIS.

MARY HOWITT to MISS MITFORD.

Nottingham, April 17, 1835.

MY DEAR MISS MITFORD,

I meant to have written you a long letter relating to ballads and tragedies, ancient and modern, on which subject I have a desire to say something; but I will not do so at this time, lest my wisdom should be thrown away, seeing this letter will reach you at a moment when you will be occupied with other thoughts. I therefore present myself before you only to assure you of our best, our kindest, wishes for your complete success on Easter Monday night.

Could I untrammel myself from circumstances which are as little controlled as the winds of heaven, I would myself be in London to witness your triumph. As it is, I can only be present in spirit, a far less satisfactory mode than in body; but you may be assured I shall be there, though not visible to your eyes.

The title of your new English opera has not yet reached us, but I have a feeling what the kind of subject will be—full of freshness, beauty, and happiness, with just enough trouble to enhance all the felicity which crowns the piece. I hear (in fancy) the English songs, the English melodies. I see the English hall, the village, the people—a peep into an English Arcadia. I see peasants haymaking, sunshine, summer flowers, trees full of leaf, and everything that gives us a sense of peace, happiness, and festivity; a wedding procession from an old hall—marriage, songs and dances, the ringing of bells heard in joyous bursts through the merry music of the village festival. All these happy images and joyful sounds are present to my mind, dear Miss Mitford, when I think of *your* English opera, and it seems to my fancy well worth a journey to London to see and hear anything so full of the amenities of human life, so fresh, so pure, so inspiriting as you would make it —such scenes and such life as many of Claude Lorraine's pictures are full of. You will laugh at me, I daresay, and tell me I am as far from the mark as I was when I, in my simplicity, took the people of your village for living men and women and children. I am half ashamed of my credulity now; I ought to have known enough of author craft to be sure all was not truth which seemed like it, but that the skill of the master consisted most in creating what looked most like truth.

Are you not delighted with the patronage Sir Robert Peel has shown to literary men and women? Here it is that the Tories are superior to the Liberals. How different was their conduct when they deprived those veteran authors—of whom Coleridge and William Roscoe were two—of the pension they received from the Royal Society of Literature. Sir Robert Peel has done great honour to himself. I grant that the pensions are small, but to persons of inexpensive habits, as some of these are, quite sufficient to make them comparatively rich. But it is the spirit of the gift which charms me. Statesmen ought to know that a part of a nation's strength, a great deal of a nation's glory, is in the hands of its literary men ; and where literature is honoured by the rulers it will also be honoured by its people. Sir Robert Peel has acted nobly; these pensions are not enough for bribes, and demand no compromise of principle. I regard them as an honour done to literature, honourable alike to the giver and the receiver.

Go on, dear Miss Mitford, with your writings, which are so entirely English, which do our English hearts good to read, and which must make our national manners, scenes, and feelings so familiar and so delightful to foreigners, and you will abundantly deserve, and assuredly shall receive, a handsome annuity from some future Premier—heaven knows! but I fear it will be long before a Whig or a Radical will do half as much. It is my honest opinion that they think us writers, who meddle neither with Church or State, Political Economy or Population, as little better than house-sparrows that the village churchwarden will buy at a farthing a head.

You honour greatly my mention of our beautiful crocuses. I wish now you could see a wild tulip, which is native to the same meadows, though it does not flower there. I saw yesterday three, which had been removed to a garden, and after three years' cultivation produced the most splendid yellow tulip I ever saw. I would fain send you a garland of such English flowers, for the love I bear your English opera.

Good-bye, and may every good fortune attend you. My husband unites in every kind wish and messages of love, if you will accept them. I write to you in town; but you must make kind remembrances acceptable to your father from my husband.

I am, dear Miss Mitford,
Yours,
M. HOWITT.

P.S.—I am sure you congratulate me on my happiness in finding myself so handsomely used in ' Blackwood's Magazine.' *You* cannot tell, you always have lived in the sunshine of public favour, how charming such a notice as this is. It is almost worth while to have sat in the darkness to experience afterwards the breaking in of light.

It may be interesting to compare the picture which Mrs. Howitt here supposes Miss Mitford to draw of a country wedding, with an actual description of one which I have found among Miss Mitford's letters, written at a later date to Miss Barrett :—

I have been to-day, for an hour, to sweet Lucy Anderdon's wedding-breakfast. My father insisted on my going. I could not go with them to church, or, rather, I could not get courage to leave him for so long. It was a beautiful scene—the bride exquisitely fair, and modest, and graceful—the bridegroom a joyous, animated young man, a very impersonation of happiness. Six bridesmaids, all so young and so pretty, and crowds of elegant men and lovely women tastefully dressed, a beautiful house and place, the very banquet a picture—bells, bands of music, village schools, children strewing flowers, and all that is pleasant to the eye and to the mind; but sweet, sweet Lucy the charm of all! May God bless her! Among our parting words—ay, when parting from the father and mother to whom she is all—she said to me, ' The moment you hear how Miss Barrett is, write to me.' May heaven bless her! I like *him;* he seems thoroughly open-hearted, good, and kind—very different from her, and perhaps the better. The father and mother approve it thoroughly, and were happier under it than I could have thought. I could not help crying; I never can when I see joy.

N. P. WILLIS *to* MISS MITFORD.

Athenæum, London, April 22, 1835.

MY DEAR MISS MITFORD,

I am anxious to see your play and your next book, and I quite agree with you that the drama is your *pied*, though I think laurels, and spreading ones, are sown for you in every department of writing. Nobody ever wrote better prose, and what could not the author of 'Rienzi' do in verse? I should like to talk over this with you.

For myself I am far from considering myself regularly embarked in literature, and if I can live without it, or ply any other vocation, shall vote it a thankless trade, and save my 'entusymussy'[1] for my wife and children—when I get them. I am at present steeped to the lips in London society, going to everything, from Devonshire House to a publisher's dinner in Paternoster Row, and it is not a bad *olla podrida* of life and manners. I doat on 'England and true English,' and was never so happy or so at a loss to find a minute for care or forethought.

I really have ten thousand things I wish to write about or talk about to you; but a letter is a needle's point to dance upon, and I must keep all my flourishes till I see you. No letter is so small, however, that I cannot express in it my happiness and pride in your friendship, and I beg you to believe, dear Miss Mitford, that your kindness is appreciated and your regard sought by no one more sensitively than,

Faithfully and always yours,

N. P. WILLIS.

[1] Enthusiasm.

Mrs. Howitt *to* Miss Mitford.

May 14, [1835?].

William is busy about his rural life, and to my mind it promises extremely well. I think you will like it. I never told you that his birthday and yours fall on the same day—the 18th of December; and last year we honoured them together, and very pleasant household festival we made, wishing many a time we had you with us.

But I meant to have told you, moreover, that the Star of Bethlehem, a few petals of which you sent, grows here in these meadows. How beautiful these wild flowers are!

Good-bye, dear Miss Mitford, I have yet a deal to say about tragedies and ballads, but that I leave to another time. God bless you!

I am, affectionately,

M. Howitt.

P.S.—William sends his love, if you will accept it, and best and kindest regards to Dr. Mitford.

Mrs. Hofland *to* Miss Mitford.

Kensington, June 14, 1835.

My very dear Friend,

Exactly as I received your very dear note I was sitting down to tell you an incident, and I must tell it you before I thank you for it, *i.e.*, for the note.

On Sunday night my good man called aloud in his sleep something which was uttered in a very exulting tone, therefore, though he awoke me in the next room, I did not think I ought to awaken him to explain it. He very seldom dreams, and, unlike me, never is sorrowful in his sleep when he does. The next morning, however, I said 'What could you be shouting about before sunrise—have you any recollection of it?' 'Oh, yes; I saw Stephen Lane at Lord's among the cricketers; he is a fine athletic young fellow, and I called out to everybody, "Look at Stephen Lane, look at Stephen Lane."' Now he had said before he went to bed, 'I shall go to Lord's ground to-morrow,' and I had answered, 'I wish Miss Mitford was going with you,' having often heard him wish you were going, and perhaps he fell asleep musing on you and the said Stephen. Be that as it may, it is evident you had given him a strong impression, indeed it is so strong he describes the Stephen of his vision as accurately as possible, which is in fact Stephen in his young days—strong, and tall, and active, and joyous. In my early life it so happened that in Sheffield we had some butchers just like him, and there was a very clever satirical poem which began:

> 'In a fair country stands a filthy town,
> By bugs and butchers held in high renown,'

and which I never recollect without seeing in my mind's eye perhaps the three very handsomest samples of *man*, as to person, I have seen in the course of my whole life, and, what is more, not one of the three was a vulgar man or of deficient manners.

I have just finished Fanny Kemble's books, and when I say that I read them the next after your most charming volumes, and was amused, and on the whole much pleased with them, I am sure they are meritorious, let the critics say what they may. When I saw her on the stage I could not admire her for the life of me, though I thought her clever; but if she can follow you, and not prove (as Mrs. Norton does) a flat, uninteresting, almost mawkish picture of fine folks, in which the truth and fine writing (however good) leave you weary and dull, she must be good, *malgré* occasional roughness and hasty conclusion, the result of youth and inexperience.

It is quite evident that on her arrival she did not like the Americans, because she had not been accustomed to a people who, full of the higher energies and better characteristics of our common nature, were deficient, not in intellect, but in forms and conventional points, who were, in fact, what we were half a century ago: but, as she goes on, you see she becomes better informed, better in conception, and, as she is evidently honest in all things, she speaks what she feels and thinks. There is in her a love for Nature, a passion for flowers, a power of rising above earth and earthly things, a contempt for the drudgery of her profession, and an estimation of the poetic character. It is her affliction to represent, not to *originate*, which bespeaks her mind superior to her station. During all the first volume I felt sorry that she lived in America, in the second I see she may live there and be happy also.

Mr. Dilke might find *sentences* and *phrases* of puerility, the repetitions are childish, and the opinions ill-formed—nay, the very language, which is that of an half-educated girl, is undeniably bad; but along with this there is a raciness, simplicity, and down-rightness very attractive.

The best account I have read of America, as it *now* is, I have found in a book written by H. Tudor, Esq. (a townsman of my own whom I knew very well in his early life some thirty years since). He is their warm admirer, but, of course, he found some things not quite *comme il faut.* Now—how should they be so in the new and peculiar state in which they stand? —to me, as the world in which the *poor* can live and *thrive*, they are all glorious.

Thank you a thousand times for the verses I have sent to New York. I think it probable the publication of ' The Pearl ' may cut my book out, but there is room for both to a certain point; at all events, I per-sonally wished them to try, but I have told them I do no more. I find Newman, who bought my stories of Longmans, has sold a great many to New York, which accounts for their being anxious to get my name as editor; but indeed my child's tales had long had a run there, which accounts for Pilbrow and Illman wishing to try the work once more. In point of fact the binding never is done well, and in that alone they failed. The book is full as good as any here, and very much more abundant in matter. I saw the other day at Mr. Linton's a journal (which sells there for four-pence English) most admirable in every respect, con-taining reviews, anecdotes, descriptions, &c., all very good, far better paper and printing than ours, with a neat back into the bargain. With Willis's Melaine, &c., I have been delighted, and indeed affected, more

than with any poetry I ever read in my life. I wonder
whether he is the gentleman I met at Mr. Wilson's
when I went to spend an evening there with Miss
Edgeworth. I remember there a young, stylish-look-
ing man (whom I set down as a nobleman or as an
Oxford man), but he was introduced to me as Mr.
Somebody, an American from Philadelphia. He was,
however, my beau-ideal of a gentleman, somewhat a
leetle too much dressed; but he was young, and handsome, and it became him well. He was a man moving
everywhere in our aristocratic circles—this is about
three or four years since.

When I used to spend a month or two at the time
at St. Leonard's, the house was always full of lords
and ladies; as one went another came. I always
found them very, very pleasant in conduct and manners, the women lively and agreeable, but the men
what I should call dull. Old Lady Cork told me, ' she
could not imagine how I got on so well, for people of
my description were always expected to *toady* or
fiddle, and she couldn't see that I took the trouble to
do either.' I told her that I was too old and too
honest for either, yet it was plain I did get on.

July 6.

The inside sheet has been written a long time,
and I could not get a frank, and I cannot re-write it,
and have nothing else to say, save that your work is
the only one going at our libraries. I am reading
Mr. Beckford's last, and am exceedingly pleased with
it. In the other sheet I was answering your question
—' did not Mr. Hofland think our aristocracy the most

amiable and sensible in manners?'—by speaking of my own experience first during a long period in which I went (when I could raise dresses) to Lord Harcourt's. He exactly agrees with you. He finds Lord and Lady Carnarvon most amiable, and to him as friendly as possible. During the time of his fever I used to receive the very kindest notes from Lord C., entering into all the particulars of his case, and telling me how his own health was, just as if we had been old friends. So far as I have seen, they are the very pleasantest people to live with. I do not know so sweet a young woman as Lady Jemima Eliot; she calls and sits with me half an hour now and then, and treats me almost with affection, purely because she fancies my books may do her children good.

The Thompsons, with whom my cousin, Miss Rolls, lives, are the best people in the world from all I can hear, and Smith tells me that, since Lord Beresford's marriage, he is become the most agreeable, kind-hearted creature that ever was born. All the world knows he used to be stiff and proud enough.

Miss Agnes Strickland was here yesterday, very wrath at the publishers of her ' Pilgrim of Walsing-ham,' being sure that a work so highly spoken of must sell well; but I think she is mistaken, for it does not always follow.

Mrs. Hall has got home, and better, from Brighton, but her left hand is still contracted.

I find Miss Landon wrote Lady Stepney's book—I never read it. She had a hundred pounds, and grumbles much, as she says it took her more time than writing a new one would have done.

Mr. Hofland bids me thank you very much for the flower-seeds. He will send you some clarkia, if you have none. It flourishes much with us, and is, I think, a very elegant flower.

My review of 'Belford Regis' is to be in next month, the 'Lady's Magazine' man says. We go to Yorkshire on the 21st. Mr. H. is exceedingly harassed with the Suffolk Street Gallery, which, by the by, many people say (those who know) is far better than the Royal Academy this year. I have not been yet to the latter, but I have heard your picture spoken of by many, and always in high terms of praise. I am glad you have heard from Miss James, and are on terms with Macready. The magazine put in all the beautiful songs I sent them from Sadak—they are very sweet ones.[1]

My master begs his kind regards to you and the doctor, to whom pray offer mine, and believe me,

Your truly affectionate friend,

B. HOFLAND.

MRS. HOWITT *to* MISS MITFORD.

July 7, 1835.

MY DEAR MISS MITFORD,

I am sure you have thought me long, very long, in replying to your last, but the truth is we are at a little loss to know best how to serve you respecting 'Belford Regis.' We live far more out of any clique, far more without connections, literary or influential, than yourself, and as the volumes had been reviewed

---

[1] 'Songs from Sadak and Kalasrade,' an opera by Miss Mitford.

both in the 'Athenæum' and 'Tait's Magazine'—the only periodicals we have any connection with, and the newspapers *here* are so utterly worthless, and move in so circumscribed a sphere that no notice they might give of your book could serve you, we felt a little at a loss to know how to do it, and yet so desirous of doing something as not to be willing to give it up. Besides, William was just about going to London, and it was thought best not to write to you till after his return. I am now doing so. He found 'Belford Regis' very much liked, and had a good deal of talk with Mr. Bentley both about it and your other works, and wherein the peculiar excellence of them lies—all new light thrown in upon the twilight of the poor publisher's brain. I expect he will look upon you henceforth as a most philosophical writer, who is to do signal service in the regeneration of English society.

I believe a set of paragraphs will go through divers provincial papers—their names I cannot tell—but William has put them in a train to do so. Unfortunately, Mr. Bentley does not send his books to our *only* London newspaper friends, so that extracts cannot be given.

But the most important thing, I think, is a paper on you and your writings, which W. is to furnish to the 'Athenæum,' and for which you may look in about a fortnight—so prepare yourself.

I am writing in great haste, having an accumulation of work on my hands, and yet being unwilling to delay writing to you any longer. I shall send you an account some day of how we spent Whitsun Monday—it would make a beautiful bit of English country life for you.

Good-bye, dear Miss Mitford, and with best wishes for you and kindest regards to Dr. Mitford, to your conservatory, your geraniums, your bay-tree, your busy bees, your village, your town, and all that appertains to you, which is about to be set forth with due honour,

I am, very truly yours,

M. Howitt.

P.S.—William is writing about you this very moment, but as yet I have not heard a word of it, so I shall tell no tales.

The following lines, written apparently by one of Miss Mitford's friends, but bearing no signature, were found among her letters :—

A Wish (too personal, perhaps).

I fain would sing before I sleep
  A little song that shall survive
The heart that gave it voice, and keep
  My memory, when I'm dust, alive.

For thee, Leona dear, I fain
  Would leave a little lay behind,
To waken up the past again,
  With all its music, in thy mind.

It's sad, sweet music—such alone
  As we on earth may hope to hear
Where mingles e'en in mirth a tone
  Of mourning—dirge-like, yet most dear.

Dear, while death's phantom shade, that lies
 O'er all, brings out some sparks divine
Within our souls, as in the skies
 Night's shadow gives the stars to shine.

Then call not my ambition vain,
 If I would shun the common lot
To be a linklet in the chain
 Of life—break off—and be forgot.

Among the many millioned throng
 Who on the world's wide stage have moved,
I fain would sing a little song
 To tell that I have lived and loved.

CHAPTER XII.

LETTERS FROM MISS SEDGWICK, N. P. WILLIS, W. HOWITT, AND
GEORGE TICKNOR.

MISS SEDGWICK *to* MISS MITFORD.

Stockbridge, August 6, 1835.

MY DEAR FRIEND,

The blanks there are in our correspondence
are not blanks in our relations, I trust, for with
me they are filled with many pleasant recollections, many flights of thoughts which, bless them!
have wings, to you, and many, many earnest desires
for your happiness and prosperity in all your doings.
Have you been conscious within the last days of
July of any particular absence of mind? Has that
spirit of yours which so loves to wander over the gifted
and *enjoyed* places of Nature and blend itself with all
that is happy and good and beautiful in the social
relations, has it not been conscious of any unseen
influence; if not, then, like poor Ophelia, I am the
more deceived, for when I was sitting with Miss
Martineau on Laurel Hill (a beautiful eminence that
rises almost from the midst of our village), and look-

ing from Sacrifice Rock (a name that our young people have bestowed on the Rocky Summit, where the poor Indian girl of my ' Hope Leslie ' lost her arm), when we were sitting there, and looking down on the lovely meadows, we talked of you, and wished for you, and when I drove our blessed friend down a beautiful ravine between a mountain and the brimful Housatonic, oh! then how we wished for you, and thought of your drives in your pony-phaeton, and when we issued from the mountain caves (a chasm between our mountains where some convulsion of Nature has piled the rocks one on another so long ago that trees have sprung from their crevices and died, and other trees have sprung from them, and the rocks are covered with mosses, and plumed with ferns), when we came out of this wild solitude and looked upon the wide-spread, smiling scene before us, the yellow harvest-fields on the hill-side, the rich meadows, our clear, little river contriving to wind in every possible way through them, so, like an ingenious child, to stay till the last minute, and the white houses of our village peeping here and there through the trees that embower each habitation, and the rustic bridge, and the little island that seems to rest there for companionship, and, but, bless me! here I am on the third page of my letter; the burden of it all is, my dearest Miss Mitford, that wherever we were we thought and talked of you. Miss M., after wandering through our southern and western states proceeded on her way to Boston. She promises to go to see you, and tell you all about us. We do not know whether to be most grieved or grateful that she whom we expected

only to admire should make us all love her, the pang
of separation comes so close upon the birth of affection! I have not yet parted from her; we are to go
to the [*torn*] Hills together in September, and I shall
see the last of her in New York.

Our little community have been delighting themselves with your ‘ Belford Regis ’; accept their united
thanks for it. Is it not good now and then during a
public career to get genuine individual gratitude?
The book is re-published rather shabbily by Carey.
I am in great hopes that we shall get our ungracious
laws altered at the next congressional session, so
that you English contributors to our advantage
shall get some remuneration for your pains. I have
a new novel, ‘The Linwoods,’ waiting till some
portion of our novel-reading public return to their
city homes, to be published. I have given directions
for a copy to be sent you. It has at least two good
lines in it—good beyond all question—the motto,
which is from your beautiful ‘ Rienzi.’ By the way,
I had the pleasure last winter of reading the very
copy you gave Miss Phillips, and by the way, too, it
is said that this young lady, with whom I have no
personal acquaintance, is about to marry one of our
rich merchants.

We are to have a visit from the Butlers shortly.
You have seen her journal, and your opinion is more
favourable than that of her English reviewers, is it
not? Its faults are juvenilities, and the consequences
of unfavourable circumstances; but are there not un-
questionable evidences of a most extraordinary mind
and a noble spirit? There should be, for she pos-

sesses them. Do not believe any of the gossip they print about her.

Your friend Theodore is here, and is to be married within a month; we are just in the midst of bridal festivities, which Miss M. stayed to help us enjoy. A pretty little niece of mine was tied on Tuesday evening to a youth towards seven feet high; but this is the only disparity between them, and disparities that can be measured are not formidable. Kate gave me a long message to you, which I have neither room nor time for. Will you offer my best wishes to your father, and believe me truly yours,

E. M. SEDGWICK.

N. P. WILLIS to MISS MITFORD.

Manor House, Lee,
Sunday, August 10, 1835.

MY DEAR MISS MITFORD,

Though, as I have said before, I am *principled* against inveigling better employed pens into correspondence, I have been longer in answering your last most delightful letter, even than 'good resolution' should exact. I have been led on from week to week, however, by the hope of fixing on a day to advise you of a flit from London and a visit to Reading, but though others have made pilgrimages to Our Village (*vide* 'Athenæum') *my* scollop-shell still hangs on the wall. I have just now decided, to the prejudice of a proposed trip up the Rhine, to pass a week or two with Sir Charles Throckmorton somewhere in the neighbourhood of Stratford-on-Avon, and one very great inducement was the *en passant* of Reading; I do

not know exactly when, but somewhere about the
first week in September I shall be on the way, and I
will write to you a few days previous, and take tea
with you in passing. I had a letter from America the
other day, wondering how I could possibly have been
a year in England without a visit to our village. It
is for the same reason I suppose that people pass
their lives within the sound of Niagara and never see
it. Your last book still rolls on, gathering golden
opinions, and I for one thank you, for I have been
passing the last fortnight in the country, and perhaps
there is no book in the world so pleasant to be on the
grass with and read to a charming woman. I have
only grudged the transfer of leaves from my right
hand to my left, and if you had heard the '*Is that all?*'
of my listener as I closed the last volume, you would
have felt that you had not lived in vain—as who has,
who has given pleasure to the world, or beguiled
weariness, or refined the aspect of life? I have been
always in the neighbourhood of London, but I have
never enjoyed life so keenly as in the variety of
excursions we have made within the last month.
What a treasure of beauty England is? What, in
other lands, is comparable to Knowle Park, Bromley
Hill (Lord Farnborough's), North Cray, and a dozen
more of these enchanting paradises? To me there is
no happier day than one passed in loitering over the
grounds of a superb English park. If I was married,
or had any 'sweet spirit for my minister,' I would
spend all my summers thus. There is no travel on
the continent that is comparable to it for enjoyment,
and objects worthy of attention. I have nearly made

up my mind to remain in England till the spring, having become rather a sun-flower in the five years' wanderings in softer climates, and dreading an American winter.

With my best respects to your father, believe me, my dear Miss Mitford (in the hope of soon seeing you),

Yours most faithfully,
N. P. WILLIS.

MR. W. HOWITT to MISS MITFORD.

Nottingham, September 10, 1835.

DEAR MISS MITFORD,

I am very glad that the paper in the *Athenæum* pleased you. Had I seen more of your pleasant neighbourhood and people it should have been much better. My peep at you was so slight that I could only hope you would pardon the great blunders and the greater omissions it must contain for the simple intention. There are various errors of the press, which make, as usual, plenty of nonsense, such as making your noble bay-tree *simple* instead of ample. All the nonsense pray lay to the charge of the printer's imp. I was tied up too about 'Belford Regis' —the *Athenæum* having given two notices of it. I felt a delicacy in making more than a passing paragraph of it, for those critics, the very best of them, are, as we people here say, 'sore chaps.' Well, I am glad it pleased you and your dear father—that is all the *pay 1 want* for it; and some other time I shall hope to be earlier in the field for you, when I can have fair play.

U 2

Well, what do you think of our Nottingham men now! I shall send you a paper to-morrow containing the account of the great cricket match played here between Sussex and Nottingham. Perhaps you may have seen in the papers that the Nottingham club challenged the Sussex, and beat them about a fortnight ago at Brighton, and now they have beaten them again here. The match commenced on Monday, and was finished yesterday (Wednesday) at about half-past four o'clock. We wished you had been there—a more animated sight of the kind you never saw. On Sunday morning, as we were dressing, we saw a crowd going up the street, and immediately perceived that in the centre of it were the Sussex cricketers, arrived by the London coach, and going to the inn kept by one of our Nottingham cricketers. They looked exceedingly interesting, I assure you, being a set of very fine fellows, in their white hats, and with all their trunks, carpet bags, and cloaks, coming, as we verily believed, to be beaten. Our interest was strongly excited, and on Monday morning we set off to the cricket ground, which lies about a mile from the town, in the Forest, as it is still called, though not a tree is left upon it—a long, furzy common, crowned at the top with about twenty windmills, and descending in a steep slope to a fine level—round which the racecourse runs, and within the racecourse lies the cricket ground, and the military ground for the troop of horse which always occupy our barracks. Each end of the cricket ground was completely enclosed by booths, and all up the forest hill were scattered booths and tents with flags flying, fires blazing, pots boiling, ale-barrels standing, and carts and asses and people bringing still more good things, ranged at the further side of the cricket ground. I had the strongest idea of an amphitheatre filled with people that I ever had. In fact it *was* an amphitheatre. Along each side of the ground ran a bank sloping down to it; and it, and the tents, and booths at the end were occupied with a dense mass of people, and all up the hill were groups, and on the race stand an eager, forward-leaning mass. There were said to be twenty thousand people, all as silent as the ground beneath them, except when some exploit of the players produced a sudden thunder of applause. The playing was beautiful. Mr. Ward, the late M.P. for the City of London, came from the Isle of Wight to see the play, and declared himself highly delighted. But nothing was so beautiful as the sudden shout and rush of the crowd when the last decisive notch was gained; to see the scorers suddenly snatch up their chairs, and run off with them towards the players' tent, to see the bat of Bart Goode, the batsman on whom the fate of the game depended, spinning up in the air, where he had sent it in the ecstasy of the moment; and the crowd, that the instant before were as fixed and as silent as the earth itself, spread all over the green space, where the white figures of the players had till then been so gravely and, apparently, coolly contending —speeding with a murmur as of a sea, and over their heads, amid all the deafening clamour and confusion, the carrier-pigeon, with the red ribbon tied to its tail, the signal of loss or gain—I know not which—beating round and round, so as to ascertain its precise situation, and then flying off to bear the tidings to some strongly interested quarter. Was it not a beautiful sight? Should you not have been delighted to see it?

My thoughts on such occasions generally fly beyond the immediate place and time, and begin to contemplate consequences, and I could not help seeing what a wide difference twenty years has produced in the character of the English population. What a contrast is this play to bull baiting, dog and cock fightings! So orderly, so manly, so generous in its character. It is the nearest approach to the athletic games of the Greeks that we have made, and the effect on the general mass of the people by the emulation it will excite must be excellent. There is something very beautiful in one distant county sending its peaceful champions to contend with those of another in a sport that has no drawback of cruelty or vulgarity in it, but has every recommendation of skill, taste, health, and generous rivalry. You, dear Miss Mitford, have done a great deal to promote this better spirit, and you could not have done more had you been haranguing Parliament, and bringing in bills for the purpose.

Mary sends her love, and wishes you could have given us the private history of all the players, their loves, their wives, and their particular characters and achievements. As Bart Goode threw up his bat, 'There,' she exclaimed, 'I hope his sweetheart or his wife sees it!' One fact you should know, for I have not got the newspaper yet, and don't know that it

will be there. A Sussex batsman—Taylor, I believe
—sent the ball straight through a tent at the end of
the ground, cutting through the canvas on each side
as clean as a cannon-shot, and smashing six bottles
of porter in its passage. With kind regards to Dr.
Mitford,

Yours very truly,
W. HOWITT.

MR. WILLIS *to* MISS MITFORD.

London, September 22, 1835.

MY DEAR MISS MITFORD,

You will think me the most perfidious of men,
for I have all but passed your door on a visit to
Warwickshire, and date, as you see, once more from
London. Having confessed my sin, extenuation is
the next step. I was later than I had promised myself, and was expected by Sir Charles Throckmorton
to join Miss Porter in a tour to Kenilworth, Warwick,
Stratford-upon-Avon, &c., &c. Miss Porter has expressed the strongest wish to know you, and I had
concocted a delightful dream of bringing her down
to Reading and taking up our abode at the nearest
inn for a week on my return from Coughton Court.
This would have been agreeable to all parties; *but*,
unluckily, I went to a picnic just before starting, fell
in love with a blue-eyed girl, and (after running the
gauntlet successfully through France, Italy, Greece,
Germany, Asia Minor, Turkey, &c., &c.,) I renewed
my youth, and became 'a suitor for love.' I am to
be married (*sequitur*) on Thursday week. Do you
excuse me for not coming to see you? I brought

Miss Porter back, but it was to chaperon me to my wedding.

The lady who is to take me, as the Irish say, 'in a present,' is some six years younger than myself, gentle, religious, relying, and unambitious. She has never been whirled through the gay society of London, so is not giddy or vain. She has never swum in a gondola or written a sonnet, so has a proper respect for those who have. She is called pretty, but is more than that in *my* eyes; sings as if her heart were hid in her lips, and *loves* me. *Voilà*, my programme in little. When you come to London, or when *we* (how delightful to write in the plural *now !*)—when *we* come to Reading, I am bent on your liking her. She already (as who does not that reads?) loves you.

We are bound to Paris for a month (because I think amusement better than reflection when a woman makes a doubtful bargain), and by November we return to London and its neighbourhood for the winter, and in the spring sail for America to see my mother. I have promised to live mainly on this side of the water, and shall return in the course of a year to try what contentment may be sown and reaped in a green lane in Kent. Will you come and live with us now and then?

What a charming book dear Miss Sedgwick has given us!

Direct to me in London still, and believe me, dear Miss Mitford,

Ever most faithfully yours,
N. P. WILLIS.

The following is a copy of some lines among Miss Mitford's papers, which may possibly have been written by Jane Porter:—

PAST IS PAST.

> Disinter no dead delight,
>   Bring no past to life again ;
> Those red cheeks with woe are white,
>   Those ripe lips are pale with pain.
>
> Vex not then the buried bliss
>   (Changed to more divine regret),
> Sweet thoughts come from where it lies,
>   Underneath the violet.

This was suggested by the circumstance of our endeavouring to revive an old amusement in the absence (by death) of one of our blithest companions—the saddest attempt at happiness I ever made.

J. P.

GEORGE TICKNOR *to* MISS MITFORD.

Clarendon Hotel, Bond Street,
October 15, 1835.

DEAR MISS MITFORD,

I received from our poor friend Kenyon, two days ago, when we reached London, your kind note and the copy of Serjeant Talfourd's 'Ion' that accompanied it.   Many thanks for both of them.

I send you with this all Dr. Channing's works, and the little series of four small volumes, in which Miss Sedgwick's 'Home' is to be found, and I send them very gladly, both because I think them good and because the last of them, 'Gleams of Truth,' is a practical illustration of the principles touching the relations of the more favoured and less favoured classes of society, which are so ably and so beautifully set forth in the separate sermon of Dr. Channing which I send with them.

In the matter of Mr. Webster, I am not so fortunate. I wanted very much to find two or three of his public addresses and two or three of his greater speeches on broad constitutional questions, that you might have judged what is the grasp of his mind. But both the booksellers and my private friends have failed me. I shall still search, and, if I am successful, I shall send you the pamphlets, or any of them I may find. But I am somewhat mortified to be obliged to say that I fear I shall not succeed.

It is not possible within the compass of a note, or even within the compass of many sheets of paper, to give you the idea I should be glad to present of the growth of Mr. Webster's mind and character. It requires detail, and would then read like a romance. But the general facts are that his father had been an officer in the war of 1756-63 against the French in America, and, after it was over, went to the very frontier of civilization, and, plunging into the forest, established himself and his household goods. There Mr. Webster was born. Schools there were none at first, and those to which he had access afterwards were humble and poor enough. But he began to rise from the first, and, though his father was always too poor to give him any substantial help, he continued to rise through all obstacles, and made his way to college, helped an elder brother to come there, and has, in short, by the mere effort of his own mind and character, raised himself to the place he now occupies in the regard of his countrymen. It has been a beautiful and a consistent course throughout, and, though I would gladly see him President of the United States, I do not think that the office would add anything to the reputation he enjoys with the wisest portion of our society.

But I am talking too much. Your kindness, of which I have already so many proofs, must excuse me. Please to give our best respects to your father, and accept Mrs. T.'s very sincere regards, and my own and my daughter's best acknowledgments.

Yours very faithfully,
GEO. TICKNOR.

P.S.—We shall none of us ever forget the truly delightful evening we spent in your cottage at 'Our Village.'

This Mr. Ticknor was the celebrated author of 'The History of Spanish Literature,'[1] and he had paid Miss Mitford a visit on the 26th of July. She writes: 'An American of the highest class and the highest talent, a charming person, Mr. Ticknor of Boston, visited me the other day, on his way to Dublin to see Miss Edgeworth.' Mr. Ticknor in his diary records this visit :—

'We found Miss Mitford living literally in a cottage

---

[1] Miss Mitford says that Macaulay admired it so much that he recommended the Queen to read it.

neither *ornée* nor poetical, except inasmuch as it had
a small garden crowded with the richest and most
beautiful profusion of flowers. She has the simplest
and kindest manners, and entertained us for two
hours with the most animated conversation, and a
great variety of anecdote, without any of the preten-
sions of an author by profession, and without any of
the stiffness that generally belongs to single ladies of
her age and reputation.'

MRS. HOWITT *to* MISS MITFORD.

November 16, 1835.

MY DEAR MISS MITFORD,

Thank you indeed for the gift of ' Ion ;' the tragedy was known to us by extracts, and our desire to
see it was great. We like it very much—it is a noble
descendant of the noble Greek tragedy. I am sure
your friend is a right-hearted, high-minded, and most
richly-gifted person—you are happy in such a friend.
I cannot believe it possible that, after the publication
of this, and the cordial manner of its reception, its
author will content himself with this one proof of
his talent for dramatic writing, a rare gift and a
glorious one, and one in which he will excel. You
will smile at me, dear Miss Mitford, but I must tell
you that I rejoice at his being a married man. It is
a blessed thing for a wife to have to sympathize and
glorify herself in the honour of her husband. From
the first poet in the land down to the successful
cricketer, my feeling always is, what a proud and
happy woman must his wife be ! I never care to be

undeceived, and told such and such a great man has a wife unworthy of him ; to my feeling it is impossible. There always is a heart that rejoices over the success and honour of the gifted, and to my mind it must be a wife ; therefore it is that I think Mrs. Talfourd must be a happy woman.

And is it your tragedy that is to occupy you this winter ? or do you begin your great story of English life ? Success to you, whatever it may be ! I am taking mine ease after my summer labours, walking out every day, and enjoying the fresh air and the autumnal landscape as much as possible. It is beautiful, and as I go along among fallen and falling leaves, and get glimpses of old halls, with their goodly roofs and old grey stateliness about them, such gushes of poetry come over me, and I long so earnestly to have written or to write something which might bring livingly to the reader such ruins and such friends. Oh ! my friend, if one could but embody one's own feelings !—but you can do so in great measure. Look at all your different country rambles, at the scenery you describe in every tale you write, at the noble sentiment and natural feeling which you scatter over every page—you have done so, and you will do so yet more. I hope, if you are writing prose, you will allow yourself space enough for the working out of a longer story than you have ever yet written. I am sure you would succeed.

Have you seen Robert Nicholls' poems ? If you are a reader of ' Tait's Magazine,' you will see the review of them ; that is a right manly and sterling volume of poetry, full of life, humour, and the noblest elements of poetry. I cannot tell you how such poems as ' Arouse the Soul,' ' I Dare not Scorn,' and others, such of which this volume has many, affect me. It is such writing as this which makes one feel that talent is nobler than birth, and high-mindedness of more worth than gold.

William unites with me in every kind sentiment towards both you and your father.

I am, dear Miss Mitford,

Yours affectionately and gratefully,

M. Howitt.

CHAPTER XIII.

LADY DACRE was a cousin of Miss Mitford. Both she and her lord had great appreciation of literature, and collected around them a circle of authors and other celebrities. In this year, 1836, Miss Mitford mentions her having dined at Lord Dacre's, and met Joanna Baillie, Mr. Harness, Bobus Smith, and Young the actor. She was first personally introduced to Joanna Baillie in Lady Dacre's drawing-room, 'where poets most do congregate.' Lady Dacre herself wrote some plays and short poems;[1] she sketched admirably, and was a perfect Italian scholar, a friend of Ugo Foscolo. She was remarkably handsome, retaining her beauty even in old age. Miss Mitford speaks of her charm of manner and magnificent figure, and adds that she was one of the best horsewomen and 'whips' in England.

The following is interesting as being the first letter written by Lady Dacre to Miss Mitford, and showing the origin of their friendship :—

[1] One of which appeared in 'The Keepsake' for 1837.

Lady Dacre *to* Miss Mitford.

The Hoo, Friday, January 1, 1836.

Lady Dacre presents her compliments to Miss Mitford, and (encouraged by Mr. Talbot) ventures to have recourse to her in her *extremity*. Lady D. has in vain tried to procure Mr. Talfourd's ' Ion ' from the London booksellers. She therefore petitions Miss Mitford to have the goodness to make interest with the author to procure her the reading of the work of which she has heard such praise. Lady D. begs to add her congratulations to Miss Mitford, the public and herself, that Miss Mitford should again be induced to write tragedy—to Miss M. herself, because there is no pleasure equal to it, even to those who do it ill; what then must it be to Miss M., whose dramatic blank verse is so incomparable ?

Lady D. hopes Miss Mitford is pleased with her beloved, honoured, and admired friend Joanna's new publication. Lady D. is delighted with many of the dramas, the serious ones; she does not think her friend equally strong in comedy.

If Lady D. is taking a great liberty with Miss Mitford, her sister and Mr. Talbot must bear the blame.

Mrs. Howitt *to* Miss Mitford.

Nottingham, February 4, 1836.

My dear Miss Mitford,

This new edition of ' Our Village ' I have been coveting ever since I saw the advertisement of it, and I will tell you why. It is one of those cheerful, spirited works, full of fair pictures of humanity, which, especially where there are children who love reading and being read to, becomes a household book, turned to again and again, and remembered and talked of with affection. So it is by our fireside; it is a work our little daughter has read, and loves to read, and which our little son Alfred, a most indomitable young gentleman, likes especially—not so much for its variety of character, which gives its charm to his sister's mind, but for its descriptions of the country. Everything belonging to the country is delicious in his eyes, and to his soul. He is as yet a bad reader, and therefore he is read to; and his cry is, ' Read me the Copse !' or ' Read me the Nutting, or a Ramble into the Country !' Such, dear Miss Mitford, being the case, when I saw the new edition advertised, I began to cast in my mind whether or not we could not buy it, for perhaps you know that *literary* people, though *makers* of books, are not extensive *buyers* thereof. You may think then what was my delight—and the delight of us all—when a parcel came in, the string was cut, and behold it contained no other than those long-coveted and favourite volumes ! Thank you, therefore, dearest Miss Mitford; you have conferred a benefit upon our fireside which will make you even more beloved than formerly, for now we shall always have you at hand. It is a pity that the volumes do not contain the whole of the five former. It is a pity also that the wood-cuts are not more worthy of their subjects. With these drawbacks, the volumes are extremely neatly got up, nicely and firmly bound, and that is something, when books in general are rather made for show than use. You are a fortunate woman to have a second or third edition, but not more fortunate than you deserve. Again let me thank you in the name of us all.

You ask me how does your friend like his aldermanic dignities.[1] Dignities there are none, not even a scarlet cloak, which, by the way, I am sure he would never have worn; the title we neither of us liked, but he was compelled into the office against his will, and now he is in he *likes* it not, because so much time is of necessity occupied, and it is so hard a warfare which he has to do, not against the Tories, but against the Whigs and even those who call themselves Radicals. I assure you I have seen more of men's selfishness and manœuvring since William has been one of the Corporation than I had any idea of. Verily, common human nature is a very common thing indeed; and these men stare and storm at him and dislike him worse by half than their most violent political enemies, because he will make them do right. We had need of your pleasant volumes to give one sunny pictures of poor human nature, after all the meanness and pettiness which it shows among the *reformers* of this *reformed* Corporation.

I have read Bulwer's 'Rienzi,' and yours also. I always thought your tragedy the best of your works, and I think so still. It is a glorious thing. I like Bulwer's too, very much, but unless there were historical ground for the love between a Colonna and the family of Rienzi, he has injured his work by its introduction. It is so palpably an imitation of the

---

[1] Mr. Howitt was an alderman of Nottingham.

tragedy, and with much less effect. Adrian Colonna and Irene in the novel destroy the unity and continuity of the story—coming in and going out, and playing at a sort of bo-peep with one another. That is the weak part of the story. The loves of Nina and Rienzi were enough for a stern, grave story like that; and their love and their characters are beautiful. To you, however, the originality belongs. Had you not written this tragedy, I question if this novel would have been written either. One thing, however, I see in it with pleasure, so much less of 'dandyism,' and of that knowing, worldly spirit which were the deformity of his Pelham novels. His mind is evidently graver, older, and wiser.

Joanna Baillie is, as you say, 'a glorious old lady.' She has a glorious mind. It is impossible for you to admire her more than I do; but one thing I must remark, you will see now the whole world of criticism exalt her to the skies, and not on the strength of her own noble intellect, but at the expense of every other woman who has written tragedy. It is the fashion of modern criticism; the idol of the day must be the head of a pyramid, erected on other men's fame. We shall have it in the quarterlies, and so echoed down to the commonest provincial papers. I saw it in 'Blackwood's' this present month, and with indignation too. I never deny the wonderful excellence of Joanna Baillie, but no one shall persuade me that 'Rienzi' is not as good as any drama by her. Do not be discouraged, dear Miss Mitford. I know how mortifying these invidious comparisons are, but everything will find its level, and thinking people will contradict by their own firesides these unjust and invidious comparisons.

I am glad that you like our friend—at least by his letters. You will like him yet more when you come to know him. For my part, I like him greatly; and, different as our tastes are in many particulars, there is so accordant and kindred a tone of spirit that we never meet without his awakening a literary inspiration. He does not suggest in words subjects, but he gives a state of mind to suggest them. You will like him too; so did Mrs. Hemans, for he, though young, was a most judicious friend and counsellor.

And now good-bye, dear Miss Mitford. Here is indeed a long scrawl for you. Give our cordial greeting to your father, and with love from my husband and Ann,

I am, yours truly and affectionately,

M. HOWITT.

Mrs. Howitt introduced Henry Chorley, to whom she alludes in the above letter, to Miss Mitford, thinking that she could assist him with letters for the 'Life of Mrs. Hemans,' which he was then preparing.

After receiving a copy of the 'Linwoods' from Miss Sedgwick, Miss Mitford sent her a critique on that work, to which the following is a reply.

MISS SEDGWICK *to* MISS MITFORD.

New York, March 9, 1836.

Thank you, my dear friend, for the kind note (with 'Ion'), and the letter that followed it; for the expres-

sions of interest and affection with which they abound.
They are, everyone of them, folded and laid away in
my heart—the right and only safe keeper of such
archives. I was very much pleased with your appro-
bation of the 'Linwoods.' Vanity (or, I would fain
hope, something better) gives us a very nice percep-
tion and discrimination in this matter of praise. We
soon get above caring for the hack reviewers, but in
so far as they affect the sale of a book. They must
review after a writer reaches a certain point in public
favour, and they must praise, but they dole it out
without one movement of the heart, as a parish officer
does his allowance to the licensed pauper. If you
get a real warm-hearted review, you may be sure it
comes from some youth whose feelings are gushing
out from a full, undrained fountain. I love young
people, and because they love immeasurably. But of
all praise, commend me to that of a friend who feels
a deep interest in your honour and success. If you
know the colouring is deeper than you deserve, yet it
is the colouring of affection, and therefore true if
everything else is false. Thank you too for your
criticisms—though very forbearing, they are valuable
to me. I have heard Fanny Butler laugh at the
Americanism 'as he used to,' but I was never before
aware that 'mother,' 'aunt,' &c., without the pronoun,
were peculiar to us. The ear soon becomes accustomed to a conventionalism of this sort, and the
omission is positively disagreeable. Yet we must
write according to the standard of our own land, if
we have had the society of no other.

We have all been delighted with the tragedy of

your friend. I wrote to Mrs. Butler (with your kind mention of her, and notice of Mr. Harness) some account of 'Ion,' and said in conclusion that if Dr. Channing could write a tragedy, it would be such a one as this. She says, in reply, 'I am reading with delight Channing's book on slavery, *but* his tragedy (whenever he writes it) will be bad, and any tragedy which is such a one as he would write, would, in my audacious judgment, be bad.' I anticipate the reversion of her opinion when she reads 'Ion.' The only fault I see in it is the fault in Scott's 'Rebecca,' the virtue is given to another faith and another race that Christianity alone could produce; the natural offspring of Christianity is given to a parentage barren of such progeny. But this is a slight fault, into which the most generous and philosophic mind would alone fall. How different is the effect of such a poem as this from Byron's—quite equal to his in vigour and beauty. Talfourd makes you love and reverence your species. Byron would make you hate, shun, and fear them.

My brother Robert says that 'Ion' is an impersonation of Jesus Christ. He certainly is an illustration of disinterestedness, and all the attributes of spirituality.

Enter Kate from her Italian lesson, laughing and shouting, her clean frock (that was) covered with mud—a fit illustration of our horrible streets at this moment. She has measured her length, some five feet, on the Broadway pavement, but nothing ever hurts or disconcerts her. I wish I could send you her picture. She is a perfect Hebe—intelligence, health, and happiness are stamped upon her.

'Those young people are English,' said a talking woman next to me at a dancing-school ball, pointing to Kate and her brother Charles, who has also the rich English complexion.

I smiled.

'Oh, they are,' said she.

' I believe not, ma'am.'

' Do you know them ?'

' Yes.'

'They must be. Are you quite sure they are not ?'

I explained their relationship to me.

'Their parents are English, then ?'

' No.'

'Well, anyhow, the girl has been brought up in England—her voice, manner, everything is English.'

I hope one day, my dear Miss Mitford, to show her to you. She is the busiest of all busy bees, and working hard at the accomplishments this winter—the piano, singing, drawing, Italian, and German—but, thank heaven, there is no expunging nature from her.

If you see Fanny Butler in England (she goes there the first of May), ask her about Kate, please, for I have a foolish desire you should know something of the child from less questionable authority than mine.

What an extraordinary acquaintance you have among the young folk ! I trust that little Howitt's productions will be published, but, as you say, ' children are wonderful now-a-days.' I am sometimes tempted to exclaim, 'Is the world all grown up?—is childhood dead?' But we have some lovely specimens of this loveliest portion of existence under our own roof—the youngest, a child of four years, the drollest little sprig of Calvinism, who, having learned the terrors of the law from her nurse, threatens us, when it suits her, with 'the wrath to come.'

Miss Martineau has been passing the winter in Boston, and is to be here in a few days. She does not leave us till August. She has proposed to me to go to the prairies, taking Niagara *en route*, and finishing at the Falls of St. Anthony. Would you not like to go with us? That would be superlative. I *feel* (as we Yankees say) as if you were a most lovable person. Even those scurrilous wretches, the Frasers, doff their caps and greet you kindly; like Satan, when he meets Uriel, 'He casts to change his proper shape.' With this I shall send, more especially for your father's amusement, the first year's publication of our 'National Gallery.' I say for his, for, as the characters are for the most part military or political, they cannot have much interest for you. I made a singular acquaintance with the person who takes my packet to England soon after the publication of 'The Linwoods.' I received an anonymous letter from a youth, communicating the disastrous fate of his love —he had addressed a cousin, she rejected him. He gave both their characters, and her letter—a most admirable one, a model—and appealed to me as a Daniel in the *cour d'amour*. He wished to know if I thought her letter final. Poor youth! the case appeared to me perfectly hopeless, and so I told him, and advised him to be satisfied with the happiness of even an unrequited love for such a woman. He took my advice, and has since been to see me and thank me for it. Still his love is so deep and true that hope is not a necessary ingredient in it.

Give my best respects to your father, and thank him for doing me the honour of reading my book.

Mrs. Butler is living a quiet domestic life, idolizing her sweet baby, and preparing for her visit home. I fear it will be hard work for her to come back again.

I have made a terrific piece of work of criticising ' Ion.' I faltered from a feeling of my presumption.

This letter is most unreasonably crammed, and yet I have left much unsaid, my dear friend, that should have expressed to you how delightful your letters are to me, and how deep an interest I take in anything that concerns you. Accept the greeting of all my tribe.

Yours truly,

C. M. SEDGWICK.

P.S.—I ought to have told you that none of my family suffered by our big bonfire this winter. The truth is, that such is the prosperity of the country, so unprecedented that of the city, that there is little apparent loss. It is shared by thousands, and ruinous to very few.

LADY DACRE *to* MISS MITFORD.

2, Chesterfield Street, March 11, 1836.

I believe I am doing an odd thing, dear Miss Mitford, in enclosing to you a letter from the glorious Joanna, in which she agrees with me in all I said of your 'Rienzi.' The *knocking your heads together* is an allusion to my saying I should wish to bring you together if you came to town, and to 'knock your clever heads together.' She agrees with me also that 'Ion' is of too highly poetical a cast for the uneducated people who form the mass of an audience. I saw her 'Separation' the other night, on the whole done little justice to, and remarked that an infinitely deeper and more breathless attention was given by an overflowing pit to that ultra abomination, 'Quasimodo.' The rack and the wheel, and the beautiful scenery, and the skipping gipsies, and the singing, and the bustle and the noise, were more their penny's worth. The scenery, I must say, was equally beautiful for the 'Separation.' I think it would be an *acting* play in good hands. At least two essential scenes are equal to anything she has ever written. I heard them read by Mr. Young, so I know what they are capable of. I am not sorry you have turned aside to a novel as infinitely a more *sure* card to play at this moment (in a pecuniary point of view); and perhaps by the time your tragedy is ready, some better actors may have turned up, and our taste may have improved. The theatre is at so low an ebb, it must mend, I think. Even our *sleeves* are coming to their senses; having crammed into them more than in our

skirts, we are going to have them the size of the
limb they are to contain. So we may find that, as
we cannot cram more bad taste and immorality into
our dramas, we shall be content to return to real
tragedy and comedy.

Excuse all this scribbling and nonsense. I am
watching a little grand-daughter's dancing lesson at
the same time.

Pray return my letter enclosed to Lord Dacre, The
Hoo, Welwyn, Herts, to which place we return to-
morrow, and believe me

Your sincere admirer,
B. DACRE.

MRS. HOWITT *to* MISS MITFORD.

Wood Leighton, June 11, 1836.

You see, my dearest Miss Mitford, by the name at
the head of this where we now are—at this, veritably
the most woodland, and quiet, and old-fashioned of
English towns. If you look for it on the map of
England, or even of Staffordshire, you will not find
it, but instead you will find Uttoxeter—a queer name,
is it not?—that is the true place, and of a truth so
exactly is the character of the town and the country
round described and depicted that I was amazed at
the fidelity. The fame of the book, if it ever reaches
this place, has not reached it at present, so I walk
among its people without exciting half the sensation
I should do if they knew that their whereabouts and,
as they would suspect, themselves figured in the three
volumes.

I wish you were here with us. The luxuriance of the whole land, even in this season of drought, is wonderful; and the whole town seems full of gardens. I was hardly aware how great a feature this was in the town, for, comparatively speaking, these gardens, or rather courts, full of shrubbery, are of recent date; and such windows full of house-plants! It is truly a most pleasant old town, but oh, so quiet—stagnant almost! I love dearly a quiet house, a large, quiet garden, but then I must feel that beyond and about are men of stirring intellects, among whom important questions are felt as such; where people read, and care about what is doing and done in the world. Here, on the contrary, for miles and miles round is an Arcadia of woods, and green hills, and deep, picturesque valleys full of the landed gentry, who have grown for generations sleek, and fat, and quiet. There is no large, influential town to call forth their energies; their quietness is shown in the very tone of their voices. Everybody talks as if they were only half awake, and they only read one newspaper for twenty miles round. You cannot think what energetic people we seem among them; one is absolutely compelled to lower the tone of one's intellectual interests amongst them. It would never do for us to live at Wood Leighton, beautiful as its country is.

Dear Miss Mitford, let me congratulate you on the success of 'Ion.' We were delighted to find that the *public* could appreciate its fine morality and its exquisite poetry. It certainly was more than we hoped for. What a disgraceful review was given of it in the *Athenæum*, the same number that treated 'Wood

Leighton' so scurvily, even after my good friend, Henry Chorley, had the week before expressed the most unqualified praise of it by letter, and led me to suppose it would win a handsome notice. The critique of 'Ion' will do the tragedy much less harm than it must do the paper in which it appeared. I have heard no one mention it—and many have mentioned it to us—who has not expressed the most perfect disgust of it. It is full of such bad taste, bad feeling, and ignorance, as well as absurdity. My husband was so indignant that he proposed writing to you immediately to express his indignation, but the winding up of his affairs occupied him so completely from hour to hour, day after day, that he never could find the spare moment, and then, when the immediate vexation was passed, we resolved to write to you from this place. And now, dear, kind Miss Mitford, if you have read 'Wood Leighton,' let me know what you think of it *honestly*. I dare say *honestly* to you, because I am sure, though you *may* not like all, you will find something to like. You will not shear me down root and branch as the *Athenæum* did. Oh, it was a cruel criticism to thrust at one at the very fag end—with a bad book tagged to one like a dog with a tin to his tail—was insulting indeed. I shall never forget the anguish of that day!

You cannot think how I enjoy this setting out on our summer ramble. The children, dear little souls! are all safely and happily disposed of, so that we dismiss anxiety for them, and we are going over the land to enjoy ourselves, and no two persons under the sun can enjoy a summer's ramble more than we.

You may fancy us, if you like, winding away over brown hills and mosses, by old ruins, over mountains, or by river sides, wayfarers clad properly for our expedition—William with a knapsack on his back containing a change of linen, and such things of every day use as civilised people cannot do without; and then you may fancy, whether gipsies, or travelling potters, or chair-menders, were ever a pair of more authentic vagabonds than we. You will hear of a vagrant poet and his wife being brought up before some worthy Dogberry or other, and you may depend upon it it will be ourselves.

William sends his love to you, and pray make our united kind regards to your father.

I am, my dear friend,
Yours most truly and affectionately,
M. HOWITT.

LADY DACRE to MISS MITFORD.

Kimpton Vicarage,
Thursday, June 30, 1836.

DEAR MISS MITFORD,

I am ashamed to present myself before you after my apparently ungrateful conduct; but I am not really ungrateful, I assure you, only a procrastinating shatterbrain, and everything most unpardonable at my age, so I have let time slip through my hands in a way I cannot account for without thanking you for your great kindness in sending me your own very beautiful opera and the wonderful production of your young friend. I wish the latter to be seen by better judges than I can be, who am no scholar, and it is thought as wonderful as you think it by those well qualified to pronounce on it. The learning she displays in the preface and the notes makes me stare, and gives me what the poor people call the 'goose skin'—a sort of vague sensation of awe to which ignorance is subject. Where is the marvellous young creature? Is it possible to get at her? And yet her sphere is so much above mine that I could but look at her as we did the other day at the eclipse, through smoked glass.

I have brought your whole parcel down here for my daughter's benefit, but when I go back to town the two books shall be faithfully deposited in Mr. Harness's hands. The opera I consider as my own, and shall, with a thousand thanks, keep it, and value it for its own sake, and your sake, and all *sorts of sakes.*

I mean soon to beg your acceptance of a little volume I am making of my translations from 'Petrarch,' but I will not insist on your reading it. Nobody reads translations who can read originals, and, as everybody reads Italian now, my work is a folly. The extreme difficulty of translating any poet, and especially Petrarch, has given my attempt a value in my own eyes, such as mothers feel for their ricketty child, who has given them more pains to rear than all their stout, chubby urchins. I am peeping out in print (*publicly*, not privately, as this is) in the shape of an interlude in one act in 'The Keepsake,' to oblige a friend—really! and also in a very trifling thing *compiled* for music the other day, which I gave Lord Northampton for a charity. I say compiled, because I wove in songs I had written long ago. I hope your novel is advancing rapidly, that you may have your mind and hands free for your tragedy, in which I take a stronger interest. Every woman who can hold a pen writes novels now, and I think the Miss B.'s stories must bring the whole thing into disrepute. Don't quote me, for their father is Lord D.'s earliest and oldest ally. And now, dear Miss Mitford, I will encroach no longer on your precious time and great good-nature. Believe me, with true esteem and admiration,

Yours truly,
B. DACRE.

The allusion at the commencement of this letter is to Miss Barrett.

END OF THE FIRST VOLUME.